CANADIAN ANNUAL REVIEW OF POLITICS AND PUBLIC AFFAIRS 2000

Canadian Annual Review of politics and public affairs 2000

EDITED BY DAVID MUTIMER

Published with the support of York University by
University of Toronto Press
Toronto Buffalo London

Toronto Buffalo London
Printed in Canada

ISBN 978-0-8020-9089-8 (cloth)
ISBN 0-8020-9089-3 (cloth)

Printed on acid-free paper

Library and Archives Canada Cataloguing in Publication

Canadian annual review of politics and public affairs.

1971–
Continues: Canadian annual review, ISSN 0068-8215.
Issue for 2000 edited by David Mutimer.
ISSN 0315-1433
ISBN 0-8020-9089-3 (2000 issue)

1. Canada – Foreign relations – 1945– – Periodicals.
2. Canada – Economic conditions – 1945– – Periodicals.
3. Canada – Politics and government – Periodicals.

FC2.C36 320.9′71′064 C71-2093

This book was published with the support of York University.

University of Toronto Press acknowledges the financial assistance to its publishing program of the Canada Council for the Arts and the Ontario Arts Council.

University of Toronto Press acknowledges the financial support for its publishing activities of the Government of Canada through the Book Publishing Industry Development Program (BPIDP).

Copies of the *Canadian Annual Review* published annually for 1960 to 1982 and 1984 to 1999 are available.

Contents

Contributors

MELVIN BAKER, Archivist/Historian, President's Office, Memorial University of Newfoundland

EMMANUEL BRUNET-JAILLY, Assistant Professor, School of Public Administration, University of Victoria

PETER EDWARD BUKER, Assistant Professor, Department of Political Studies, University of Prince Edward Island

KEN COATES, Dean of Academics, Sea to Sky University, Squamish, BC

ROBERT DRUMMOND, Associate Professor, Department of Political Science, York University

ROBERT EVERETT, University Secretariat, York University

ROBERT FINBOW, Associate Professor, Department of Political Science, Dalhousie University

JOSEPH GARCEA, Associate Professor, Department of Political Science, University of Saskatchewan

CAREY HILL, Doctoral Candidate, Department of Political Science, University of British Columbia

HAROLD JANSEN, Assistant Professor, Department of Political Science, University of Lethbridge

GEOFFREY LAMBERT, Professor, Department of Political Studies, University of Manitoba

WARREN MAGNUSSON, Professor, Department of Political Science, University of Victoria

PETER NEARY, Professor, Department of History, University of Western Ontario

GREG POELZER, Associate Professor, Department of Political Studies, University of Saskatchewan, and University of the Arctic

DANIEL SALÉE, Professor of Political Science and Principal of the School of Community and Public Affairs, Concordia University

CHRISTOPHER SPEARIN, Deputy Director of Research and Assistant Professor of National Security Studies, Canadian Forces College, Toronto

RICHARD WILBUR, Fundy Promotions, St Andrews, New Brunswick

Preface

In last year's edition of the *Canadian Annual Review*, I indicated that we would be gradually introducing a series of changes to the organization and content of the volume, following last year's inclusion of the newly created Nunavut. This year we continue with a discussion of the politics of Nunavut, together with the other two northern Territories, and make three other changes to the text.

The first is that we have decided to eliminate the separate chapter on federal–provincial relations, which has long been a staple of the *Review*. This change reflects our judgment that it no longer makes sense to pull this issue out of the broader discussion of politics and public affairs, for two reasons. The first is that ongoing debate about the future of Canada and Quebec, which has dominated federal–provincial relations for so long is, for the moment at least, not taking the form that it has done. The second is that the scope of these relations, as the provinces take ever-greater responsibilities, has spread to the point that it is found in most, if not all, issues. On behalf of the *Review*, I would like to take this opportunity to thank Michael Howlett, who has written this section since 1987, and has provided a valuable contribution to our understanding of Canadian politics.

The second is that we have introduced a chapter on Municipal Affairs. This decision reflects the growing importance of municipal governance in Canada. Both as a result of the very high level of urbanization in the country – at 77 per cent one of the highest in the world – and of the downloading of services, municipal government is more important today than at any time in our history. While technically municipalities are creations of the provinces, the issues that are faced at this level of government are quite distinctive, and, of course, are often the most relevant to the day-to-day lives of Canadians.

The changes in Canadian life that have given rise to the first two changes to the *Review* have also led us to the third. The clear division between federal and provincial perspectives around which the volume has long been organized no longer makes the kind of sense it once did. The federal and provincial governments both overlap increasingly on important issues and act independently in similar spheres. We have, therefore, removed these divisions from the organization of the text. Furthermore, the tacit importance given to provinces by their ordering within the text seems to us out of keeping with the tenor of the times. We have opted in this edition for an essentially geographic ordering of the provincial and territorial chapters.

We see the *Review* as a work in progress, and so intend to introduce further changes in the years to come, guided by our goal of reflecting as clearly as possible the issues and practices of government that are of greatest importance to Canadians.

Together with these changes, this volume also sees comings and goings of a more usual nature, as authors leave and join the excellent group that brings you the *Review*. I would like to take this opportunity to thank those leaving and welcome those joining us. Jocelyn Coulon is leaving, having provided the chapter on Quebec in the 1997, 1998, and 1999 editions. We are fortunate to be joined by Daniel Salée of Concordia University. Since 1987 James Lawson authored our sections on the northern Territories, and is succeeded this year by Ken Coates of the Sea to Sky University and Greg Poelzer of the University of Saskatchewan. Christopher Spearin of the Canadian Forces College is also joining the *Review* this year, contributing the chapter on Canada's foreign affairs and national defence, a chapter that has been authored by Dean Oliver since 1992. The addition of a new chapter gives us the opportunity to welcome two other new authors to the fold: Emmanuel Brunet-Jailly and Warren Magnusson, both of the University of Victoria, have jointly authored the new Municipal Affairs section. To all those leaving, our heartfelt thanks for your sustained efforts on behalf of the *Review*; and to those joining, a hearty welcome.

In closing, I would like to say a special word of thanks to Marshall Beier of McMaster University, who has compiled the Calendar and Obituaries. As anyone who has had reason to assemble a calendar of events knows, it is a painstaking and often thankless task.

Canadian calendar 2000

JANUARY

2 Objecting to the pension and severance package offered by the federal government, miners at the Cape Breton Development Corp. begin a wildcat strike. It is a year since Ottawa announced that it will be getting out of the coal-mining business.

5 The federal government announces that it is closing down the monitoring and coordination centre set up to deal with feared computer system failures associated with the so-called Y2K bug, confirming the success of efforts to resolve the widespread date-format problem before the roll-over to the year 2000.

– With total sales in excess of 1.5 million cars, 1999 is reported to have been the best year for automakers in a decade and the second best ever.

11 The future of the Voisey's Bay nickel-mining megaproject is put in question as Inco Ltd rejects the Newfoundland government's call for a firm commitment to process the ore in the province.

– A U.S. court rejects a bid by the Grand Council of the Cree and a U.S. environmental group to prevent the sale of power to the United States by Hydro-Québec.

12 With the easing of fears of a millennium-related terrorist attack, heightened security measures along the Canada-U.S. border are relaxed.

13 The Canadian Radio-television and Telecommunications Commission unveils its plans for the gradual introduction of specialty digital television channels that will revolutionize signal delivery to consumers.

– Defence Minister Art Eggleton confirms that Canada

will withdraw its peacekeeping troops from East Timor.

14 In order to evade protests, and against the objections of community leaders, plutonium from decommissioned U.S. nuclear weapons is secretly flown to the Atomic Energy Canada labs at Chalk River, Ontario, to be evaluated as a fuel for Candu nuclear reactors.

18 The Federal Court of Appeal rules that suspected terrorists can be deported to another country even if they might face torture.

– Ontario Premier Mike Harris announces that anyone convicted of cheating the province's social welfare system will thenceforth be permanently denied access to welfare support.

19 Federal Human Resources Minister Jane Stewart releases an audit showing that her department may have mismanaged as much as $1 billion in grants for job creation, training, and literacy.

– Federal Health Minister Allan Rock unveils gruesome images of tobacco-related illnesses that will accompany new warnings on cigarette packages by the end of the year.

24 The Ontario Public Service Employees Unions warns that provincial government plans to privatize jails holding the province's most dangerous youth offenders will put the public at risk.

26 BCE announces that it will spin off most of its stake in high-performing Nortel Networks to its shareholders.

29 A United Nations–sponsored conference in Montreal crafts an agreement on the trade of genetically modified products that will allow countries to refuse imports they judge unsafe.

30 Reform Party leader Preston Manning wins the support of 75 per cent of delegates to the party's biennial convention in Ottawa. The strong endorsement of his leadership is read as a mandate to proceed with plans to 'unite the right' through what will be called the Canadian Reform Conservative Alliance.

31 The federal government approves the $8 billion takeover of Canada Trust by the Toronto Dominion Bank.

FEBRUARY

1 The federal government announces that it will give compensation to civilian sailors who gave wartime service in Canada's merchant marine.

– Quebec Anglo-rights group Alliance Quebec announces a constitutional challenge to a provincial language law requiring that all companies in the province conduct internal communications in French.

3 The Newfoundland government offers a $3,000 incentive to new nurses who remain in the province.

– A report on homelessness in Toronto finds that it is on the rise and will continue to grow without a significant commitment from both the federal and provincial governments to subsidized housing.

4 Four years after Casino Rama began operating near Orillia, an agreement is reached on the distribution of revenues among Ontario Native groups.

7 Defence Minister Art Eggleton says his department will make testing available to members of the military who believe they might have been exposed to depleted uranium while on postings abroad.

11 Foreign Affairs Minister Lloyd Axworthy reacts angrily to U.S. Senator Diane Feinstein's suggestion that lax Canadian laws and poor border control have raised the spectre of a terrorist threat emanating from Canada.

– Justice Minister Anne McLellan introduces legislation that will give same-sex partners equal access to, among other things, child-care tax breaks and pension benefits.

14 Rejecting the suggestion that a renewed federalism should be his party's objective, Quebec Premier Lucien Bouchard reaffirms his commitment to Quebec sovereignty.

15 In response to American criticism of Calgary-based Talisman Energy's involvement in the Sudanese Civil War, Foreign Affairs Minister Lloyd Axworthy says Canadian policy will not be dictated by Washington.

17 The federal government announces that it will recognize post-traumatic stress disorder as a disability

among military veterans of wars and peacekeeping operations.

– Two Saskatoon police officers are suspended in connection with allegations that police drove a Native man to the edge of town and left him to walk home without his coat. The practice is linked to the freezing deaths of four other aboriginal men.

20 British Columbia's governing New Democratic Party elects Ujjal Dosanjh as its new leader and the province's premier.

24 Quebec Intergovernmental Affairs Minister Joseph Facal says the province will simply ignore the federal government's Clarity Act, which is designed to make a pro-sovereignty referendum outcome more difficult to achieve.

27 The RCMP opens a second investigation involving federal job-creation grants to Prime Minister Jean Chrétien's St-Maurice riding.

28 Federal Finance Minister Paul Martin tables a balanced budget with good news for individual and corporate taxpayers, all of whom are promised tax reductions over the next several years.

– Statistics Canada reports that the Canadian economy grew by 1.1 per cent in the final quarter of 1999, continuing the longest sustained period of growth since the 1960s.

29 Following on Prime Minister Jean Chrétien's refusal to testify, three main complainants withdraw in protest from the inquiry into RCMP conduct at the 1997 Asia-Pacific Economic Cooperation summit in Vancouver.

– The Y2K computer bug hits Montreal belatedly as the city's taxation computer system is confounded by the leap year, unexpectedly reading the date as 1 March 1900.

MARCH

1 Honouring his campaign pledge, New Brunswick Premier Bernard Lord puts an end to widely unpopular tolls on a section of the Trans-Canada Highway between Fredericton and Moncton.

2 Ward Elcock, director of the Canadian Security Intelli-

gence Service, tells the Commons immigration committee that Canada is not a haven for terrorists.

– British Columbia drops a suit in a U.S. court alleging that the United States was in violation of conservation provisions in the 1985 Pacific Salmon Treaty.

9 The federal government is forced to take over the Canada Student Loan program after the Bank of Nova Scotia, the Royal Bank of Canada, and the Canadian Imperial Bank of Commerce withdraw.

– 'The Vancouver Agreement: An Urban Development Agreement between Canada–British Columbia–Vancouver regarding Economic, Social and Community Development in the City of Vancouver' is signed.

15 The federal government's Clarity Act on Quebec secession overwhelmingly passes the Commons by a vote of 208 to 55.

– A report by the International Joint Commission recommends that Canada and the United States impose a ban on bulk water exports in order to protect the Great Lakes ecosystem.

– The Alberta government passes legislation banning same-sex marriage.

– An Ontario Superior Court decision puts an end to tycoon Conrad Black's suit against Prime Minister Jean Chrétien, brought after Mr Chrétien blocked Mr Black's appointment to the British House of Lords last year.

– Quebec Health Minister Pauline Marois announces legislation that will make it illegal for hospitals in the province to run budget deficits. The intention is to curb spiralling health-care costs.

17 A U.S. moratorium on railway mergers frustrates Canadian National's plans for a $6 billion merger with Burlington Northern Santa Fe.

21 Statistics Canada reports that Canada's trade surplus reached a new all-time high in January.

22 In a speech at Carleton University, Foreign Affairs Minister Lloyd Axworthy says that American plans to build a national missile defence system will put the U.S. at greater risk by undermining existing multilateral arms-control agreements.

– The British Columbia Supreme Court overturns the ban on smoking in all workplaces that went into effect in the beginning of the year.

23 Ted Moses, Chief of the Grand Council of the Cree, says that Quebec's legislative claim to the right of self-determination denies aboriginal peoples the very right the province seeks to affirm for itself.

– The Canadian Human Rights Commission reports that disabled, poor, and aboriginal people are among the groups that continue to suffer discrimination in Canada.

– A Commons committee proposes that the traditional definition of marriage should be upheld in federal legislation to extend rights and duties to same-sex couples living in common-law situations.

24 Troubled Canadian Airlines International receives court-sanctioned protection from its creditors as it works with parent Air Canada to restructure its $3.5 billion debt.

25 A new federal party, the Canadian Reform Conservative Alliance, is born from the union of the Reform Party and disaffected Tories.

31 Citing continuing concern for groundfish stocks, the federal government cuts the catch quota for Newfoundland's cod fishery by one third.

APRIL

4 The Commons passes new privacy legislation designed to give Canadians more control over how their personal information is gathered, used, and distributed.

– The Canadian Centre for Policy Alternatives reports that 2.2 million Canadian women live in poverty. According to the report, more than half of single mothers and nearly one half of woman aged 65 and older are poor.

6 Immigration Minister Elinor Caplan introduces changes to the Immigration Act designed to crack down on people smuggling and refugee claimants with criminal records.

7 Appointing two Liberals to fill Senate vacancies,

Prime Minister Jean Chrétien cements his party's majority in the upper house, bringing to 55 the number of Liberals sitting in the 105-seat chamber.

11 The federal government's controversy-plagued same-sex bill passes third and final reading in the Commons.

– Nova Scotia Finance Minister Neil LeBlanc delivers a budget that seeks to combat the province's debt with a range of new user fees and the elimination of some 1,600 public sector jobs.

12 Alberta's private health-care bill passes second reading.

13 A 113-year land-claim settlement effort is brought to fruition as the Nisga'a Treaty passes a Senate vote and receives speedy royal assent from Governor General Adrienne Clarkson.

14 North American stock markets suffer their worst-ever one-day point drop, losing more than $1 trillion in value. The Toronto Stock Exchange loses more than 5 per cent on the day.

17 Prince Edward Island Premier Pat Binns's Conservatives win a landslide majority government, taking 26 of the province's 27 seats.

– A study by the Canadian Council on Social Development puts Montreal's poverty rate at 41 per cent, making it the poorest city in the country.

– Citing rising energy prices as the main culprit, Statistics Canada reports that inflation hit 3 per cent in March, resulting in the largest one-month increase since the 1991 introduction of the federal Goods and Services Tax.

18 Judicial independence is called into question with the introduction of a private member's bill by Ontario Conservative MPP Marilyn Mushinski. The bill, which has the support of Premier Mike Harris, calls for performance reviews that would single out judges who regularly fail to impose stiff sentences.

20 Gold miners in Red Lake, Ontario, vote to end a four-year strike that is one of the longest in Canadian history.

25 Media baron Conrad Black's Hollinger International announces that it will sell off most of its newspaper

publishing empire in an effort to shore up share prices and reduce its debt.

27 Canada imposes diplomatic sanctions on Vietnam after a Canadian citizen is executed by firing squad on drug-smuggling charges. Canada was not given warning of the execution of Toronto seamstress Nguyen Thi Hiep, despite the fact that Toronto police had recently uncovered compelling exculpatory evidence.

– Pat Duncan's Liberals win a majority government in Yukon, prompting the resignations of the leaders of the NDP and the Yukon Party.

28 Ontario's Conservative government reveals plans to allow private universities to operate in the province.

MAY

2 Statistics Canada reports that foreign control of the Canadian economy grew steadily through the 1990s, with the largest share taken by U.S. firms.

– Ontario Treasurer Ernie Eves delivers a balanced budget with new spending for health, education, and policing, as well as rebates to taxpayers.

5 Charges of insubordination against former air force sergeant Mike Kipling are stayed. Sergeant Kipling faced the charge for his refusal to be vaccinated against anthrax while on deployment in Kuwait in 1998.

– Federal Health Minister Allan Rock calls for bids on a contract to provide marijuana to the government for distribution to persons who have been granted permission to smoke the drug for medical reasons.

8 A study of spousal abuse in the Canadian military finds that a serious problem exists and that officers have sometimes allowed abusers to go unpunished while victims have been harassed.

10 With a view to thwarting transnational crime and terrorism, new cooperative measures are announced for control of the Canada-U.S. border.

11 Federal Finance Minister Paul Martin suggests that tobacco taxes could be increased by as much as fifteen dollars a carton because rising prices in the northern

U.S. will work to curb the smuggling problem that moved Ottawa to cut its cigarette tax in 1994.

– Ontario's Conservative government introduces changes to the province's Education Act that, among other new provisions, will enable the government to take control of school boards that do not follow its new rules.

15 In what is widely regarded as a test of Joe Clark's leadership of the federal Conservatives, Tory Loyola Hearn narrowly wins the Conservative safe seat of St John's West in a by-election.

– The premiers of Canada's four Atlantic provinces sign an agreement establishing the Council of Atlantic Premiers, a collective body for the advancement of regional concerns in dealings with Ottawa.

17 U.S. President Bill Clinton announces that new technological solutions will be employed in order to increase control of the Canada-U.S. border in the wake of a terrorist plot to carry out bombings in the U.S. on New Year's Eve.

24 The Fisheries Resource Conservation Council delivers more bad news to Atlantic fishers, revealing that cod stocks are not recovering as quickly as expected and recommending further cuts in the allowable catch.

– A Statistics Canada report shows that the number of university-educated Canadians joining the so-called brain drain to the U.S. is more than offset by the arrival of new immigrants with university degrees, but many of the latter are unable to work in their fields because their credentials are not being recognized in this country.

29 Human Resources Minister Jane Stewart announces the planned dismantlement of a massive government database of Canadians' personal information brought to light in the annual report of the federal privacy commissioner.

30 In a report to the Commons, acting federal Environment Commissioner Richard Smith says that the problem of air pollution is not being taken seriously enough even though it kills more Canadians annually than car accidents, breast cancer, or melanoma.

31 The *Globe and Mail* reports that documents obtained through access-to-information requests show that Quebec has received the lion's share of federal sponsorship monies from Public Works Canada over the last two years, while the West has received very little by comparison.

– The World Trade Organization upholds a ruling against the Canada-U.S. Auto Pact, finding that the 35-year-old arrangement violates international fair trade rules.

– Defence Minister Art Eggleton promises a full investigation following reports that Canadian soldiers deployed to Croatia in the early 1990s poisoned their platoon leader's coffee, leaving him visually impaired and confined to bed.

– Ontario's chief coroner announces that his office is investigating the deaths of nine people following an outbreak of E. coli in the water supply of the town of Walkerton.

JUNE

2 The Council of Ministers of Education reports that the science scores of Canadian children have improved considerably over the results shown in 1996 testing.

4 A World Health Organization study ranks Canada twelfth in the world in terms of 'healthy' life expectancy.

6 A Senate subcommittee report recommends that Canadians who take leave from work to provide palliative care to loved ones should be given job rights and protections similar to those given to new mothers.

8 The Ontario government announces a multi-million-dollar compensation package for Walkerton residents affected by the E. coli outbreak in the town's water supply, but they will be required to waive their right to sue.

9 Prime Minister Jean Chrétien enlarges his party's majority in the Senate with the appointment of another two Liberals to the upper house.

13 Alberta Treasurer Steve West announces the payment of $2.7 billion against the provincial debt, leaving some $12 billion outstanding.

15 The Supreme Court of Canada unanimously upholds the federal government's right to pass gun-control legislation in the interest of public safety.

– A protest against homelessness turns ugly in front of the Ontario Legislature. Riot police make twenty-nine arrests amidst dozens of injuries.

20 Chief of Defence Staff General Maurice Baril announces that the case of soldiers alleged to have poisoned their platoon leader in Croatia in the early 1990s will be handed over to Ontario Crown prosecutors.

22 Almost a decade after the Oka Crisis, Kanesatake Mohawks and the federal government sign a tentative agreement on the control of disputed lands in the area.

– Nova Scotia Premier John Hamm announces a deal that will see the Swiss Duferco Farrell Corp. buy the perennially troubled Sydney Steel Corp., saving almost half of the 500 jobs at stake.

27 The federal departments of Justice and Immigration report that Canada has been making strides in the effectiveness of efforts to keep accused war criminals out of the country.

29 The federal government's controversial Clarity Act on the terms of any future referendum on Quebec secession passes the Senate.

– For the seventh year in a row, the United Nations Human Development Index declares Canada the best place in the world to live. The news is tempered, however, by a fall from eighth to eleventh place on the poverty index.

– Prime Minister Jean Chrétien announces a $700 million Atlantic Investment Partnership, designed to foster economic development in the region.

– Seeking to restore voter confidence amidst a persistent budget-deficit scandal, British Columbia's NDP government passes balanced-budget legislation.

JULY

5 The Royal Canadian Mounted Police open Canada's new DNA bank, which will hold samples of genetic material from persons convicted of violent crimes.

– The Ontario Superior Court upholds as constitutional the right of parents to use moderate physical force in disciplining children.

6 American firm Oxbow Carbon and Minerals Ltd announces plans to buy the assets of the Cape Breton Development Corp, saying it will rehire as many as 500 coal miners who lost their jobs as a result of the federal government's decision to close its mines.

– Imperial Tobacco and two other companies file suit in the Quebec Superior Court in an effort to overturn federal legislation requiring new graphic health warnings on all cigarette packages.

– The British Columbia Court of Appeal upholds the right of the federal government to grant a separate commercial fishery to Native fishers.

7 A report prepared for the Organization of African Unity credits retired Canadian Lieutenant-General Roméo Dallaire with having tried to prevent the 1994 Rwandan genocide in the face of apparent international indifference.

8 Ontario Attorney General Jim Flaherty announces that the province will join the federal government in appealing a court decision awarding an additional $20 million to the lawyers who successfully represented Canadians who contracted hepatitis C from infected blood.

11 In what is believed to be the work of radical anti-abortionists, a Vancouver gynecologist suffers a second near-fatal attempt on his life as a masked attacker stabs him in the back outside his office. Dr Garson Romalis was also hit by a shot fired into the kitchen of his home in 1994.

12 Grand Chief of the Crees of Northern Quebec Matthew Coon Come is elected National Chief of the Assembly of First Nations.

– Former Alberta Treasurer Stockwell Day becomes the first elected leader of the new Canadian Reform

Conservative Alliance Party, beating Reform Party founder and erstwhile Opposition Leader Preston Manning.

14 With winds of up to 300 kilometres per hour, one of the worst tornados in Canadian history cuts a more than one-kilometre-wide swath through a crowded Alberta campground, killing ten people.

21 Following the collapse of its merger plans with American rail giant Burlington Northern Santa Fe, Canadian National announces a rail-sharing agreement with its long-time rival, Canadian Pacific.

24 The British Columbia Supreme Court thwarts a bid by the province's Opposition Liberals to overturn the historic Nisga'a Treaty.

25 The International Joint Commission recommends that residents of the Great Lakes region be warned that high levels of toxins present in fish caught in the lakes and consumed could result in birth defects and other health problems.

26 Half a century after Canada sent troops to join the United Nations contingent in the Korean War, Foreign Affairs Minister Lloyd Axworthy announces the normalization of diplomatic relations with North Korea.

27 Responding to an Innu request for an injunction from the Federal Court of Canada, the Department of National Defence announces the suspension of plans to conduct supersonic test flights over Labrador.

31 CanWest, Canada's second largest private broadcaster, joins with Conrad Black's Hollinger newspaper empire in a $3.5 billion deal that creates a multimedia giant of unprecedented print and electronic reach.

– Ruling unconstitutional the law criminalizing marijuana possession on the grounds that some people are allowed to use marijuana for medicinal purposes, the Ontario Court of Appeal gives the federal government one year to clarify the law or it will be struck down.

AUGUST

2 Despite the objections of northern residents, Native people, and environmentalists, Toronto City Council votes 36 to 20 to ship millions of tons of municipal

garbage by rail for disposal in an abandoned mine in the northern Ontario town of Kirkland Lake.

4 Bombardier Inc. announces that it will buy Daimler-Chrsyler's railway division for $725 million, making it a world leader in the production of railway locomotives and train cars.

10 Moved by concerns over safe drinking water in particular, Ontario Municipal Affairs Minister Tony Clement announces $240 million for smaller municipalities to help them upgrade their health and safety infrastructure.

11 Speaking in a panel discussion in Vancouver, Canadian Alliance MP John Mykytyshyn makes comments suggesting Atlantic Canadians are unwilling to work, preferring to receive handouts.

16 A protester makes his way past bodyguards and hits Prime Minister Jean Chrétien in the face with a pie in Charlottetown, Prince Edward Island.

– The Ontario Court of Appeal rules that the requirement that political parties field at least 50 candidates in order to enjoy the benefits of registered status is not discriminatory.

17 The federal government announces plans to replace the military's aging fleet of Sea King helicopters.

18 Statistics Canada reports that Canada's trade surplus hit a record $5 billion in June, propelled by rising energy prices.

21 In an effort to shame governments into putting more resources into legal aid programs, the Canadian Bar Association says it will begin to publicize accounts of some of the worst cases of Canadians who are unable to access the justice system.

– Statistics Canada reports that retail sales hit an all-time high in June, with growth in the auto sector and higher gasoline prices moving consumer spending to a record $22.9 billion.

– Alberta-based Telus Corp. acquires the Clearnet Communications national mobile telephone network with an offer of $6.6 billion.

24 British Columbia Finance Minister Paul Ramsey says better-than-expected economic performance has

increased government revenues, replacing a projected deficit with a surplus of $52 million.

25 The federal government announces that it will remove tariffs from a wider range of goods imported from the world's poorest countries.

27 Some 250 protesters storm a Parti Québécois national council meeting to voice their disapproval of the provincial government's municipal reforms, which could result in job losses to contracting out as the number of local governments is reduced.

28 The World Trade Organization authorizes Canada to impose $2.1 billion in retaliatory trade sanctions against Brazil over six years in answer to subsidies enjoyed by Brazilian commuter jet manufacturer Embraer that give it an unfair advantage over Canadian manufacturer Bombardier.

29 A clash between federal fisheries enforcement officers and Native fishers over the disputed Burnt Church lobster fishery in Miramichi Bay off New Brunswick leaves one Native boat damaged and two others sunk.

31 Federal Fisheries Minister Herb Dhaliwal refuses to meet with Burnt Church Natives as long as they continue to set traps in the disputed Miramichi Bay lobster fishery.

– Crediting rising energy prices, gambling revenues, and personal tax revenues, Alberta Treasurer Steve West says Alberta could wipe out its accumulated debt in just three years.

SEPTEMBER

1 Vietnam releases 75-year-old Tran Thi Cam four months after executing her daughter on questionable drug charges. A landed immigrant to Canada, Tran Thi Cam had been sentenced to life imprisonment in connection with the same allegations.

5 Leaders from four of Canada's churches win the approval of Newfoundland Natives by apologizing for years of abuse in church-run schools and other facilities.

6 Speaking at a book signing in Montreal, former prime minister Brian Mulroney says that free trade is his

greatest legacy and suggests that Canada and the U.S. should work toward a customs union without border posts or other restraints on the free flow of people, goods, and services.

11 Canadian Alliance Leader Stockwell Day and federal Conservative Leader Joe Clark each win by-elections, gaining seats in the Commons.

– Prime Minister Jean Chrétien reaches a historic-health care agreement with the provincial premiers that will see billions of dollars in increases in transfer payments to the provinces over the next several years.

14 Foreign Affairs Minister Lloyd Axworthy announces the establishment of the International Commission on Intervention and State Sovereignty, which will report on humanitarian intervention on the working assumption that state sovereignty cannot be used as a shield for gross violations of human rights.

– Former Ontario Premier Bob Rae accepts an appointment by federal Fisheries Minister Herb Dhaliwal to mediate the Miriamichi Bay lobster fishing dispute.

– Statistics Canada reports that full-time working women still earn only 72.5 cents for every dollar a man makes. The gap is even wider when the whole of the workforce is considered, since women are more likely to be employed in low-paying part-time positions.

15 Foreign Affairs Minister Lloyd Axworthy announces a new aid package aimed at protecting children from human-rights abuses.

– Another multimedia colossus is formed as telecom leader BCE strikes a deal with Thompson Corp., bringing together Bell's Sympatico Internet portal, the CTV television network, and the *Globe and Mail*.

18 Foreign Affairs Minister Lloyd Axworthy announces that he is ending nearly three decades in politics to join the Liu Centre for Global Issues at the University of British Columbia. Among other highlights of his political career, he will be remembered for his central role in the process leading to the Ottawa Convention banning antipersonnel landmines.

20 Immigration Minister Elinor Caplan says a plan is in the works for mandatory HIV and hepatitis B testing

of prospective immigrants with the aim of disallowing the applications of those who test positive.

21 An Ontario Court of Appeal decision strikes down the Conservative government's 'spouse-in-the-house' rule cutting welfare benefits for single mothers who cohabit with a man for less than three years.

25 After more than three decades in politics, Saskatchewan Premier Roy Romanow announces his resignation.

26 Statistics Canada sets Canada's population at 30,750,000 as of 1 July 2000, pushed forward primarily by an increase in the number of new immigrants.

– A shipment of plutonium from decommissioned Russian nuclear weapons is flown into the Atomic Energy Canada facility at Chalk River, Ontario, under such secrecy that opponents of the shipments are unable to mobilize a protest.

27 New Brunswick Finance Minister Norm Betts reports that increases in federal transfers have resulted in an even rosier than predicted fiscal picture for the province, its projected $12.3 million surplus having grown to $62.7 million.

– A national pump-price survey finds that despite a significant drop in the price of crude oil, gasoline prices are at an all-time-high average of 76.4 cents per litre.

OCTOBER

1 Nova Scotia's Water Resources Protection Act comes into effect, outlawing bulk water shipments with a ban on the removal of water in quantities larger than 25 litres.

3 A two-hour state funeral is held in Montreal's Notre Dame Basilica for former prime minister Pierre Elliott Trudeau, who died of prostate cancer on 28 September at the age of eighty.

4 Federal Industry Minister John Manley confirms that the Canada-U.S. Auto Pact will die in February 2001 in compliance with a May ruling by the World Trade Organization.

5 Criticizing federal and provincial governments alike, federal language commissioner Dyane Adam says the

implementation of bilingualism has fallen short of what is called for in the Official Languages Act.

6 Prime Minister Jean Chrétien says he has sent a letter to the new president of Yugoslavia offering the lifting of trade sanctions and assistance with post-war reconstruction now that former president Slobodan Milosevic has accepted electoral defeat.

11 Two weeks after announcing a $300 million investment in its Oshawa, Ontario, plant, General Motors commits a further $440 million for retooling its St Catharines, Ontario, plant for the production of next-generation engines.

12 The Supreme Court of Canada upholds the controversial 'rape-shield' law that prohibits the raising of details of a woman's prior sexual history in sexual assault cases.

– In his annual report, Alberta Auditor General Peter Valentine criticizes Premier Ralph Klein's government for one-time spending announcements following the spring budget. Mr Klein's response is that 75 per cent of any surplus must be spent on debt reduction, but the balance can be used for one-time funding decisions.

13 Canada and the U.S. announce a bilateral agreement on smog reduction that, it is hoped, will reduce levels of airborne pollutants in Eastern Canada.

16 Just twenty months into his second provincial mandate, Brian Tobin resigns as Newfoundland premier to return to federal politics, seeking the Liberal nomination for the Newfoundland riding of Bonavista Trinity Conception.

18 Statistics Canada reports that the national homicide rate fell to its lowest level in three decades in 1999, at 1.76 murders per 100,000 population.

19 Ontario Colleges and Universities Minister Dianne Cunningham introduces legislation allowing private universities.

20 Citing unacceptably high liability, Toronto abandons its planned $1 billion scheme to ship municipal garbage north for disposal in an abandoned mine in Kirkland Lake, Ontario.

– Former British Columbia premier Glen Clark faces

fraud and breach-of-trust charges laid by the RCMP in connection with a casino licence application by a friend and neighbour who undertook improvements to Mr Clark's home.

22 Prime Minister Jean Chrétien calls a general election for 27 November, drawing immediate criticism from opposition parties for taking voters back to the polls after only three and a half years.

23 Canada takes delivery of the first of four used British Upholder-class diesel-electric submarines, which will replace the Canadian navy's aging Oberon-class subs over the next two years.

25 The Alberta Court of Appeal upholds a 23 October Alberta Court of Queen's Bench ruling suspending the Canada Elections Act spending limits imposed on third parties during federal elections.

– A two-day meeting of the G-20 finance ministers and central bank governors wraps up in Montreal with promises of a new global social safety net to help the world's poor deal with the harsher effects of globalization.

– An audited statement shows that New Brunswick's projection of a larger-than-expected budget surplus just four weeks ago will come to naught. Instead of the reported $62.7 million, payouts to civil servants taking early retirement will reduce the surplus to an anticipated $8.1 million.

NOVEMBER

7 The Canadian Alliance is faced with a serious public-relations problem when a policy manual for candidates is found to have a number of discrepancies with the party's official platform. Critics charge that this is evidence the Alliance has a hidden agenda.

8 The British Columbia government agrees to pay $6.5 million in compensation to people who contracted hepatitis C through tainted blood but are not covered by a previous settlement agreement.

9 The Supreme Court of Canada rules that rent increases charged to non-Native leaseholders on the Musqueam reserve in Vancouver are excessive and must be reduced.

– Newfoundland Energy Minister Paul Dicks unveils a plan to scale back the $12 billion Churchill Falls hydroelectric project that was to have involved both Labrador and Quebec. Under the revised plan, Quebec's only role is as a potential consumer of the electricity to be produced.

10 The Supreme Court of Canada upholds the Canada Elections Act, reinstating a provision limiting campaign spending by third parties in federal elections.

– The federal Finance Department reports a sharp increase in the federal surplus for the first six months of the year, up $5.4 billion over the same period last year to an estimated $13.5 billion.

14 A prominent Prince Edward Island potato producer says the industry's survival is being threatened by a U.S. ban on Island potatoes that has been in place since a fungal disease was discovered in one field several weeks ago.

– The Quebec Superior Court rules against ten francophone families who had been pressing for the right to have their children educated in English-language schools.

– Ontario Social Services Minister John Baird unveils a plan that would require welfare recipients to submit to a drug test in order to receive benefits.

15 Quebec Premier Lucien Bouchard's Parti Québécois government tables legislation to amalgamate the City of Montreal and surrounding municipalities.

26 Following on the broadcast of disturbing images of children sniffing gasoline in the remote Labrador Innu community of Davis Inlet, the federal government promises a detoxification centre and moves to extend the Indian Act's provisions to the Innu in order to give them better access to social programs.

27 Prime Minister Jean Chrétien's Liberals win a third consecutive majority, deepening their hold on power as the government caucus grows to 172 seats from the 155 won in 1997. With 66 seats, the Canadian Alliance forms the official Opposition while the Bloc Québécois, NDP, and Conservatives take 38, 13, and 12 respectively.

– An inquest report into unexplained infant deaths at Winnipeg's Health Sciences Centre concludes that as many as ten of the twelve tiny heart patients might have lived if the quality of care had been better.

29 Talks between Canada and Brazil aimed at resolving an ongoing trade dispute over Brazilian subsidies for commuter jet production collapse, setting the stage for Canadian retaliation authorized by the World Trade Organization in August.

– Tobacco giant Rothmans Benson & Hedges responds to new restrictions on tobacco advertising by cutting its support for major Canadian film and fireworks festivals.

– The board of directors of bookseller Chapters Inc. scoffs at a takeover bid by Indigo Books and Music Inc. and Onex Inc. According to Chapters executives, the Indigo-Onex offer does not reflect the true value of the company.

30 Statistics Canada reports that despite expectations it would cool off, the Canadian economy is growing at a rate of 4.8 per cent, double the rate in the U.S.

DECEMBER

3 Citing health care as a priority, Quebec Premier Lucien Bouchard says he cannot justify spending millions of dollars on a sovereignty referendum that would have no chance of succeeding.

4 Ontario Finance Minister Ernie Eves says the province will deliver a $1.4 billion budget surplus for fiscal year 2000–1.

6 Speaking at a Liberal fundraising dinner in Toronto, Prime Minister Jean Chrétien says his government will work toward achieving social justice in place of the 'Third World conditions' on Native reserves.

11 Ontario Consumer Minister Bob Runciman says the province's Conservative government will not be pressured into recognizing gay marriages.

– Days after arresting fifteen members of the Rock Machine motorcycle gang, Quebec police announce the arrest of seven members of another gang connected to the Hell's Angels. Law-enforcement officials in the province have stepped up anti-gang efforts since the attempted murder in September of a Montreal crime reporter believed to have been targeted by bikers.

14 Saying the monies are already owed under existing agreements, Grand Chief Ted Moses of the James Bay Cree rejects a $170 million offer by the Quebec government to settle an ongoing forest-management dispute.

– Driven by soaring energy prices, the national inflation rate hits a nine-year high of 3.2 per cent, Statistics Canada reports.

– Prime Minister Jean Chrétien telephones U.S. President-elect George W. Bush to offer his congratulations. According to Mr Chrétien, Mr Bush claims to know a good deal about Canada on the strength of trips he made to Toronto for baseball games when he owned the Texas Rangers.

– Ontario's Conservative government tables legislation that would allow the province to seize all profits made by convicted criminals who sell their stories.

15 Canada signs a United Nations protocol to halt illegal immigration and another to fight international crime.

18 The *National Post* reports that low voter turnout for the 27 November federal election has prompted chief electoral officer Jean-Pierre Kingsley to comment that Parliament might have to consider passing a mandatory voting law.

19 Prime Minister Jean Chrétien says his government has not yet decided whether to participate in the controversial U.S. ballistic-missile defence scheme that is being pushed by the incoming Bush Administration.

– Federal Finance Minister Paul Martin says Canada will place a moratorium on loan repayments by some of the world's poorest countries and confirms plans to eventually forgive such debts entirely.

20 Lobster fishers in southwestern Nova Scotia report that stocks have risen to levels unseen in recent memory, showing the effectiveness of conservation measures and making this a banner year for those whose livelihoods depend on the fishery.

21 A land governance accord, ratified by a narrow margin, is signed by leaders of Oka's Mohawk commu-

nity. The ratification process is complicated by the fact that traditionalists do not recognize the legitimacy of the elected band council.

22 While absolving commanders of responsibility for discipline problems with Canadian peacekeepers in Bosnia, a military report recommends study of the impact of stress on soldiers who serve multiple tours on overseas peacekeeping missions.

29 The National Gallery of Canada moves to find the rightful owners of a number of works in its possession that might have been stolen by the Nazis during the Second World War.

– Police sources say that the Quebec Hell's Angels have begun moving into Ontario, marking increased competition between rival biker gangs.

31 Canada completes a two-year term of membership on the United Nations Security Council, its fifth term since the founding of the body.

CANADIAN ANNUAL REVIEW OF POLITICS
AND PUBLIC AFFAIRS 2000

EDITOR'S INTRODUCTION – THE YEAR IN REVIEW

The year 2000 began with a whimper. By itself this might not seem overly surprising for, except for fireworks, the beginning of January is not often marked by exciting public events. Nevertheless, the all too usual calm of the first of January this year was notable, because of the widespread concern that it would be anything but calm. For several years there had been a growing chorus of voices warning of the dangers of 1 January 2000, or, as our ever-contracting world would have it, Y2K. The problem was that computers, which had become ubiquitous only in the past twenty years, had not been programmed to recognize the year 2000. The fear was that on the first of January the computers would 'think' it was the year 1900. While this might be amusing on a personal desktop system, the concern was that the computers that ran the world's infrastructures – air, rail, and sea traffic, energy and telecommunications grids, for example – would stop working. The threat was taken seriously, for example, by the Canadian military, which mounted Operation Abacus, the largest-ever country-wide military operation, to cope with the potential chaos. As it happened, the world did not end ...

The serenity of the beginning of the year largely, if not entirely, set the tone for the year to follow. In 2000 the Canadian economy was in rude health, the federal fiscal house seemed to be in order, and so attention was turned to distributing surpluses rather than managing deficits. With a growing economy and money to distribute, it is not surprising that the federal government chose to renew its mandate this year, with an election in November. The call capitalized not only on the government's economic position, but also on the convolutions of the right-wing opposition. In February the Reform Party met and voted itself out of existence, forming at the same moment the Canadian Reform Conservative Alliance, or Canadian Alliance. After an extended campaign, the new party chose former Alberta cabinet minister Stockwell Day as its first leader, rejecting in the process Reform founder Preston Manning. But for all that the process was designed to 'unite the right,' and despite calling itself a Reform Conservative Alliance, the new party was little more than the old Reform Party with a new logo, as the Progressive Conservatives under Joe Clark refused to join in. The Liberals, therefore, faced a new party with a new leader, and a continued split on their right. The result in November was that, while the Alliance gained a higher proportion of the vote than Reform had in 1997, it was almost entirely taken from the Tories, and the Liberals were able to return with a strengthened majority.

The reverberations of the 1995 Quebec Referendum came to an important close in 2000 with the passage of the Clarity Act. The Act was the culmination of the federal government's Plan B response to the referendum. Plan A had focused on convincing Quebec of the benefits of confederation, and in altering the division of responsibilities in favour of the provinces, but without constitutional amendment. Plan B was the iron fist inside this Plan A velvet glove. The centrepiece of Plan B had been the constitutional reference to the Supreme Court, on which the Court ruled that unilateral secession was illegal, but that the federal government would be bound to negotiate separation in response to a clear majority on a clear question. As the Court pointedly refused to define the clarity of either question or majority, Parliament would have to, and the result was the Clarity Act. The Act set out the process by which Parliament would determine whether or not the question and the majority were clear, and therefore whether negotiation on separation would occur. While the Act sets out no detailed criteria, importantly it does establish that it is the Parliament of Canada that will uniquely determine the clarity of question and majority in the case of any future separation referendum. Not surprisingly, the Bloc Québécois was livid.

Plan A had resulted, in 1999, in the Social Union agreement, but little, if anything, was advanced under its aegis following the agreement. Nevertheless, the issue that seemed to engage Canadians more than any other was one of social policy, specifically the future of health care in Canada. The debate over the future of health care continued throughout the year. While the federal government provided more money for health in the February budget, the provinces insisted it was not enough. In particular, Alberta's Ralph Klein challenged the federal government directly by introducing legislation to expand private, for-profit clinics in the province, in a way that seemed a direct violation of the Canada Health Act. A first ministers meeting was finally convened on the issue in September, and it concluded with a new accord on funding. It seemingly satisfied no one. The provinces did not think that there was enough money in the deal, while those concerned with the way provinces spend health-care money were not satisfied with the watered down provisions on reporting and monitoring.

September also saw the end of a notable era in Canadian politics, with the death of Pierre Elliott Trudeau. Pierre Trudeau had been a signal presence in Canadian politics from the time of Trudeaumania in 1968 to his interventions in the constitutional debates around the Meech Lake and Charlottetown Accords. While he was far from universally loved, or even admired, few Canadians have had as significant an impact on the country as Mr Trudeau. A combative politician and a rigorous intellectual, itself an odd mix, Mr Trudeau ultimately transformed the country. The Charter of Rights and Freedoms, which he had championed from his early days in politics and finally achieved soon before his (second) retirement, has influenced the nature of Canadian public life more, perhaps, than any other single act. In death, particularly following so soon after the 1998 loss of his son Michel, the strong emotions Mr Trudeau inspired turned to a remarkable outpouring of grief, with people lining the railway tracks through the woods of Quebec as the train carrying his coffin travelled between Ottawa and Montreal for his funeral.

A quiet year domestically, 2000 was also relatively quiet in terms of Canada's international engagements. It marked the second year of our two-year term on the UN Security Council, and we used the opportunity to try to advance the human security agenda, which had marked Canada's foreign policy under the tenure of Foreign Minister Lloyd Axworthy. Most notably, following the UN Millennium Summit, Canada announced the creation of the International Commission on Intervention and State Sovereignty (ICISS). ICISS was to explore the relation between sovereignty and the humanitarian imperative, looking to set out the scope for humanitarian intervention in an era in which state sovereignty was, increasingly, no longer considered sacrosanct. It is possible that the formation of ICISS will mark the climax of the Canadian human security agenda, whose future was put into doubt soon after ICISS was announced. Lloyd Axworthy, the minister so closely associated with human security, decided not to seek re-election in 2000, leaving Parliament to become the head of the Liu Institute for Global Issues at the University of British Columbia. He was replaced by John Manley.

The UN was not the only focus of Canada's international activity, of course. In June, Windsor was host to a meeting of the Organization of

American States. Security was tight, given, in particular, the recent unrest in Seattle at the World Trade Organization meetings in 1999. There were anti-globalization protests in Windsor, and again when Finance Minister Martin hosted a meeting of G20 finance ministers, at which he attempted to advance the issue of debt relief. His call for an immediate moratorium was not well received in all quarters, particularly by the United States, which had not been consulted in advance.

Canada's relations with the United States, always high on the foreign policy priority list, focused in 2000 on movement across the border. In mid-December 1999, Montreal resident Ahmed Rassam was caught trying to cross into the United States with the makings of explosives. It was later determined that he was part of a plan to bomb Los Angeles airport around the New Year. Canada's immigration and refugee policies were attacked in several quarters in the United States, and unfavourable comparisons were drawn between the security of the northern and southern U.S. borders. The Canadian case was not helped by the ongoing fallout of the shiploads of illegal Chinese migrants that had landed in British Columbia in the summer of 1999, most seemingly intent on travelling on to the United States. Canada worked to assuage the U.S. concerns, for tightening controls along the Canada-U.S. border can have a devastating effect on the Canadian economy, given its reliance on the U.S. market.

This edition of the *Canadian Annual Review* marks a change in the way we present the organization of politics and public affairs in Canada. To this point, the *Review* has reported on public life in Canada under the headings of the federal government and the various provincial and territorial governments. Governance, and thus both politics and public policy, has increasingly exceeded these two levels of government, even within our federal structure. Perhaps of greatest significance to the largest number of Canadians is the importance of municipal government, particularly the influence of the large Canadian cities. Canada is one of the most heavily urbanized countries in the world, with 77 per cent of our people living in urban centres. What is more, changes in the global economy in the past thirty years have tended both to load ever-greater responsibility on cities for the provision of services and to create a network of so-called global cities at the heart of the world's economy. For the first time, in this edition of the *Review*, we report directly on municipal affairs. Because there are literally thousands of municipalities in Canada, and no central voice, the chapter is rather different from the others. Nevertheless, we are convinced that it is an important and timely addition to the volume.

The timeliness of a chapter on urban politics is seen in the three most significant events related to municipal governance in 2000. The first was a shocking reminder of both the importance of municipal responsibilities and the dangers of restricting the resources available for the provision of their services. In mid-May it became clear that the water supply of a small municipality in southwestern Ontario, Walkerton, had been contaminated with *E. coli* bacteria. With the death of several residents, questions were raised about the capacity of municipalities to manage their responsibilities, particularly in light of the provincial government's downloading of more and more responsibilities to municipalities without any concomitant resources. In the Walkerton case, this was exacerbated by cutbacks at the provincial level, so that there were no checks on what appeared to be local incompetence and, perhaps, malfeasance.

One attempt to cope with balancing the resources and responsibilities of Canadian municipalities has been to amalgamate smaller cities into single 'mega-cities.' Toronto was, perhaps, the most high-profile amalgamation, but it was by no means the only one. In 2000, the city-merger craze reached Quebec, and while the mergers were controversial wherever they were announced, none was more so than Montreal's. While the mayor was committed to 'one island, one city,' Montreal remained divided in a potentially explosive fashion, as the questions of suburban autonomy that are always raised by urban amalgamation overlapped in this case with French-English divisions. The Montreal merger, therefore, raised the most explosive issue in Quebec politics at a time when the fire seemed to have been going out of the language debates at the provincial level.

Finally, the disjuncture between governmental responsibilities and resources, which was most evident in the long-term deterioration of urban infrastructure, seemed to make a mark on the national political agenda in 2000. Following sustained lobbying by the Federation of Canadian Municipalities, the federal government announced a $2 billion urban infrastructure program in its February budget. The next month, an agreement was signed that might show the way forward for achieving the goals of such an investment. The Vancouver Agreement was an initiative of the federal Department of Western Economic Diversification. It was signed by the federal and provincial governments as well as the municipality of Vancouver, and recognized for the first time the importance of all levels of government coming together in an urban development plan.

The year 2000 is the sort of year Canadians should hope to have more of. Unlike in 1999, we went to war against nobody. The economy grew at a healthy rate, and at least one level of government had organized its finances in a way that generated surpluses and the possibility for renewed social spending. We were able to advance an international agenda aimed at providing security and future prosperity to others in the world. Our own politics never seemed particularly serious in 2000, with the high point reached when the Leader of Her Majesty's Loyal Opposition arrived at a press conference on a jet ski, and in a wet suit. Cocktail debate raged over whether this was the first year of a new millennium, or the last of the old. We will have to wait and see whether 2001 follows 2000's suit, or marks a new beginning for our country and its newly returned government.

ROBERT EVERETT

The federal government, politics, and national institutions

In search of a third successive victory at the polls, the Liberal Party under Jean Chrétien met the voters on 27 November. It was an early election. The Liberals were only three and a half years into the customary four- to five-year mandate earned in 1997. As is always the case when a government chooses to accelerate the electoral process, the timing was controversial. It was also understandable. In opinion polls taken before the election, the Liberals were far ahead of their main rivals. At the same time, the official opposition party, Reform, had barely finished the process of acquiring a new name and an even newer leader. Re-christened as the Canadian Conservative Reform Alliance, and now headed by former Alberta cabinet minister Stockwell Day instead of Reform founder Preston Manning, the party posed the biggest threat to the Liberals. Mr Chrétien and the Liberal campaign team were determined to engage the electorate before Mr Day was able to establish a winning persona and his re-branded party was in a position to challenge. The gamble paid off handsomely. The Liberals were returned to power for the third time in a row, and emerged with an increased majority in the House. Ironically, the twelve months of 2000 represented one of the most challenging and potentially debilitating periods that Mr Chrétien and his colleagues had faced since they were first elected in 1993. Consequently, the triumph at the polls was especially gratifying to the Liberals, and particularly galling to opposition parties. A decisive verdict also meant that the Liberals had defied prognosticators, including some uneasy backbenchers, who thought that the party would be punished for the early election call or for appearing to coast into the election on an outpouring of affection for former Liberal prime minister Pierre Trudeau, who had passed away in late September.

Although the Alliance managed to increase its share of the popular vote and seats, it failed to realize its core tactical objective of making genuine breakthroughs in parts of the country that had shunned Reform in elections past. This was not surprising in itself. The Alliance's principal strategic purpose was to 'unite the right' against the centrist Liberals. However, the refusal of the Progressive Conservatives under Joe Clark to merge with the Alliance or even enter into an electoral coalition on the right meant that precious votes were once again split. At least the Alliance managed to hold its own. The fortunes of the aloof Tories plummeted as the party only just retained official party status in the House after winning the minimum dozen seats.

Disappointing fates befell the other major parties contesting the election. Like the Progressive Conservatives, the New Democratic Party of Alexa McDonough just managed to keep its official party status in the wake of the latest in a lengthening string of electoral setbacks. The NDP lost eight seats in the process. An unexpected twist saw the Bloc Québécois shed a half-dozen seats in its Quebec bastion despite retaining its traditional share of the popular vote in the province. The Liberals, out of favour in Quebec since the constitutional crises of the 1970s and 1980s, captured a plurality of votes.

The Prime Minister justified an early election on the grounds that Canadians needed to be 'consulted' on how to apportion annual budgetary surpluses. The government was in an enviable position on this score. The Liberals had succeeded in ending a string of staggering annual deficits that were the legacy of Brian Mulroney–era Progressive Conservative governments. On the other hand, the Liberals' vaunted balancing act had been accomplished by sacrifice, steep spending cuts, and, some critics said, fiscal sleight of hand. It was possible that alternative visions of how to manage the government's finances would resonate with the electorate in the changed circumstances. Entering the election the Liberals extolled an approach to surpluses that involved a nearly proportional combination of debt reduction, tax breaks, and new spending. Parties on the left favoured more modest tax breaks (especially for the affluent) and enhanced social spending. On the right, the Alliance and Tories were predisposed to greater tax relief and faster debt repayments. In the end the ruling party succeeded in convincing voters to endorse its middle way.

According to Mr Chrétien, the campaign was also about fundamental political 'values.' Had this been borne out, the election might have provided the opportunity for the kind of sober, sustained discussion of the most pressing issues of the day that elections are supposed to promote. Yet the consensus among political savants was that the exercise was wholly unedifying and even unsavoury. The *Toronto Star*'s William Walker was left wondering what sort of mandate the Liberals had actually received after a campaign that was 'saturated with hostility and attacks' (28 November). One of the deans of national political punditry, Allan Fotheringham, used words like dismal and cynical to describe the unbecoming spectacle on the hustings (*Globe and Mail*, 28 November).

With so much of the focus falling on the run-up to the election, and the campaign proper, the spotlight was trained away from the House of Commons. The legislative calendar was thin and few major initiatives came to fruition. The Commons did provide the backdrop for a full budget in February and an unusual, scaled-down second version in October. On both occasions Finance Minister Paul Martin gifted taxpayers with dividends from the federal government's burgeoning surpluses while keeping spending on social programs in check. The lower chamber also echoed with bitter exchanges between cabinet ministers and opposition critics over a number of controversies, including the alleged mismanagement of programs by Human Resources Development Canada and the questionable ethics of Mr Chrétien's personal involvement in a bid to secure loans for businesses in his constituency.

Federal–provincial relations continued to be strained in the year 2000. Although provincial governments benefited from Ottawa's propitious financial position, there was never enough in the way of transfer payments to satisfy peevish premiers. The government also engineered passage of a 'clarity bill' aimed at setting the terms of any future referendum over the status of Quebec. The move was daring, and the achievement considerable, but the process was punctuated by strident and potentially wounding opposition. Ottawa and the provinces also squared off over aid to farmers stricken by drought and caught in an escalating global subsidy battle.

The policy arena was not quite entirely vacated. The issue that commanded the most attention during the year was health. Public opinion polls showed, consistently and significantly, that health care was highest on the list of concerns among Canadians. Health initiatives, including increased allocations to the provinces, featured prominently in the February budget. Despite injections of additional money, the federal government's role was the subject of an ongoing and often vitriolic debate between Ottawa and the provinces, and was the main topic at a first ministers' meeting held in September. In addition, the issue provided a soupçon of substance for an otherwise shallow campaign.

Election 2000

Early hints of a fall election

Members of the Liberal Party gathered in Ottawa for their biennial convention on 15 March. There was much to keep conference-goers occupied between policy sessions. The media had been obsessing about the timing of the next election, and the corridors were alive with speculative chatter. Although the Liberals appeared to be an unassailable electoral force, party members and pundits were also fixated on the question of who would lead the governing party during the next campaign.

The prominence of the leadership issue was remarkable given Mr Chrétien's estimable record of campaign victories since he had become leader. Would the Liberals really consider jettisoning a proven leader while they continued to enjoy such popularity? Still, on the eve of the convention, the *Globe and Mail* published the results of an Angus Reid survey indicating that two-thirds of Canadians believed that Mr Chrétien should step aside in favour of Finance Minister Paul Martin (13 March). Mr Martin was the apparent beneficiary of the Liberals' highly regarded economic achievements, and carried little of the baggage accumulated by Mr Chrétien over the course of three decades on Parliament Hill. Long thought to be the likely heir, Mr Martin publically denied rumours of his impatient quest to replace the Prime Minister. However, already tepid relations between the Martin and Chrétien camps cooled considerably when it was learned that key Martin advisers and supporters had met on 10 March at a suburban Toronto hotel to plot strategy for the convention. Alarmists suspected a coup was in the making, and the Prime Minister's most ardent defenders derided Mr Martin for his supposedly waning loyalty and integrity.

The Prime Minister was defiant. On the day the Angus Reid poll was released he did the rounds of newspaper editorial boards, taking the opportunity to express his determination to lead the party in the next election. Despite having reached sixty-five, the age of mandatory retirement for most citizens, he vowed that his political career had not ended. The Prime Minister's energetic performance during the convention week tied Mr Martin's hands. So skilful was Mr Chrétien in exploiting the convention to affirm his stature that doubt was cast on Mr Martin's future in government. Writing in the *Toronto Star*, Mark McKinnon recounted 'theories' that included the possibility that Mr Martin would leave Parliament in order to seek a senior position with the International Monetary Fund (14 March). For his part, Mr Martin vowed to remain in cabinet and seek re-election no matter what happened.

Against this backdrop, the Prime Minister commented on the eternally tangled history he shared with Mr Martin during a widely reported press conference on 19 March. In one of his typically convoluted pronouncements, Mr Chrétien noted that the finance minister has 'said he is supporting me. All the delegates said "four more years" so I'm feeling good. Those people are supporting me because I am here. When I am gone they might support Paul but that is a long time from now' (*Toronto Star*, 20 March). The Prime Minister also used the occasion to sketch the outlines of the Liberals' strategy in the next election. The coming campaign, he insisted, would end up in a fundamental debate over the country's destiny. Under his leadership, the Liberals would defend universal health care and other social programs against the 'Americanizing' tendencies of right-wing parties. Only his party could effectively protect the weakest members of Canadian society while managing a robust economy.

With the convention behind them, House and Senate Liberals gathered for their weekly Wednesday caucus meeting. It was at this point that backbench MPs were advised that the election call would come sooner rather than later. Party insiders were also quoted to the effect that the major substantive issue of the campaign would be health care. If anonymous sources were correct, the Liberals were planning to position themselves, in the coming fight about 'values,' not only against conservative parties at the federal level but against right-wing provincial governments, notably those of Ontario and Alberta, who were threatening to undermine the principles of the Canada Health Act through incremental privatization and de-listing of services.

Birth of the Canadian Conservative Reform Alliance

In February 1999 members of Reform voted their party out of existence, at least in principle. At the so-called First United Alternative Convention, and with the support of a smattering of Tories, party members embraced leader Preston Manning's dream of uniting conservative-minded partisans under a single electoral banner. Notwithstanding the urging of some of its members and the pleading of many right-wing media columnists, the federal Progressive Conservative Party remained officially and implacably hostile to the merger. The reluctance of the Tories was disappointing, but this stance did not deter Reformers from moving forward with the project. Without a partner the idea of unification seemed dubious somehow, but the process moved toward the formal establishment of a 'new' party. United Alternative supporters reconvened at a second conference held in Ottawa on 28 to 30 January. Once again the delegates enthusiastically endorsed the project. Mr Manning was delighted by this vindication, and received another boost when 75 per cent of those in attendance rejected a leadership review. But what name should the new party adopt? Members were offered five options: Reform Party of Canada (Reform), United Reform Alliance (United Reform), Canadian Reform Party of Canada Alliance (Canadian RFP Alliance), Canadian United Reform Alliance, and Canadian Conservative Reform Alliance Party. In a show-of-hands vote necessitated by a computer glitch, Canadian Conservative Reform Alliance Party won out over Canadian United Reform Alliance by a count of five hundred and twenty-nine to four hundred and one. Media wags could not help but notice that the winning name translated into a rather unfortunate acronym.

While the party's name was being sorted out, delegates also worked on its ideological orientation and identity. The convention floor was largely populated by Reform members, and it was unthinkable that party policy would be dramatically revamped. As a result, delegates approved platform planks in a 'Declaration of Policy' that affirmed the primacy of heterosexual marriage and traditionally defined families. Convention goers also endorsed the familiar neo-conservative dream of a flat tax on income (in this case, at a rate of 17 per cent). Other recognizable principles included the election of senators, the sanctity of private property, support for business and free trade, debt reduction, and a 'restoration' of provincial government powers. The party did vote to respect official bilingualism in a symbolic effort to distance itself from charges that Reform had been anti-Quebec and anti-bilingual, and adopted other objectives (such as affirming the principle of equalization payments to less well off provinces) that were closer to the current mainstream.

A referendum on the proposal concluded on 25 March. The creation of a new party had to be endorsed by at least two-thirds of the membership and a majority in each of the provinces and territories. Both tests were met. With 66.5 per cent of eligible voters casting ballots, 91.9 per cent of the delegates agreed to fold Reform and launch the successor. The party quickly applied to Elections Canada to formally change its name to the Canadian Conservative Reform Alliance on 27 March. Chief electoral officer Jean-Pierre Kingsley approved the change, prompting Tory leader Joe Clark to denounce the decision. Professing himself 'astonished' by the 'cavalier' nature of the decision, Mr Clark vowed to fight the abrogation of the term 'Conservative' in the federal court of Canada. The point became moot. The official short form of the name was Canadian Alliance, and the party was almost universally referred to as the Alliance.

A new day dawns

The next order of business for the Canadian Alliance was to select a leader. Founding leader Preston Manning was so closely associated with the ideological framework and evolution of Reform/Alliance that it was difficult to imagine another in his place. But militants had other factors to consider. For example, if their goal was to distance Alliance from Reform, it might be preferable to find a leader with roots outside of Reform's western base. Mr Manning was a known commodity, and he had presided over the birth of Reform and husbanded its most memorable successes. Yet a mature movement hoping to reach a higher plateau might need to consign Mr Manning's singular contributions to history. After years of exhausting effort Mr Manning was not fluent in French, a drawback that begged the question of whether or not a party hoping to broaden its appeal across a bilingual country could afford to keep a virtually unilingual leader. Heading into a leadership campaign it was certain that Mr Manning could count on the unstinting admiration of many longtime followers. It was less clear that he would measure up according to the cold political calculus demanded by the Alliance's heated-up aspirations.

Mr Manning did have momentum coming out of the convention that gave birth to the Alliance and he declared his intentions swiftly. Just one day after the party was created he stepped down from his posts as head of the party and leader of the official opposition in order to pursue a leadership bid. Control of the parliamentary party passed to veteran MP Deborah Grey. As Jean Chrétien quipped, Ms Grey became the fifth leader of the opposition he had faced. Ms Grey was the most seasoned member of the caucus, having been the first Reform MP ever elected, and she was one of the most respected champions of right-wing causes in the precincts of Parliament Hill.

Other candidates followed in short order. The first to challenge Mr Manning was the treasurer of the province of Alberta, Stockwell Day. A favourite of Alberta Premier Ralph Klein, and a seasoned advocate of the unite-the-right initiatives, Mr Day had served in the provincial legislature for fourteen years. Before his career in electoral politics, the Ontario-born, Quebec-raised hopeful had held a variety of jobs ranging from auctioneer to lay preacher. By the time Mr Day confirmed his candidacy, he had rounded up support from within the old Reform caucus (recruiting MP Jason Kenney to run his campaign), from rural parts of the west, and, it was conjectured, in the eastern half of the country that had proven so barren for Reform. Younger and more naturally suited to media performance than Mr Manning, Mr Day also appeared to possess personal attributes that might go down well with the public.

Joe Peschisilido, an Ottawa attorney, and Keith Martin, the Canadian Alliance MP for Esquimalt – Juan de Fuca in British Columbia, followed into the fray. A physician in private practice before entering the political ring, Dr Martin lacked visibility, caucus support, or realistic hopes. He billed himself as a social moderate and in that sense at least staked out relatively unoccupied ground within the Alliance. Next in line, or so it was thought, was Ontario MP Frank Klees. Mr Klees did everything but formally announce his bid, and boasted that he enjoyed significant support from within the Progressive Conservative cabinet and activist caucus of his home province. As an outsider to the Reform family, and a central Canadian, he seemed capable of personifying the unity bid, and appeared to have a plausible chance despite his relative obscurity. Yet on 4 April he announced that he would not proceed. Mr Klees said that he had been put off by the fact that one prospective donor had tied his campaign donation to a promise that Mr Klees would throw his support behind another (unnamed) candidate on the second ballot. It was an unlikely feint by Mr Klees in the first place, but an even more curious end to the dalliance.

Into the vacuum created by Mr Klees' reticence stepped the final credible candidate, Tom Long, who announced his candidacy on 27 April. Mr Long was best known as a principal architect of the winning electoral strategies employed by the Progressive Conservatives in Ontario. He was also in line to serve as Mr Klees' campaign chair. The entry of the Toronto-based lawyer hastened the departure of Mr Peschisilido. Mr Long became a controversial figure during the late stages of the campaign when his team claimed to have signed up the undoubtedly inflated estimate of 2,800 new party members in the Gaspé region of Quebec where support for sovereignty ran high and interest in Reform-Alliance was minuscule. This and other claims made by candidates led to calls for an audit of membership signing efforts, and enlivened a campaign often judged to be lackluster given the essentially undifferentiated outlooks of the contenders.

The first of three televised debates was held 30 May. The major competitors were joined on stage by a long-shot latecomer, John Stachow, a staunch proponent of complete income tax repeal. There were few sustained bouts of disagreement or disagreeableness during this and subsequent debates. The candidates were generally agreed on the pet right-wing topics they were asked to discuss. The contenders did cautiously express varying degrees of enthusiasm about the possibilities of more private health-care services to shift some of the burdens on the public system; but this proposition was broadly consonant with the thrust of right-wing thinking in North America. With health-care reform such a sensitive topic, talk of privatization was largely suppressed.

When the first-round tally of votes was concluded on 24 June, Mr Day emerged as the front-runner. With 44.2 per cent of the vote, he finished comfortably ahead of Mr Manning's 36.1 per cent and came very near to the required 50 per cent threshold. Mr Long placed third with 18.2 per cent. Dr Martin trailed badly, garnering just 1.4 per cent. Mr Stachow's total was infinitesimal. Adding to Mr Day's confidence was the fact that he was ahead in every province west of Quebec (with the exception of a narrow defeat in British Columbia). Mr Manning was shaken and puzzled by the results. He was left to cite low turnout by his supporters, together with glitches with the telephone voting system, as the chief reasons for his poor showing.

Although the top three candidates carried on to the next round, a rapid change of heart led Mr Long to withdraw. In doing so he endorsed Mr Manning. Mr Long's quick departure from the race not only narrowed the field, it changed the dynamic in Ontario. Whereas a significant number of Tory members of the provincial legislature publicly backed Mr Long while he was in the contest, only a handful declared for one of the two finalists. Interest had receded, a warning sign that the right-wing unity effort could be unravelling.

A special debate between Mr Manning and Mr Day was held in suburban Ottawa on 5 July. Mr Manning adopted a more offensive approach than in previous campaign appearances, but he could do little to stall Mr Day's ascent. On the second ballot, Mr Day cruised home with 63.3 per cent of the 114,000 votes cast. Mr Manning was gracious in defeat and pledged to stand by the new leader's side. Although a general election was in the offing, the new leader's priority was to find a seat in the House. The Prime Minister said he would act expeditiously if a sitting Alliance member resigned in order for Mr Day to run in a by-election. Mere hours after the Canadian Alliance leadership campaign had ended, Conservative leader Joe Clark challenged Mr Day to go head to head in the riding of Calgary Centre. Mr Day declined. Soon enough both leaders earned their entry into the House.

By-elections: enter the leaders

Three by-elections were held during the year. The first resulted when Progressive Conservative MP Charlie Power resigned the seat of St John's West in Newfoundland. The vacancy was filled on 15 May when Loyola Hearn of the Tories narrowly defeated the NDP's Greg Malone. The Tories retained the seat by a slim margin of 35.5 per cent to 34.4 per cent. The Liberal candidate attracted just 25 per cent of the vote, while the Canadian Alliance trailed with 4.1 per cent.

Writs were issued on 5 August for two important races involving leaders. Tory leader Joe Clark, an ex–prime minister, had been criticized for steadfastly refusing to seek a seat in the House following his election as party leader in 1998. After investing heavily in the effort to rebuild the party outside the House, he was finally ready to take his chances. With a feisty Stockwell Day so anxious to win a seat and appear in the House as leader of the official opposition, Mr Clark had little choice but to seek elected office again. The resignation of two sitting members paved the way for by-elections. In the British Columbia riding of Okanagan-Coquihalla, Jim Hart stepped aside for Mr Day. On the east coast, Mr Clark contested the riding of Kings-Hants in Nova Scotia after sitting MP Scott Brison resigned. The by-elections were scheduled for 11 September

The Liberals chose not to field a candidate in either by-election. The Tories did not run against Mr Day. Facing a field of seven rivals, Mr Day coasted to victory with 70.3 per cent of the votes cast in Okanagan-Coquihalla. The NDP candidate finished a distant second with 12.6 per cent, while the Green Party earned a credible (and to the New Democrats a potentially worrisome) 7.7 per cent. Mr Clark also won with ease. He took 53.4 per cent of the vote in Kings-Hants. The runner-up NDP banner holder finished well back with 27.1 per cent.

Fine-tuning the cabinet

On 18 September Foreign Affairs Minister Lloyd Axworthy announced that he was leaving politics to return to academic life. He was slated to take up a position at the Liu Centre for Global Studies at the University of British Columbia. This created an opportunity for Prime Minister

Chrétien to tinker with his cabinet before the election. On 16 October one-time federal cabinet minister Brian Tobin resigned as Liberal Premier of Newfoundland. The very next day Mr Tobin returned to the federal scene as minister of industry. His predecessor at the industry portfolio, Ottawa-area MP John Manley was moved to the foreign affairs slot vacated by Mr Axworthy. With Mr Tobin on board, it was decided that there was only room for one Newfoundland MP around the cabinet table. As a result, George Baker was unceremoniously returned to the back benches from Department of Veterans Affairs. Finally rewarded for long-time loyalty in August 1999, the long-time MP's stay in cabinet was brief. His precipitous demise reportedly deflated morale among many Liberal backbenchers. Mr Baker's place at Veterans Affairs was handed to Manitoba's Ron Duhamel, who was also named political minister for his province and assumed responsibility for western diversification and La Francophonie. The government leader in the Senate, Bernie Boudreau, replaced Mr Baker as secretary of state for the Atlantic Canada Opportunities Agency.

Crossing the floor: expulsions and defections

The year 2000 proved to be volatile when it came to the composition of the five caucuses. Some changes were voluntary. Others were not. Jake Hoeppner, who had been suspended from the Reform caucus in July 1999 over his opposition to the alliance campaign, sat as an 'Independent Reformer' for the first months of 2000. Finally, on 4 April, he declared himself a true independent. Another erstwhile Reform member, Jack Ramsay, also had his caucus privileges stripped in 1999 after being found guilty of sexual assault charges. On 6 April he declared himself an independent Canadian Alliance member. Two months later he dropped the Alliance tag altogether. The Canadian Alliance did pick up one new member in the person of Markham MP Jim Jones. The jump from the Progressive Conservatives was no surprise. Mr Jones' professed interest in a united right-wing alternative to the Liberals led to a steadily chilling relationship with Mr Clark, and he was suspended from the Conservative caucus on 5 July for insisting on trying to run as a 'Tory-Alliance' candidate in his constituency. Mr Jones switched to the Alliance on 14 September.

All of the other conversions advantaged the Liberals. The most noteworthy new Liberal was André Harvey. On 28 April he abandoned the Tories to sit as an independent. It was suspected that the member for Chicoutimi would ultimately drift across the floor, and he joined the

Liberals on 4 October. Two other Quebec MPs had already bolted the Tories by the time Mr Harvey finalized his decision. On 12 September Shefford MP Diane St-Jacques confirmed speculation when she cast her lot with the Liberals. Compton-Stanstead MP David Price followed Ms St-Jacques into the fold two days later. The Liberals welcomed another defector on 27 September when Rick Laliberte, the MP for Churchill in Saskatchewan, left the New Democratic Party. Commenting on Mr Laliberte's arrival in the Liberal ranks, Mr Chrétien urged others to move over from the NDP fold (or, more bluntly, suggested that the NDP should simply fold) to form a 'centre-left' coalition with real prospects of forming a government and instituting cherished social democratic policies.

The election call

The week of 16 October was packed with the kind of political manoeuvring that suggested nothing if not a prelude to an election. Mr Chrétien shuffled his cabinet (and in the process welcomed back a fierce campaigner in former Newfoundland premier Brian Tobin). Finance Minister Paul Martin unveiled a mini-budget on 17 October that accelerated the timetable for tax cuts announced in February. The week brought some bad news for the Liberals, too, when Auditor General Denis Desautels issued a damning report on the state of affairs at Human Resources Development Canada. Nothing, however, was going to derail plans for an election.

Mr Chrétien visited the Governor General at her official residence on 22 October to dissolve the House. Voters would head to the polls on 27 November. Mr Chrétien argued that Canadians needed to be consulted on fundamental political values and the more tangible question of how best to manage budgetary surpluses. Because the election call came on the conventional Christian Sabbath, the devout Mr Day waited until the following day to respond. Travelling around the potentially fertile electoral ground of eastern Ontario, Mr Day, who had promised to restore dignified debate to national politics, immediately attacked Mr Chrétien over his record of disdain for Parliament, softness on crime, and a spendthrift approach to the public purse. Other leaders criticized the Prime Minister for calling the election as a way of shoring up his legacy. In the words of Mr Clark, it was a 'vanity election' for Mr Chrétien (*Toronto Star*, 23 October).

At dissolution the party standings in the House were as follows: Liberals 161, Canadian Alliance 58, Bloc québécois 44, New Democrats 19, Progressive Conservatives 15, and independents 4.

The field forms

A total of 1,808 candidates were certified by Elections Canada for the 2000 campaign. Only the Liberals fielded candidates in all 301 ridings, with the NDP and Alliance running in 298 constituencies. The Tories contested 281 seats. The Bloc Québécois confined itself to the seventy-five ridings in Quebec. The total number of official parties stood at eleven (up one from 1997). In addition to the five parties represented in the House, the campaign was fought by the Green Party, the Canada Action Party (headed by former Liberal cabinet minister and Conservative leadership candidate Paul Hellyer), the Communist Party, the Marxist-Leninists, the Natural Law Party, and, making its debut, the Marijuana Party. In addition, twenty-eight candidates ran as independents. As always, the media spotlight fell almost exclusively on the five parties represented in the House at dissolution.

Parties and platforms

The Liberal platform was announced on 23 October. Entitled 'Sharing Opportunity' the document recalled the broad policy directives set out in the 1993 and 1997 editions of the so-called 'red book' of promises. In a slender twenty-six pages the party reiterated promises made in past campaigns or foreshadowed by various ongoing policy initiatives. There was one key plank that drew special attention from the media. The party said it would continue to embrace a 'balanced' approach to surpluses, but would no longer be bound by a strictly formulaic division between tax cuts, spending increases, and debt reduction. This was widely understood as a signal that tax cuts and debt payments would trump investments in social programs in the future.

The Alliance manifesto, 'A Time for Change,' was issued on 5 October. Organized around twelve key planks, the manifesto contained a controversial promise to introduce, over time, a flat tax of 17 per cent. Mr Day subsequently retreated somewhat from the seemingly unequivocal party line by insisting that further study would be conducted before this rate was extended to the 3 per cent of taxpayers earning in excess of $100,000. The Alliance also called for an increase in child-care benefits to $3,000 (approximately $600 more than the Liberals had promised in their 2000 budget) and the elimination of taxes altogether for low-income individuals and couples. Debt reduction would be sped up, with some three-quarters of any excess revenue used to pay down the debt. The party would also cut capital gains taxes as a way of stimulating the economy and would curtail market-distorting, politically motivated subsidies to businesses in various economic sectors and regions. The platform also promised a tougher approach to criminals, including and especially youthful offenders. Alliance also planned to increase military spending.

On 30 October the NDP unveiled its platform. The party emphasized the need to enrich funding for health care and the creation of a national plan for ensuring prescription drugs. The NDP also highlighted a number of environmental initiatives and pledged to build the nation's stock of affordable housing. In terms of future budgets, the NDP proposed to restrict tax cuts to low- and middle-income earners in contrast to the across-the-board approach favoured by the Liberals. There would be new premiums for the wealthy in what was dubbed by the media as a 'millionaire's tax' and higher rates for corporations earning 'excess profits' (*Globe and Mail*, 31 October). The cost of the NDP's spending plans was estimated at $30.3 billion annually. Although the party promised to make significant investments in health, education, and infrastructure, it was confident that there would be enough left in the kitty to pay down the national debt by up to $5 billion annually.

The Bloc Québécois platform was approved at a special conference on 21 October. The document ran to 177 pages. There were few references to the Quebec sovereignty project that was so fundamental to the Bloc's very existence, and the length and density of the document fostered a widespread perception that the party's strategy in this campaign pivoted around downplaying its most important political objective. The party's slogan was 'Quebec wins by voting Bloc,' but Gilles Duceppe noted that he and his colleagues were prepared to represent all Canadians if they were to form the official opposition. Like the NDP, the Bloc favoured income tax cuts concentrated on lower income earners. The party would also press for greater investment in social housing and the environment. In the case of the latter, the manifesto stressed the importance of protecting the St Lawrence River basin of Quebec. Not surprisingly, the Bloc wanted to grant Quebec greater freedom to act independently on the international stage. The Bloc had an anti-crime plank of its own: a call for legislation aimed at curbing the activities of biker gangs that had fostered so much violence within the province as a result of a protracted turf dispute.

The Progressive Conservatives rolled out their platform at intervals during the year. A draft document was issued on 12 April and reviewed at a policy convention in May. Highlights included calls for an elected Senate and run-offs in elections to ensure that successful candidates for seats in the Commons had earned a majority of votes in their ridings. In addition to parliamentary reform, the Tories pledged to institute tax cuts across the board while reinstating health-care funding to the provinces. The Progressive Conservatives' motto was 'Change You Can Trust,' an obvious play on the title of the Alliance manifesto.

On the hustings

Even before the campaign opened in earnest, the unfolding narrative focused on the debate over 'values.' As it happened, substantive issues were often obscured as the contest turned toxic at times. Ms McDonough and Mr Duceppe earned kudos for trying to maintain a focus on serious matters, and Mr Clark won high marks for experience and aplomb. Mr Chrétien wanted to take on the Alliance. He got his wish. With the support of the media and Mr Day, the election became a testy two-party showdown.

For Mr Day, the campaign began as an ordeal. He was dogged by protesters from the outset, and compounded his troubles with self-inflicted gaffes and policy reversals. The media made hay out of an early slip when Mr Day, trying to illustrate a supposed exodus of educated workers to the United States at a stop in Niagara Falls, wrongly likened the brain drain to the southerly flow of water from Lake Erie (it actually drains north). Mr Day retreated from an informal commitment to authorize national referenda over the signature of just 3 per cent of the electorate (a threshold he considered too low upon reflection) and the official party stance of instituting a flat tax of 17 per cent. Alliance supporters did not forsake the party, but the leader's confusing campaign offered scant incentive to voters inhabiting the supposedly broad centre-right spectrum.

The *Toronto Star*'s James Travers prophesied that the Liberals would play upon fears about the Alliance and Mr Day's views (24 October). He was proven right by events. Shortly after the campaign began the Prime Minister warned, dimly, that the Alliance would threaten the Charter of Rights. Other prominent Liberals joined in. For example, Immigration Minister Elinor Caplan complained that the Alliance sheltered bigots. Liberal ads homed in on Mr Day's supposed character flaws and perceived policy extremes. The Alliance leader's religious views (his Christian theology ran to creationism) also fuelled sceptical media scrutiny.

Mr Day was not above hurling barbs himself. For some commentators a defining moment of the campaign occurred on 17 November. The previous day Mr Chrétien admitted that he had contacted the president of the Business Development Bank of Canada on behalf of constituents seeking a loan for a leisure property that the Prime Minister had once partly owned. This was the latest revelation in a controversy that had dogged Mr Chrétien for months and even years. Mr Day's reaction was extraordinary. In what Paul Adams of the *Globe and Mail* described as a 'desperate' act that might have been propelled by increasingly distressing polling results (18 November), the Alliance leader implied that Mr Chrétien's behaviour in the affair might be in violation of the Criminal Code. Later Mr Day joined Mr Clark in calmly requesting a formal review of the Prime Minister's conduct by the government's ethics commissioner, Howard Wilson; but his original outburst may have cost him votes, especially when Mr Chrétien was cleared of conflict of interest at the end of the campaign by Mr Wilson.

The debates

There were four televised leaders' debates during the campaign. The final one, on 20 November, was sponsored by the National Action Committee on the Status of Women. Only Ms McDonough and Mr Clark appeared in person. The other leaders delegated lesser lights for the occasion. Ms McDonough and Mr Day debated alone on another occasion when abortion rights emerged as the key differential. The main debates were held in mid-campaign. All five of the parliamentary party leaders came together for nationally televised debates in French on 8 November and in English the following day.

Two leaders were overshadowed in the opening French-language debate. Ms McDonough continued to experience difficulties in her second language and was often shunted aside by her male counterparts. Mr Day also struggled. It was evident that he was not as fluent in French as advertised. The discussion on 8 November tackled issues such as health care (Mr Clark accusing the Prime Minister of 'betraying the tradition of Lester Pearson' over his handling of medicare in one ear-catching sound bite), but the debate also afforded an opportunity for other leaders to direct criticisms at Mr Chrétien for sundry economic, constitutional, and personal misdeeds.

The English-language debate of 9 November was a spirited affair.

Party preferences (%):
selected polls conducted by Environics

	3 November	9 November	18 November	24 November
Liberals	45	48	46	46
Canadian Alliance	29	26	23	24
Bloc Québécois	11	9	11	11
Progressive Conservatives	7	8	10	10
New Democrats	7	8	9	9

The leaders fenced over a number of questions and formed fleeting alliances as they alternately joined forces against the others (especially Mr Day or Mr Chrétien). The previous evening's exchanges over health care were clearly on Mr Day's mind. In anticipation of further attacks on Alliance's plans, he came prepared with a disallowed prop (a sign reading 'no two-tier health care,' which Mr Clark promptly snatched away), and a sound bite aimed at Mr Chrétien: 'Either call me a liar or pull those [negative] ads.'

Electoral outcome

On the eve of the election the Liberals were preparing to celebrate. There was a slim chance that the party would fail to earn a majority in the House (a hope that was harboured by those who fancied a minority government, such as the NDP), but there was no doubt that it would capture the most seats. The result was a majority. Strength in eastern and central Canada, especially in Ontario, sealed a victory that was, if anything, stronger than forecast. With 172 seats the Liberals had surpassed their showing in 1997.

The dimensions of the triumph were underscored by a number of results. The only party to field candidates in all 301 ridings, the Liberals were also alone in garnering significant support in every region of the country. Votes came hardest west of Manitoba. Even so, the party still harvested around 21 per cent of the popular vote in both Saskatchewan and Alberta. The best showing was in Ontario: more than 51 per cent of the vote, and all but two ridings, fell into the Liberal column in Canada's most populous province. The party also rebounded in the east, upping its total by seven in the Maritime provinces and Newfoundland. Unexpectedly, the Liberals fared well enough in Quebec to surpass the Bloc Québécois in votes if not seats. The Liberals lost but two cabinet ministers. Bernie Boudreau was defeated in New Brunswick after stepping down from the Senate to run for office. In British Columbia, Secretary of State (Asia-Pacific) Raymond Chan fell to an Alliance candidate after two terms in the House.

As the Liberal share attested, there was a decidedly regional cast to the returns. The Alliance came within a fraction of taking half of the votes cast in Saskatchewan and British Columbia and picked up 58.9 per cent of the vote in Alberta. In the Atlantic provinces the party failed to win a single seat, and Alliance candidates seldom received even 10 per cent of the vote. Overall, the Alliance did increase both its share of the popular vote and seat total. Nevertheless the result was bitterly disappointing for Mr Day and the party. The effort to reposition the movement under a new partisan banner and leader had not reaped the rewards expected. The biggest blow was the failure to make substantive headway in Ontario. Despite extraordinary exertions, the party picked up just two seats and its share of the popular vote rose fractionally, from just over 19 per cent to 23.6 per cent.

For the Progressive Conservatives the evening of the election began well enough. The Tories captured 30 per cent or more of the vote in Newfoundland and the Maritime provinces. The Atlantic tide receded quickly once results came in from Quebec, and the party failed to take more than 14.5 per cent of the vote in any other province while shedding eight seats overall. The Tory rebound in the east hurt the New Democrats, especially in Nova Scotia. The NDP had pockets of success across the country (notably in the northern territories, Saskatchewan, and loyal but widely scattered ridings elsewhere), but tumbled to a total of thirteen seats. The Bloc Québécois was stunned by the results in Quebec. While the party's share of the overall vote in the province actually rose two points to 39.9 per cent, it lost six seats to the Liberal resurgence.

The election offered a stark glimpse into the state of Canada's democracy. It was not a rosy picture. Other parties and independents accounted for 2.2 per cent of the vote. Just fifty-six women were elected in 2000, down from sixty after the previous general election. Voter turnout continued to fall. Only 62.1 per cent of those eligible to vote cast ballots in 2000 compared to 67 per cent in 1997 and 69.6 in 1993. Participation rates had fallen by more than 13 per cent since the high-water mark of 75.3 per cent recorded in the 1988 election, which featured a debate on free trade with the United States. In terms of provincial trends, turnout was highest in Prince Edward Island at 72.7 per

Party standings at election, 1993–2000

Party	2000	1997	1993
Liberals	172	155	177
Reform	66	60	52
Bloc Québécois	38	44	54
New Democrats	13	21	9
Progressive Conservatives	12	20	2
Independent	0	1	1
Total	301	301	295

Party share of popular vote, federal elections 1993–2000

Party	2000	1997	1993
Liberals	40.8	38.5	41.3
Reform / Alliance	25.5	19.4	18.7
Bloc Québécois	10.7	10.7	13.5
New Democrats	8.5	11.0	6.9
Progressive Conservatives	12.2	18.8	16.0
Independent / Other	2.3	1.6	3.6

cent and lowest in Newfoundland at just 57.1 per cent. The total was even lower in Nunavut and the Northwest Territories. Just 58 per cent of electors voted in Ontario. The downward trend had been the object of a special Royal Commission on Electoral Reform and Party Financing. Recommendations adopted after the commission reported in 1991 had done nothing to reverse a troubling spiral. Some commentators took smug satisfaction from the contrast between the disputatious presidential election in the United States and the more decorous proceedings north of the border. Others were chagrined by the tone of the campaign and the apathetic reaction of prospective voters.

Fund-raising and expenditures

In a gross way the results reflected campaign expenditures. The Liberals budgeted approximately $13 million for the campaign, a figure that was more than half of the expenditures of the other four major parties combined. The Alliance invested some $9 million, while the NDP had about $7 million at its disposal and the Progressive Conservatives about $5 million. The Bloc's campaign budget amounted to around $3 million.

The Liberals trumped all other parties in fund-raising during the election year. The party received donations totalling $21 million from 33,900 individuals and corporations. The Alliance trailed at $19.6 million (three times the amount raised in the previous year). The NDP total was $16.4 million (a figure that included donations at both the national and provincial levels). The Tories raised just $6.2 million and, as a result, saw their debt rise to $10.3 million from $7.2 million in 1999. The Bloc managed to raise $2.3 million during the year.

Aftermath

The healthy majority earned by the Liberals should have settled the question, at least for a spell, of who would lead the party in the near future. This was Mr Chrétien's third win in a row, and the 2000 results nearly matched the Liberals' impressive results of 1993. Yet the polls had barely closed when the media began to speculate again about the timetable for the Prime Minister's departure and the ascendency of Finance Minister Paul Martin. For the moment, however, Mr Chrétien was secure.

Contemplating the electoral results, Alliance leader Stockwell Day concluded that the electorate had decided 'not yet, not this time' for his party. His campaign performance was almost universally panned and top officials at party headquarters quietly resigned soon after the campaign ended. Mr Day was adamant about staying on as head of the Alliance and leader of the official opposition. He was forced to attend to more immediate, personal matters after the election, especially the resolution of a lawsuit brought against him by an Alberta attorney.

Questions about the future of the Bloc emerged soon after the polling results were finalized. The party had fought against the substance and principles of the Clarity Bill for more than a year, but had not been redeemed at the polls. Although the party suffered a shocking fall in its seat total, leader Gilles Duceppe insisted that the turnabout could be explained. He was convinced that the Bloc suffered a backlash from voters displeased with the municipal amalgamations organized by the ruling provincial Parti Québécois. As a result, the Bloc lost votes in key ridings around metropolitan areas. Overall the Bloc's vote total was actually up over 1997 by some 2 per cent. Although the party downplayed sovereignty during the campaign, or perhaps because of this fact, Mr Duceppe said it would be wrong to infer that the results could be interpreted as a setback for the sovereignist movement. Like other opposition party leaders, Mr Duceppe pledged to stay on in his post.

After Rick Laliberte bolted the NDP for the Liberals, Prime Minister Chrétien mused about the cloudy future of social democracy in Canada and the desirability of a grand 'centre-left' coalition. Mr Chrétien might have been overly bold to predict the demise of the NDP, but there was little doubt that the election results had a sobering impact on the traditional party of the left in Canada. Caucus was trimmed to the point where the NDP's status as a recognized party hung by a thread, and the poor showing emboldened critics. Media pundits assayed various explanations about why a proud heritage had eroded. Writing in the *Toronto Star*, Richard Gwyn opined that 'trade unionists in Ontario and the West [where Reform/Alliance had made inroads] quit the NDP because they felt it had become so politically correct it no longer represented the interests of workers' (8 December). Academics tended to point to a fundamental shift in the political spectrum, beginning with the advent of neo-conservatism, which had stranded social democracy at the edge of the political space. The NDP had recognized such 'new realities' when it launched an (unsuccessful) effort to woo small business in 1998.

Although her leadership was faulted, Alexa McDonough was brave in defeat and upbeat about the NDP's prospects. Her plan was to stay on until the next national convention in the autumn of 2001, if not longer. This did not stop party insiders like Buzz Hargrove of the Canadian Auto Workers and veteran MP Lorne Nystrom from averring that the party's prospects would be enhanced with a new standard bearer. They and others also argued that the NDP should return to its roots. It was furthermore suggested that the party should reach out to younger activists galvanized by the anti-globalization movement or find a new name.

The dismal outcome for the Tories did nothing to dispel speculation about the future of the party or end talk about a merger with Alliance. However, in an interview with the Canadian Press, Joe Clark resisted any talk of a merger that narrowed the PCs to a 'right-wing' coalition or blended fiscal and social conservatism (*Toronto Star*, 9 December). These sentiments were reprised by former prime minister Brian Mulroney, who insisted that only a 'socially progressive' party of the right would attract support in the eastern half of the country (*Globe and Mail*, 11 December). Mr Clark did not disclose his plans, but advised the party that they should not count on him to be at the helm two years hence.

National institutions

Senate

The Liberal majority in the Senate continued to climb as Mr Chrétien appointed six more of his party adherents to the upper house. The first two appointments were announced on 7 March. A vacant Alberta seat was given to Tommy Banks, an award-winning musician and television performer. He was joined by Saskatchewan's John Wiebe. A one-time lieutenant-governor of his native province, Mr Wiebe, best known for his involvement in farming circles, had also served two terms in the Saskatchewan legislature.

The month of June brought a total of four more appointments on two separate dates. On 9 June Mr Chrétien tapped Jane Cordy, an educator and local politician, to represent Nova Scotia in the red chamber. Also entering the Senate that day was Raymond Squires of Newfoundland. At the age of seventy-three, Mr Squires would be eligible to serve for less than two years. Later in the month another appointment went to an individual nearing the mandatory retirement age of seventy-five when former broadcaster Betty Kennedy was named to the Ontario seat. That same day Raymond Setlakwe, a lawyer and entrepreneur based in Quebec, was elevated to the Senate.

Up until the late autumn a smattering of five independents faced an ever-growing majority of Liberals and a dwindling band of Progressive Conservatives in the Senate. The opposition party in the House, the Canadian Alliance, had never had a senator. The party that favoured senatorial elections finally staked a claim in the Senate when Jerry St Germain, a former MP, switched allegiance from the Tories. On 29 June he declared his independence, and four months later he cast his lot with the Alliance. With this change, and the appointments made during the year, the party standings in the Senate at the end of December were as follows: Liberals fifty-seven; Progressive Conservatives thirty-five; independents five; and Canadian Alliance one.

Auditor General

As he prepared for his final months in office, Auditor General Denis Desautels prepared a three-volume regular report to Parliament. The December release of the third volume was postponed to February 2001 because of the election. The first report was presented on 11 April. In it Mr Desautels reviewed progress made by the government in improving the quality of services to Canadians. Although many departments had lived up to their commitments, others were lagging. In its 12 April coverage of the report the *Ottawa Citizen* highlighted findings that the government's scientific research credits, which cost approximately $2 billion annually, had done little or nothing to boost Canada's relatively poor international standing in research and development. Companies and individuals had produced just $55 million in concrete results out of this investment. The Royal Canadian Mounted Police was faulted for poor management of its crime laboratories and a backlog of forensic investigations. Among other issues emphasized by the *Ottawa Citizen* were the following:

- antiquated and overly complicated management systems that were impeding renewal of an aging and depleted public service;
- insufficiently rigorous screening of immigrants, some of whom entered the country with criminal backgrounds or infectious diseases;
- an abysmally managed and meanly funded educational system for aboriginal children.

The second volume, issued 17 October, highlighted problems at Human Resources Development Canada. The Auditor General had previously testified on HRDC issues before a Commons committee and authorized a special audit of the agency. In his foreword to the volume, Mr Desautels wrote: 'I find our audit observations in Chapter 11 on grants and contributions at HRDC disturbing in the light of good public administration principles. Our work confirmed the findings of the Department's 1999 internal audit, and more. We found breaches of authority, improper payments, limited monitoring, and approvals that had not followed established procedures. Beyond the immediate corrective action it has taken, HRDC needs to make today's extraordinary effort tomorrow's routine and fundamentally change its day-to-day approach to the delivery of grants and contributions.' The report identified violations of government contract rules at the Canadian International Development Agency (responsible for $1.8 billion annually), with irregularities reported in close to half of the contracts examined. Mr Desautels also expressed concern about the process of privatizing Canada's major airports. Ottawa had been too lax, according to the report, when it came to ensuring that the transfer to local authorities resulted in solid business plans (*Ottawa Citizen*, 18 October).

Economic indicators and issues

Economic indicators

Despite worrisome trends in some sectors of the economy, Canada continued to compare well with other industrialized nations. Gross domestic product rose by 3.3 per cent during 2000. The economy continued to expand, but at a lower rate of growth than in previous years. Overall growth was reflected in higher employment. For the fourth straight year, and with the exception of Saskatchewan and Newfoundland, the national economy produced more jobs. Unemployment ranged from a high of 7.1 per cent to a low of 6.6 per cent during the year, and ended at 6.8 per cent in December, the same level as January 2000. Job creation was greatest in the service sector. The manufacturing sector continued to grow, but again at a slower rate than in 1999 (2.7 per cent compared to 5.9 per cent). Building permits, key measures of economic activity and consumer confidence, reached their highest monetary value since 1989.

These relatively impressive results were partly attributable to near-record surpluses in merchandise trade. Exports exceeded imports by $54 billion for the year. The situation was particularly favourable for energy exporters. Manufacturers of machinery and high-technology equipment also enjoyed a solid year, even though manufacturing slowed dramatically as the year unfolded. Exports into the vital U.S. economy were up by 16.2 per cent despite a slowdown south of the border. Growth translated into higher inflation. In December the consumer price index jumped to 3.2 per cent, the highest month-over-month increase recorded since December 1990. The annual average of 2.7 was also the highest recorded since 1990.

Budget 2000

On 29 February Finance Minister Paul Martin rose to deliver his annual budget speech. A beaming Mr Martin declared that individual Canadians were entitled to their share of budget surpluses as he announced a series of tax reduction initiatives. The biggest news was the restoration of full indexation for personal income tax rates and the end of so-called 'bracket creep.' Tax brackets had not been cushioned against inflation increases since the Mulroney government lifted protection in 1985. Mr Martin also announced that the middle tax rate would be reduced from 26 to 23 per cent over five years, with the first planned reduction, to 24 per cent, to take effect on 1 July. At the same time, the floor for middle and upper tax rates were increased to $35,000 and $70,000. The surtax imposed on income up to $85,000 was eliminated. Additional taxes on income above $85,000 would be phased out more gradually. There were also bonuses for corporations in the tax package. The most highly taxed companies would see their rates cut to 21 per cent from 28 per cent over five years. The tax on capital gains was dropped from 85 per cent to 66 per cent.

In addition to lower rates, the government introduced a number of related measures. The first $8,000 in earnings was fully exempted from tax. Child tax benefits were set to rise to $2,400 over five years. The annual deduction for families with children with disabilities went from $7,000 to $10,000, while the general disability tax credit was boosted by $500 per year. Parental leave was extended to up to a full year. The proportion of foreign content in registered retirement savings plans was increased to 25 per cent in 2000 and 30 per cent starting in 2001.

Transfers to the provinces were also increased, with an infusion of $2.5 billion for post-secondary education and health care. The equalization fund for provinces with lower revenue would be raised by approximately $500 million in fiscal 2000–1. Ottawa would also set aside $1 billion for infrastructure projects over six years, with nearly half released in the first twenty-four months of the program.

In the latest round of initiatives in research, Ottawa pledged $900 million to universities for the creation of two thousand endowed chairs through the Twenty-first Century for Research Excellence program. A similar amount was invested in the Canada Foundation for Innovation. Post-secondary students or their parents would be able to claim a $3,000 exemption on scholarships and bursaries, up from $500. As always, Mr Martin tucked some of the surplus into a contingency reserve. The figure for 2001 was $3 billion, an amount that would likely be used to pay off debt given positive revenue forecasts.

Although taxes and education were high on the billing, Mr Martin (and later his cabinet colleagues) insisted that health spending was the real 'priority.' Opponents found the Liberals wanting on this score. Within the precincts of Parliament Hill other parties called the new investment a pittance. Provincial premiers also complained, and there was sharp disagreement with the government of Ontario in particular.

The mini-budget

In the final run-up to the election, Mr Martin's customary autumn financial statement before the House finance committee was transformed into a 'mini-budget' delivered on the floor of the House on 17 October. Amid rampant speculation that an election would soon be called, members of the opposition upbraided the Liberals for dangling goodies in front of taxpaying voters. In the main, Mr Martin was offering an accelerated timetable for the distribution of surplus-derived dividends. Among the highlights of the package announced by the finance minister was a reduction in tax rates for lower income earners from 17 to 16 per cent beginning 1 January 2001. For middle income earners the rate would drop to 22 per cent from 24 per cent. The 29 per cent rate for upper-middle income earners was dropping to 26 per cent. Soaring energy costs had become a hot political issue, and the government chipped in a $250 rebate for less affluent consumers. Capital gains taxes were dropped to 50 per cent from 66 per cent, and the surtax was finally and fully eliminated for all taxpayers, including those earning in excess of $85,000. When combined with cuts announced in February, the accelerated tax-cutting initiative exceeded $100 billion. Mr Martin expected annual surpluses of more than $10 billion for the next five fiscal years. The debt would also be reduced at a faster pace.

The mini-budget received mixed reviews. It was difficult for conservative politicians and pundits to be parsimonious in their praise for the principle behind tax reductions. As a result, they complained about the pace or boasted that the centrist Liberals had finally seen the light.

The Bank of Canada

The search for a replacement for retiring Bank of Canada governor Gordon Thiessen ended on 20 December with the appointment of David Dodge as his successor. In some respects the new governor was something of a surprise. Mr Dodge was the first individual from outside the bank to be named governor. Although he left the post of deputy minister of health to move to the bank, Mr Dodge was better known for his work as deputy minister of finance. At the finance department he served as the principal adviser to Paul Martin. It was anticipated that the new governor would continue to be vigilant in monitoring and addressing inflationary pressures.

Shake-out in mass media and telecommunications

The year 2000 witnessed major changes in the ownership structure of Canada's mass media and telecommunications systems. A series of transactions resulted in the creation of two giant media enterprises and consolidation elsewhere in the industry. The changes in Canada followed on the heels of the 'convergence frenzy' in the United States that had also produced several giant media conglomerations.

The two key players were CanWest Global, owned by the Asper family of Winnipeg, and BCE Enterprises, the holding company that had grown on the foundation of the Bell Canada telephone monopoly. Early in the year CanWest finalized a major restructuring resulting from the acquisition of television assets from Western International Communications (controlled by Shaw Communications, a smaller but ambitious player in the industry). The deal, overseen by the Canadian Radio-television and Telecommunications Commission, involved a series of trades between CanWest and WIC together with a CRTC-ordered investment of $84 million in television programming. One result of these transactions was to create a third over-the-air national television network under the Global brand. On 25 February BCE Enterprises launched a successful bid for CTV, Canada's other private television network. In a deal that cost BCE some $2.3 billion, BCE acquired CTV plus a sufficient number of speciality cable channels to become the largest television enterprise in the country.

Meanwhile, two major newspaper corporations announced plans to sell off their holdings. In January the storied Thomson Corporation revealed that it would shed all of its newspapers, except the prestigious *Globe and Mail*, in order to concentrate on new media. A more stunning announcement came on 25 April. That day Hollinger Incorporated, controlled by media magnate Conrad Black, hung a for-sale sign on three hundred Canadian daily and weekly newspapers (along with papers in the United States and elsewhere). On 31 July CanWest reached agreement to purchase thirteen of Hollinger's domestic daily newspapers together with a number of weeklies, trade publications, and Internet portals. Hollinger retained a half-interest in the *National Post* (Mr Black's pet project) and, for the time being, several other holdings. The deal was valued at $3.5 billion. There were ironic partisan overtones to the deal. Mr Black was a constant critic of the Chrétien Liberals and had founded the *National Post* as a strident right-wing editorial voice. Mr Asper was closely connected to the Liberals and Mr Chrétien, even serving as leader of the Manitoba wing of the party in the past.

Not to be outdone, BCE entered into negotiations with Thomson. In a deal cemented on 15 September, BCE would gain control of just over 70 per cent of the shares in a new entity (eventually dubbed Bell Globemedia), with the remaining stock held by Thomson Corporation and the personal investment company of Ken Thomson. For an investment of $385 million Mr Thomson would continue to chair the board of the *Globe and Mail*. As in the case of the CanWest-Hollinger settlement, the BCE-Thomson venture included special channels and an assortment of Internet companies. The merger was subject to CRTC authorization. In a December ruling the commission required that Bell Globemedia invest some $230 million (roughly 10 per cent of the transaction) in its broadcast holdings. Approximately 60 per cent of the total was to be funnelled into programming, the vast majority commissioned from domestic independent production companies. Bell Globemedia was also obliged to auction off Sportsnet, one of Canada's two main speciality sports channels.

Yet another takeover was announced on 13 September. In this instance the diversified media company Quebecor gained control of the cable company Groupe Videotron. In February the Videotron board had accepted a bid from Toronto-based Rogers Cable to sell its cable interests in the province of Quebec. The transaction, if finalized, would have given Rogers a sea-to-sea cable network. Quebecor had other ideas. In an alliance with the powerful financial institution Caisse Populaire it upped the ante for Videotron's purchase and consummated a deal worth $4.9 billion.

All of this reawakened concerns about the degree of concentration in Canadian media ownership, which had been the subject of a special Senate committee in 1970 and a royal commission in 1981. Critics of the transactions decried the unprecedented degree of concentration. Many renewed calls for a special government inquiry. Mark Kennedy in the *Ottawa Citizen* reported that there was concern among members of the Liberal Party (4 August). He quoted from a letter to Prime Minister Chrétien in which Ontario MP Dan McTeague asked, 'Is this kind of media oligopoly the place where we, as a society, want to end up?' Convergence also handed the CRTC a thorny public-policy issue. Among BCE's assets was Bell ExpressVu, a direct-to-home satellite distribution system that was growing in subscribers. In a submission to the CRTC, Rogers Communications argued that BCE's acquisition of CTV and its related cable services violated the spirit behind a rule against the simultaneous ownership of content providers and distributors (29 August). Rogers asked that the CRTC rescind the policy and allow conventional cable operators to acquire speciality channels. If the CRTC agreed, it would undoubtedly lead to even more concentration within the broad media sector. The CRTC's review of the policy was expected to conclude in 2001.

Bailout for NHL teams?

Just three days after announcing a subsidy plan for Canadian-based National Hockey League teams, Industry Minister John Manley was forced to drop the idea amid a growing furor over handouts to the affluent. The move was well intentioned. In the previous decade two Canadian teams had relocated to the United States, and four of the remaining six clubs were finding it difficult to compete with player contracts escalating and the dollar stubbornly pegged at an unfavourable exchange rate. Ottawa Senators owner Rod Bryden, a former national president of the Liberal Party, had been vociferously pleading for government assistance for many months. On 18 January Mr Manley offered to provide up to $20 million in overall aid to teams as part of an aid package. There was a catch, however. Provinces and municipalities would also have to contribute toward the subsidy. The other levels of government balked, and talk-show lines lit up with callers pillorying the government for ignoring the needs of ordinary Canadians in order to support wealthy sports proprietors. Even Liberal MPs were publicly critical of the government. In the face of this opposition, the reversal came swiftly. A chastened Mr Manley tried to salvage the situation by emphasizing that the government had listened to the voices of the people.

Federal–provincial relations

The Clarity Bill

On 13 December the federal government introduced bill C-20, 'An Act to give effect to the requirement for clarity as set out in the opinion of the Supreme Court of Canada in the Quebec Secession Reference.' The legislation was a follow-up to the 1997 ruling by the Supreme Court on the matter of how a referendum on Quebec sovereignty should be conducted. The Parti Québécois government in Quebec continued to insist that the bill was irrelevant, and that the question of the province's future would be decided by the popular will rather than through legal avenues or political manoeuvring. Inside Ottawa, opposition came from the Bloc Québécois and most of the Progressive Conservative caucus.

The bill moved quickly during the preliminary stages. On 28 February, in an effort to stymie the government, the Bloc introduced 1053 separate amendments to the bill in a bid to delay passage. In the event, the House was compelled to vote on, and defeat, 400 amendments in recorded votes. The government did accept two amendments sponsored by the NDP that would grant aboriginal organizations a say in determining the federal government's response to a referendum.

The bill passed the House on 15 March. The vote was lopsided at 208 to 55. Members of the Bloc Québécois taunted Liberal cabinet ministers as the votes were recorded, and Bloc leader Gilles Duceppe prophesied that the Liberals would pay dearly for their audacity. The spotlight turned to the Senate, where there was concern that passage would not be smooth. Anxiety was provoked by rumblings from some Liberal senators that the bill was nothing more than a 'blueprint' for secession. The final outcome was closer than in the House, and a handful of Liberal senators abstained, but the government prevailed by a vote of 52 to 34 (29 June).

Health-care accord

The year was punctuated by federal-provincial debates over health-care principles and funding. In early January, the media covered a crisis in emergency care across the country. Partly owing to an influenza outbreak, emergency wards filled to overflowing and ambulances were turned away as hospitals struggled to keep up. Against this backdrop, the February budget set aside additional monies for provincial health care. The premiers were dissatisfied. Collectively and individually they petitioned for a greater share of federal surpluses to help defray the growing costs of health care. Pressure mounted for a special summit on the issue. For most of the year Prime Minister Chrétien rebuffed these overtures, and insisted that Ottawa had done more than its share to help revive an ailing health system.

Ontario Premier Mike Harris was prominent among critics of the federal government. Another foe, Alberta's Ralph Klein, took action that appeared to challenge basic tenets of the Canada Health Act. On 2 March his government introduced legislation that would permit more private, for-profit 'clinics' for surgery and overnight stays. Federal Health Minister Allan Rock was in the forefront of those warning the Alberta government away from the scheme, which opponents charged would pave the way for 'queue jumping' by those who could afford private care. Mr Rock's threats were vague enough to leave Mr Klein wondering if the federal government was sufficiently serious to contemplate imposing sanctions against Alberta, as had happened in the past for violations of the Act. The Prime Minister said that Ottawa would withhold comment until the legislation passed. Following a face-to-face encounter between Mr Chrétien and Mr Klein on 23 October the Prime Minister insisted that he 'did not blink' when the topic came up. In the event, and to the disappointment of public-health-care advocates, Ottawa did not act when the province's legislation was approved.

Finally, a first ministers' meeting was arranged for 11 September. The gathering ended with a new accord on funding. Ottawa would increase health-care transfers from $15.5 billion in 2000–1 to $18.3 billion in 2001–2. This figure would rise to a minimum of $21 billion by the year 2005–6. In addition, the provinces would receive $2.3 billion for infrastructure, health information technology, and primary-care initiatives. These changes would require parliamentary approval. With an election looming, the legislation was drafted and accelerated through the approval process. Unhappy with the outcome, but reluctant to publically refuse the injection of new money, many of the premiers described the accord as a welcome but partial first step. Meanwhile the federal government was criticized for seeming to surrender over the issue of its involvement in health care. The provinces were required to publish annual reports on health-care expenditures, but this fell far short of direct accountability to Ottawa.

It was clear that the accord had not fully resolved the ongoing debate. Indeed, as John Ibbitson reported in the *Globe and Mail*, the conference was a likely prelude to an even more acrimonious debate over the broader issue of equalization (12 September). The debate over health care appeared to overshadow an attempt by the wealthier provinces to limit equalization payments to the 'have-not' provinces, an initiative that would test the traditional tenets of federalism.

Major policy fields

A thin legislative agenda

The Liberals were once again targeted by opposition parties for taking a desultory approach to governance. Many of the bills introduced since the autumn of 1999 were allowed to lapse when the House was prorogued before the election. Writing for the Canadian Press, Nahlah Ayed compiled an inventory of stranded bills (21 October). Among the most prominent legislative initiatives that were cut short were bills to amend the Young Offenders Act (Bill C-3), revamp the Citizenship Act (Bill C-16, which was stalled in the Senate), provide consumers with greater protection in dealings with financial institutions (Bill C-38), change immigration rules (C-31), deter cruelty to animals and increase penalties for disarming police officers (C-17), and stiffen the penalties for stalking and home invasion as well as clarify the role of ministerial review in the case of unlawful convictions (C-36). On 28 September Human Resources Development Canada Minister Jane Stewart introduced Bill C-44, which was intended to relax employment insurance regulations (or make them 'less punitive' in the words of the minister). Critics charged that the move was a pre-election sop to Atlantic Canada's seasonal workers, who had found it more difficult to obtain benefits under reforms approved in 1996.

Several important environmental initiatives also came to naught. The government's long-awaited Species at Risk Act (Bill C-33, read for the first time on 11 April) had not moved out of the committee stage by the election. This was also the fate of the Marine Conservation Areas Act (Bill C-8). Although the bill, which would create protected areas in the Great Lakes and the coasts of all three oceans, surfaced in October 1999, it did not proceed to final reading. One of the last new bills to reach the floor of the House before dissolution was C-46, an act creating the Canada Foundation for Sustainable Development Technology. The bill, designed 'to address climate change and air quality issues' through technological innovations, did not reach committee stage.

Some pieces of legislation were rushed through on the eve of the election. On 19 October the House approved legislation sealing the health-care accord between Ottawa and the provinces signed in September (Bill C-45). Earlier, on 6 October, approval was given to a bill granting benefits to civilian veterans of the Second World War such as merchant mariners (C-41). During the year the House also passed other government bills, including the following:

- Bill C-5, which established the Canadian Tourism Commission
- Bill C-18, containing amendments to the Criminal Code raising the maximum sentence for impaired driving causing death to life imprisonment
- Bill C-19, the Crimes Against Humanity and War Crimes Act, which formally ratified the Rome Statute setting up an International Criminal Court

Airline industry rules

When Air Canada completed its controversial takeover of Canadian

Airlines in 1999 the federal government promised to ensure that the new entity would not exploit its near monopoly over domestic service. Transport Minister David Collenette introduced legislation on 17 February. Under the terms of Bill C-26 the Competition Bureau and the Canadian Transport Agency would enjoy increased powers to monitor and police monopolistic practices. The CTA would be permitted to launch independent investigations of airlines practices without awaiting customer complaints, while the Competition Bureau would enjoy greater anti-monopolistic powers. The thrust of the legislation was to ensure that Air Canada complied with promises to divest some regional carriers and do nothing to block access by other domestic airlines to terminal space and routes. Failure to comply could result in jail terms of up to five years and fines of up to $10 million. Mr Collenette also promised to monitor the situation carefully and authorize more foreign competition within Canada if domestic companies did not establish a foothold. The House committee on transport added an amendment to establish an air-travel complaints commissioner. As Heather Scoffield and Oliver Berton reported in the *Globe and Mail*, these initiatives were widely hailed by consumers and competitors (18 February). Even Air Canada itself welcomed the ensemble of policies. The bill was passed by the House on 16 June.

Licensing of the Canadian Broadcasting Corporation

In 1999, the Canadian Radio-television and Telecommunications Commission launched a process leading up to the renewal of the licence of the English- and French-language services of the Canadian Broadcasting Corporation. Although the CBC's legislated mandate meant that the CRTC could not suspend its licence, there were hints during the hearing phase of the renewal that strict conditions would be attached. By mid-December the CBC had been briefed on the outline of the CRTC's thinking. Executives of the corporation, including newly installed president Robert Rabinovitch, were allegedly upset by what they heard. Heather Scoffield of the *Globe and Mail* wrote that the two agencies appeared to be on a collision course, and that the CRTC was planning to add stipulations that the CBC felt were antipathetic, intrusive, and thoughtless (6 January).

The CRTC's decision was announced on 6 January. The public broadcaster was ordered to institute a number of changes that were at odds with the CBC's internal planning. By 2002, said the CRTC, the corporation would have to stop airing non-Canadian feature films in prime time. Starting as soon as practical, the CBC was expected to provide five hours of regional public affairs and entertainment fare each week (rising to six hours by 2002). The CRTC also ordered a reduction in professional sports programming and an increase in the coverage of amateur sports. French-language television would be responsible for delivering additional arts programs, while the English-language services would have to boost their regional content. The CRTC blocked the CBC's plans to reintroduce a modest amount of advertising on radio but, at the same time, required that the corporation invest funds to boost the quality of radio services. In one of the few welcome decisions, the CBC's all-news and public-affairs cable services, Newsworld and Le Réseau de l'information, were granted fee increases of eight and ten cents respectively.

Elements of the CRTC's decision pleased private broadcasters, especially the elimination of blockbuster imported films and the reduction in professional sportscasts. Initially the CBC and its supporters were irate. Mr Rabinovitch blasted the commission for saddling the CBC with costly new responsibilities for regional broadcasting while attempting to eliminate revenue from popular programs. The corporation estimated that the CRTC's conditions would cost $250 million over the seven-year renewal period. 'We will not ignore the CRTC,' said the president, 'but when I say ignore I didn't say implement' (*Globe and Mail*, 7 January). The CBC had already given an undertaking to lessen its professional sports programs. Under the circumstances, Mr Rabinovitch was inclined to take all voluntary measures 'off the table.' Anticipating a hostile reaction, the CRTC ruling advised the CBC to make better use of available funds and improve its strategy for marketing abroad.

Same-sex legislation

In 1999 the Supreme Court ruled that the Ontario government had wrongly denied social and taxation benefits to cohabiting same-sex couples. This ruling resulted in the federal government revisiting its own legislation. On 11 February Justice Minister Anne McClellan introduced a comprehensive act 'to modernize the Statutes of Canada in relation to benefits and obligations.' In essence, the changes would end discrimination against homosexual couples.

Bill C-23 had a rocky ride to passage. Critics on the opposition benches and within the ranks of the ruling Liberal Party charged that the legislation would undermine the institution of marriage and weaken the family. Meanwhile delegates to the Liberal Party's March policy convention pointedly rejected same-sex marriages. These concerns were addressed in an amendment approved at the committee stage. As a result, the legislation went forward with a clause stipulating that nothing in the legislation would impinge on the legal meaning of marriage as the 'lawful union of one man and one woman to the exclusion of all others.' Despite this codicil, seventeen Liberals broke with their party to join the Canadian Alliance and some Conservatives to vote against the bill. The measure passed by a still-comfortable majority of 174 to 72, with the NDP and Bloc solidly behind the initiative. Time allocation was imposed on debate by the government to ensure passage. The Senate approved the measure on 14 June.

The passing of Pierre Trudeau

On 28 September former prime minister Pierre Elliott Trudeau passed away at his home in Montreal at the age of eighty. Canada's fifteenth prime minister succumbed to prostate cancer and Parkinson's disease. Mr Trudeau's passing was announced by his surviving children (son Michel having predeceased him in 1998) shortly after they had revealed his illness. A sombre parade of citizens paid their respects as the former prime minister lay in state on Parliament Hill in the bleak days before his funeral. Others remembered him in more private ways. Perhaps no death had ever moved the Canadian public to such a profound degree.

For the media, it took a torrent of words to do justice to the extraordinary life led by Mr Trudeau and to assess his impact on Canadian politics. He arrived in Ottawa in 1965 along with his close friends Jean Marchand and Gérard Pelletier. All were passionate foes of Quebec nationalism, but Mr Trudeau, schooled in the teachings of Lord Acton, was best able to articulate the theory and practice of federalism. He soon emerged as the dominant of these 'three wise men' by virtue of intellect, savvy, joie de vivre, charm, and dynamism. At the convention that elected him to succeed Lester Pearson, and during his first campaign as leader of the Liberal Party, Mr Trudeau's 'charisma' dominated the scene. His tenure as prime minister lasted from 1968 to 1984, a span interrupted only by the short-lived Progressive Conservative government of Joe Clark. Mr Trudeau was known for accomplishments that included passage of the Official Languages Act and the arduous negotiations culminating in the Charter of Rights and Freedoms and the modernization of the constitution.

Although many Canadians were swept up by 'Trudeaumania' at the beginning of his federal career, Mr Trudeau was by no means universally adored. The bloom went off his trademark rose as early as 1972 when the Liberals clung to power in a minority government. Members of the press gallery soured, and some of his personality traits, once perceived as positive, were seen by some as negative, evidenced by charges of arrogance, negligence, and churlishness. Always a complex figure, Mr Trudeau inspired strong feelings in friends and adversaries alike.

Crowds lined the tracks as a special train carried his body to Montreal and a state funeral. Dignitaries from across Canada and around the world attended the service, including former U.S. president Jimmy Carter and Cuban prime minister Fidel Castro. Eulogies were delivered by Jacques Hébert and Mr Trudeau's law partner Roy Heenan and, in a moving tribute, Justin Trudeau. Mr Trudeau was laid to rest in a family crypt in St Rémide-Napierville.

Scandals and controversies

Management of Human Resources Development Canada

As the year 1999 came to a close, the government came under fire after disclosures of sloppy administration of the myriad assistance programs under the aegis of Human Resources Development Canada. The department was responsible for administering a wide variety of programs, including pensions, old age security, and employment insurance. It was a 'transitional job fund,' designed to help create long-term employment in areas of the country with high unemployment rates, that attracted the interest of and criticism from the opposition. Reform MP Diane Ablonzy was especially arduous in pursuit of the government. She and others in the House accused the government of essentially operating a slush fund that benefited government-held ridings, lacked accountability, and operated under capricious or non-existent accounting standards. The minister in charge, Jane Stewart, faced withering attacks in the House. Mr Chrétien weighed in on behalf of the beleaguered minister, who was something of a protégé of his.

Ms Stewart insisted that she was not apprised of problems within the department until 17 November 1999. At that point she ordered a random internal audit of 459 projects representing about one-third of the $3 billion fund. On 19 January Ms Stewart released the report and was obliged to confess that the department's management of the grants program had been seriously flawed. The audit concluded that more than 80 per cent of the files had not been properly supervised or subjected to due diligence. Many of the applications – 72 per cent according to auditors – had not been accompanied by appropriate business plans. Indeed one-quarter failed to describe the precise nature of the project. It fell to the minister to apologize for the systemic problems identified in the report.

The problems at HRDC also attracted the attention of the police. On 1 March Ms Stewart said that she was aware of nine separate investigations by police. The confession caught her staff off guard. Previously the department had admitted that as many as four probes were under way. Eventually the controversy would lead to twenty separate investigations and numerous charges.

In addition to the internal probe and police investigations, Auditor General Denis Desautels launched his own review of affairs at HRDC. In testimony before the House committee on human resources development he complained that past warnings of poor administration had gone unheeded. In 1991 and 1994 his predecessors had pointed to major problems (23 March). He planned to conduct the most comprehensive independent review of a government agency ever undertaken. A formal report was released on the eve of the election. In an eighty-three page critique, Mr Desautels pointed to carelessness in day-to-day administration and little sense of overall direction. 'Our findings show that up to December, 1999, there were unacceptable weaknesses in the control framework for the management of grants and contributions at Human Resources Development Canada.' Moreover, the discrepancies were found to be 'systematic' rather than 'sloppy.' On the positive side, the Auditor General was pleased by the steps taken by the department since the scandal first broke.

The Prime Minister's riding

Prime Minister Chrétien prided himself on being an active and effective Member of Parliament for the riding of St Maurice despite the burdens of high office. To members of the opposition the Prime Minister was helpful to a fault. Over the course of the year 2000 they assailed him for using his office to exert illegitimate influence on government agencies. Questions about Mr Chrétien's actions intensified during the year and led to an (exculpatory) investigation by ethics commissioner Howard Wilson.

The convoluted story actually began after Mr Chrétien made his return to public life in 1990 as Liberal Party leader. In April 1993 the future prime minister and two business associates sold their shares in a local hotel and restaurant facility, the Auberge Grand-Mère, to another colleague, Yvon Duhaime. Later in the year Mr Chrétien arranged to sell his stake in an adjacent golf course (acquired in May 1988) to Jonas Price of Toronto. Early in 1996 it came to light that Mr Price had not concluded the transaction. As a result, the Prime Minister (or rather the blind trust established after he took office) still effectively held the shares. More crucial to the story was a telephone call Mr Chrétien placed to François Beaudoin, the president of the federal government's Business Development Bank of Canada. Mr Duhaime, hoping to renovate and enlarge the Auberge, had enlisted the Prime Minister in seeking a loan of some $2 million from the bank. Mr Chrétien raised the matter again in a private conversation at the Prime Minister's official residence in May of that year. In September the bank turned down Mr Duhaime's request because the business plan was too weak to warrant such a sizeable loan.

Mr Duhaime persisted. After working out a more modest plan for the Auberge, he put together a request for a loan from the bank of $615,000 while submitting a proposal to Human Resources Development Canada for a grant of $164,000. In February 1997 Mr Chrétien agreed to contact Mr Beaudoin at the Business Development Bank. In September the loan was approved. The grant was also approved on 28 May. None of these details were known when, in May 1999, ethics commissioner Howard Wilson ruled that the Prime Minister did not violate conflict-of-interest rules when one of his aides lobbied on behalf of Mr Duhaime. Early in 1999 the derailed golf-course transaction came to light. In October 1999 a buyer was found for the golf-course shares once owned by Mr Chrétien. Mr Wilson was again asked to rule on the propriety of the transfer. Once again he concluded that there had been no violation of cabinet guidelines on conflict of interest.

Mr Chrétien's name also surfaced in connection with the dealings of Claude Gauthier. In September 1996 Mr Gauthier purchased land adjacent to the golf course for just over a half million dollars, a deal that may have enhanced the facility's prospects. In November 1997 a company controlled by Mr Gauthier, Transelec, won a sizeable contract from the Canadian International Development Agency. Then, in March 1998, Human Resources Development Canada transferred the sum of $1.2 million to a plastics manufacturing company called Placetoco, another of Mr Gauthier's holdings. The deal resulted in an investigation by the Royal Canadian Mounted Police into allegations that the money was used to cover a bank loan rather than to create jobs. Then opposition leader Preston Manning was among those who peppered the Prime Minister with questions about his relationship with Mr Gauthier to the point where Mr Chrétien intemperately threatened to sue.

The issue would not go away, especially when it was learned that Mr Chrétien himself had interceded on behalf of Mr Duhaime, which came to light on 14 November when Mr Beaudoin implied that his departure from the bank was related to efforts to recall the Auberge loan. To the opposition this smacked of a conflict of interest and undue exercise of power. Mr Day and Mr Clark pounced. Both demanded an investigation by the RCMP. They also wanted to hear from Howard Wilson. On 21 November, less than a week before the election, ethics commissioner Wilson forwarded his conclusions to Mr Day. In his letter and in public pronouncements Mr Wilson exonerated the Prime Minister of wrongdoing. Since Mr Chrétien had 'no personal interest' in the Auberge, he could not be in a conflict of interest.

Lawsuit against Mr Day

In April 1999, while he was member of the legislature in Alberta, but more importantly a cabinet minister, Stockwell Day wrote a letter to the editor of the *Red Deer Advocate* criticizing a local attorney for defending an individual arrested on pedophile charges. The lawyer, Lorne Goddard, filed a defamation suit against Mr Day seeking $600,000 in damages. In his action Mr Goddard argued that Mr Day had insinuated that defending an alleged pedophile was tantamount to defending the crime. Mr Day drew criticism for appearing to condemn the sacrosanct principle that all criminal defendants are entitled to appropriate counsel. He was also condemned for drawing on a provincial government risk-management fund to cover his legal bills. The trial was slated to begin on 6 November, but the presiding judge permitted a delay until 27 November, after the election campaign was concluded. In the meantime Mr Day's lawyers assayed a unique defence of their client's actions. During the course of the pre-trial motions they argued that Mr Day's speech should be protected because, as a politician, he should be free to express his views in the public interest. On 21 December Mr Day settled out of court. Details of the settlement were not released, but it was suspected that Alberta taxpayers would be on the hook for significant sums.

Without peer: Mr Black's lawsuit against the Prime Minister

In February 1999 the leader of the Progressive Conservatives in the United Kingdom, William Hague, nominated one of Britain's leading media proprietors for a life peerage and a place in the House of Lords. British Prime Minister Tony Blair transmitted the name to the Queen. When the Prime Minister's office in Ottawa was consulted, the peerage was blocked. The nominee was none other than Conrad Black, the right-wing Canadian newspaper owner and founder of the *National Post*. Mr Black had made no secret of wanting to join in a tradition that had seen other British-based Canadian media magnates, like Lord Beaverbrook and Lord Thomson of Fleet, take their place in the House of Lords. He was incensed by Mr Chrétien's action.

In recommending against the peerage, the Prime Minister cited an obscure resolution adopted by the House of Commons in May 1919 named after its mover, William Nickle. The resolution asked the Crown to 'refrain from conferring any title of honour or titular distinction upon any of your subjects domiciled or ordinarily resident in Canada.' Although he spent much of the year in London, Mr Black remained a Canadian citizen. Aggrieved, in August 1999 Mr Black filed a $25,000 lawsuit for the Prime Minister's 'abuse of power.' Mr Black also cited in his filing the embarrassment caused by the Prime Minister's intervention. Partisan opponents chided the Prime Minister for indulging in petty politics and seeking revenge for hostile coverage in the *National Post* and Mr Black's other newspapers (charges Mr Chrétien denied).

On 15 March Justice Patrick Lesage of the Ontario Superior Court dismissed the suit. In his judgment Mr Lesage found that the Prime Minister had exercised his prerogative to advise the Crown on matters of honours. Mr Black announced he would appeal the decision and arguments were heard in the Ontario Court of Appeal on 12 September. With the ruling up in the air, Mr Black also threatened to revoke his Canadian citizenship if his appeal was dismissed.

CHRISTOPHER SPEARIN

Canada in the world: foreign affairs and national defence*

The year 2000 started with Canadians holding their breath, given the hype the Y2K bug had received for at least two years before the start of the new century. In the end, vital computer systems did not shut down and, consequently, the feared social and economic chaos did not ensue. As for the Department of National Defence (DND) and the Canadian Forces (CF), they had launched Operation Abacus, the largest ever country-wide military operation. During the lead-up to 1 January 2000, the military ensured that not only were its essential systems Y2K-compliant, but that it had sufficient capacity to deal with the negative repercussions should any of the civilian critical infrastructure fail. Over 2,500 CF personnel were deployed across the country to see in the new year and an additional 25,000 regular and reserve force personnel stood ready to respond if necessary. On 7 January, the Minister of National Defence, Art Eggleton, ordered the CF to stand down and revert to its standard domestic/emergency response posture. For Mr Eggleton, the success of Operation Abacus was a feather in the hat of both his department and the government of Prime Minister Jean Chrétien: 'The Government of Canada and the Department of National Defence took the Year 2000 challenge very seriously and worked hard with federal, provincial, and municipal authorities to safeguard the health, safety, security and economic well-being of Canadians' (*DND News Release*, no. 4, 7 January).

The year 2000 also ended with great uncertainty, albeit in different fields, with respect to Canadian foreign and defence policy. The year brought to a close the second and final term of the Clinton administration in the United States. During President Clinton's eight years in office, not only were Ottawa's relations with Washington relatively calm and the personal relations between the American president and

* The author would like to thank Abhinava Kumar, Cathy Murphy, and Donald Spearin for their assistance in the preparation of this chapter.

the Canadian prime minister fairly strong, Mr Clinton had also championed many of the multilateral initiatives and forums salient in Canadian foreign and defence policy-making. In late 2000, it became clear, after a lengthy recount process, that the American people had selected the Republican Party's nominee, Texas Governor George W. Bush, to be their president. The advent of the Bush Administration evoked many questions and concerns for Canadian policy-makers. How would Ottawa's relations fare with Washington, given that during the presidential campaign, Mr Bush seemed to stress a more southern-oriented continental policy towards Mexico? How would Canada's international endeavours be affected by an American government more interested in global retrenchment and assertive bilateralism rather than in multilateralism? On a personal level, how would Mr Bush, the son of former president George H.W. Bush, who was a close friend of former Conservative prime minister Brian Mulroney, feel about Prime Minister Chrétien? Given that Raymond Chrétien, the Prime Minister's nephew and the Canadian Ambassador to Washington, had suggested publicly that Canada would have preferred an American government run by the Democratic Party's presidential nominee, Senator Al Gore, one could hypothesize, as 2000 drew to a close, that Ottawa's relations with the new regime in Washington would likely be rocky in the coming year.

The future direction of Canadian foreign and defence policy was also uncertain at the end of 2000. The 27 November federal election returned Canada's third straight Liberal majority government, with the Canadian Alliance party keeping its role as the official opposition. The Liberals won 172 seats, while the Canadian Alliance, the Bloc Québécois, the New Democratic Party, and the Progressive Conservatives won 66, 38, 13, and 12 seats respectively. As in most federal elections, foreign and defence affairs played only minor roles in the campaign platforms of the major political parties. What the federal election did herald, however, was the departure of Foreign Affairs Minister Lloyd Axworthy from the political scene. Since 1979, Mr Axworthy had served as the MP for the riding of Winnipeg South Centre. He decided to bow out of political life shortly before the election in order to pursue an academic opportunity at the University of British Columbia. Hence, Prime Minister Chrétien appointed John Manley as Mr Axworthy's replacement on 17 October. Minister of International Trade Pierre Pettigrew and National Defence Minister Art Eggleton were re-elected and maintained their respective cabinet posts. Despite the continuity inherent with a new Liberal majority and the continued presence of key ministers, the departure of Lloyd Axworthy posed many questions regarding the future direction of Canadian foreign policy given the level of investment, under his guidance, Canada had made in the pursuit of the human security agenda. Would Foreign Affairs Minister Manley follow in Mr Axworthy's footsteps, or would he chart a new course in Canada's foreign relations? Would he embrace Canadian participation in traditional multilateral forums and champion Canadian human security initiatives, or would he concentrate more on Canada's international economic activities and Canada's relations with the United States, files of secondary importance during the Axworthy era?

Foreign affairs

United States

Issues pertaining to the 6,500-kilometre-long border and its crossing by people and material played a considerable role in the relations between Canada and the United States in 2000. It was only in mid-January that American officials ended an unprecedented heightened state of alert following the arrest of an Algerian-born Montrealer, Ahmed Ressam, at Port Angeles, Washington, on 14 December 1999. American officials charged Mr Ressam with making false statements and smuggling explosive materials when they found him in possession of sophisticated bomb-making equipment after arriving by ferry from Vancouver Island. Subsequent investigations revealed that he was linked to Osama bin Laden, the leader of the terrorist organization al Qaeda, and that Mr Ressam was but one component in a plot to disrupt millennial celebrations in the United States with mass bombings. Canadians officials, for their part, were embarrassed that Mr Ressam, who had been denied refugee status because of his links with Algeria's Armed Islamic Group, had been on the lam and been recently left unmonitored by the Canadian Security and Intelligence Service due to a lack of resources.

American officials accused Canada of having lax standards in antiterrorism and immigration policy and made unfavourable comparisons of the Canada-U.S. border with the heavily fortified 2,000-kilometre border the United States shares with Mexico. Noting that at least thirteen known terrorists had entered the United States from Canada during the 1990s, Senator Dianne Feinstein of California argued that '[t]he situation on the northern border in some ways is more serious than on the southern border' (*Globe and Mail*, 11 February). She also contended that Mexicans seeking illegal entry into the U.S. were actually coming to Canada in hopes of obtaining easier access. In this vein, the

U.S. Customs Service increased the work hours of its staff along the Canadian border and reinforced its presence by adding 500 inspectors. Also, Michael Sheehan, American ambassador at large and coordinator for counterterrorism, asserted that Canadian activism too was required: 'They [the Canadians] understand they are going to have to ramp up some of their activities and we have had talks with them about that' (*Globe and Mail*, 11 February). Canadian officials responded to U.S. concerns by striking a cautious balance between removing U.S. security concerns on the one hand and keeping the border open to trade and maintaining Canadian sovereignty on the other. Foreign Affairs Minister Axworthy contended, in the face of U.S. criticism, that '[t]his is something that's not going to be resolved by putting big fences along the 49th parallel' (*Globe and Mail*, 12 February). In 2000, Canadian officials did begin to share with their U.S. counterparts fingerprint records of deported criminal aliens and information on illegal aliens charged with criminal offences. In an effort to remove congestion and expedite border crossings for low-risk travellers and goods, Revenue Minister Martin Cauchon introduced the 'pre-approved' Canpass system in April. New immigration legislation, introduced by Immigration Minister Elinor Caplan in May (analysed below), was also designed with both security concerns and ease of border crossing in mind.

Another cross-border issue in 2000 was the entry into Canada from the United States of plutonium from the American nuclear arsenal. On 14 January, 119 grams of bomb-grade plutonium arrived by air in Chalk River, Ontario, having been shipped by truck to Michigan from the U.S. nuclear laboratory in Los Alamos, New Mexico. The material was sent to Canada to test if Canadian-designed nuclear reactors could use this material as fuel, thus making it possible for Canada to serve as a disposal option for weapons-grade nuclear material from the Cold War era. As argued in the House of Commons by Natural Resources Minister Ralph Goodale, '[T]he rationale for the testing is to make this world more safe and secure from the nuclear threat of those plutonium stockpiles that are in existence in the United States and Russia' (*Globe and Mail*, 22 September). In addition, if the tests proved to be successful, the results could serve as a marketing tool for Canada's Candu nuclear reactors.

However, many groups were upset by the shipment, even though plutonium is a relatively safe element. According to John Sutherland of New Brunswick Power, plutonium 'is a strategic material, and subject to the predictable emotionally inspired antics of certain groups' (*Globe and Mail*, 19 January). Local residents, municipal officials, and aboriginal groups in Ontario were upset that they had not been informed in advance of the flight, having earlier taken steps not to have the material shipped by truck through their communities. Indeed, if the flight had occurred in the United States, it would have been deemed illegal given the amount of material transported. As well, Canada's Atomic Energy Control Board chose not to inform Mr Goodale of the air shipment, one that Transport Canada had turned down before later approving it. The Ontario Public Service Employees Union filed charges in court in February, claiming that Ontario's Natural Resources Ministry had failed to inform them about the shipment and appropriate safety precautions. As for environmental groups, they too were displeased. Greenpeace was against Canada getting 'into the plutonium business' (*Globe and Mail*, 15 January) and the Canadian Coalition for Nuclear Responsibility suggested negligence on the government's behalf with respect to the initiative: '[T]he whole idea of responsible government, the whole idea of responsible environmental assessment, is to look at even improbable accidents and see what the consequences could be' (*Globe and Mail*, 3 August). Despite this array of concerns, Atomic Energy Canada in July submitted to the Chrétien government a plan to conduct further tests by burning Russian nuclear material. On 26 September, 15 kilograms of nuclear material arrived by air at CFB Trenton in order to avoid protests.

Finally, other events in 2000 similarly highlighted the 'permeability' of the Canada-U.S. border to wildlife and humans alike. In March, the provincial government in British Columbia dropped its appeal, made in U.S. courts, of the Salmon Treaty. This brought to a close a lawsuit, initiated in 1997, that accused the United States of violating the conservation and equity provisions indicated in the 1985 treaty. In May, a joint investigation conducted by Canadian and U.S. officials cracked a multi-million-dollar criminal smuggling network involving weapons brought back from overseas to be smuggled into the United States via Toronto or Montreal. Also in May, charges were laid against six Americans and six Canadians as investigators shut down one of the largest liquor smuggling rings in the history of both countries.

Illegal immigration

In parallel with the border concerns noted above, 2000 saw the Canadian government continue to grapple with the arrival by sea in 1999 of approximately 600 Chinese migrants. In light of Australia's strict stance towards illegal migration and Canada's perceived lax immigration and refugee policies, coupled (again) with the seeming permeability of the Canada-U.S. border, Canada over the course of the 1990s had become a destination of choice for Chinese migrants. These individuals were willing to take the risk and pay criminal gangs upwards of U.S.$60,000 per person for the passage to Canada. The start of 2000 proved to be no different, with twenty-five more Chinese migrants arriving by sea, in this case by container ship, on 6 January.

In order to deal with the issue and deter criminal organizations and potential migrants alike from attempting such dangerous travel to Canada, Ottawa took several steps both domestic and international. In January, the RCMP laid charges against members of the Walpole nation Native reserve located along the Canada-U.S. border in Ontario, a known conduit for the smuggling of Chinese migrants into the United States. In March, a parliamentary committee recommended not only the construction of permanent detention facilities in British Columbia, but also the automatic detention of any individual thought to arrive in Canada by means of human trafficking. Other recommendations were for the quicker removal of illegal migrants and the imposition of harsher penalties for those convicted of human smuggling. Immigration Minister Caplan followed suit in April when she introduced a new immigration act designed to 'close the back door to those who would abuse the system' (*Globe and Mail*, 26 May). Similarly, Canada signed on 15 December a new United Nations protocol to deter and curtail illegal immigration.

Though Canada returned to China close to 250 migrants before the end of 2000, Canadian governmental activism on this issue did face some challenges. Many Chinese migrants who arrived in 1999 started to claim in 2000 that they were members of the outlawed falun gong sect, making it much more difficult for Ottawa to return these individuals to China for fear of harsh treatment. In August, Korean sailors accused of bringing one boatload of Chinese migrants in 1999 were found not guilty of smuggling illegal aliens, a major setback in the government's efforts to deter human trafficking.

World Trade Organization

The year 2000 marked the end of the thirty-four-year-old auto pact between Canada and the United States. Initiated by the Pearson government and the Johnson administration in 1965, the pact's rationale, from the Canadian perspective, was to attract investment into the auto industry in Canada. The pact required the 'Big Three' American automakers – General Motors, Ford, and Chrysler (now Daimler-Chrysler) – to produce as many cars in Canada as they sold here. In return, the Canadian subsidiaries of the Big Three were excused from a 6.1 per cent tariff on cars for sale in Canada originating from anywhere else in the world. This tariff, however, raised the ire of the European Union (EU) and Japan who turned to the World Trade Organization (WTO) for redress. In 1999 the WTO issued an interim report indicating that the pact violated international trade law in at least seven different ways. In February 2000 the WTO issued its final report, which indeed found that the pact favoured the Big Three at the expense of European and Japanese automakers. The WTO ordered Canada and the United States to dismantle the pact within ninety days of its ruling.

Though the WTO very rarely ever reversed decisions on appeal, the Chrétien government nevertheless did make an appeal, if only for the political importance of the issue. The official rationale for the government's decision, according to International Trade Minister Pettigrew, was to 'seek and clarify the reasoning and scope of the panel's findings' (*Globe and Mail*, 12 February). The Canadian subsidiaries of the Big Three supported the government's decision to appeal the WTO ruling, as did the Canadian Auto Workers union, which feared that its 52,000-strong membership working for the Big Three would be affected adversely by cyclic downturns in the automotive industry should the auto pact be abolished. Moreover, given that voters in seat-rich Ontario, the primary base of Canada's automotive industry, might take unkindly to the demise of the auto pact, an appeal of the WTO ruling was virtually assured.

The WTO's appellate body issued its report on 30 May, and in the end Canada lost its appeal. To soften the blow, federal officials argued that in many ways the North American Free Trade Agreement had superseded the guidelines laid down by the auto pact. Indeed, 85 per cent of the cars purchased in Canada would not be affected by the auto pact's demise. Similarly, then Industry Minister John Manley implied that Canada would not feel substantial negative repercussions because of the inherent strengths of the Canadian automotive industry: 'The auto pact was based on the fundamental premise that we should produce one vehicle for every one that sold in Canada, and we're now producing two for every one that's sold' (*Globe and Mail*, 5 October). A small victory for the Chrétien government regarding its appeal could be found in the timing of the auto pact's termination. Whereas the EU and Japan wanted the pact to end ninety days after the appellate board's decision, Canada argued that, because of the complexities of the North American automotive sector, it should have fifteen months to dismantle the pact. The WTO elected to make a compromise and ordered Canada to comply within eight months, thus effectively removing the auto pact as a potentially contentious issue in the fall federal election campaign.

In the face of this loss at the WTO, Canada also had to manage the implications of an ongoing trade dispute with Brazil regarding the lucrative and highly competitive regional jet marketplace. At issue were Ottawa's use of Canada Account Funding and the Technology Partnerships Canada (TPC) program to support Bombardier Inc. and Brazil's own Proex financing program, which provided foreign buyers with a 15 per cent rebate on Embraer jets – programs that the WTO ruled in 1999 contravened international trade regulations. In an interim ruling issued in April 2000, the WTO found that Canada had made sufficient changes to the TPC, while the Proex program and the much more modest Canada Account Funding needed more retooling. For both countries, the regional jet marketplace was a critical trade battleground, not only for financial reasons, but for symbolic and political reasons too. For Madelaine Drohan, the stakes could not be higher: 'If Canadians see regional aircraft manufacture as a high-tech boost to a low-tech image, that is true in spades for the Brazilians' (*Globe and Mail*, 1 July).

For Canada, achieving the benefits of this 'win' at the WTO proved to be an illusory undertaking. The fear in Ottawa was that Brazil would not comply because it viewed the WTO ruling as fundamentally unsound; Brazil should be allowed to offer subsidies, and substantial ones at that, because of its status as a developing country. Ottawa, for its part, was fearful that the implementation of sanctions of up to $10 billion against Brazil, allowable under the WTO ruling, would not make much of an impact as it would necessitate an end of trade with Brazil for up to seven years. Moreover, an additional worry was that Brazil, in retaliation, might stymie Canadian investment endeavours in Brazil and elsewhere in South America, a much more important marketplace for Canadian business. As stressed by Jean Daudelin at the North-South Institute, 'If we are at all serious about the Americas, it's very difficult not to be serious about Brazil ... We should play our other cards very, very carefully' (*Globe and Mail*, 6 April).

In the face of Canadian pressure, such as Ottawa's decision in April to investigate Brazil's dumping of stainless steel in Canada, Brazil elected in May to enter into negotiations with Ottawa to offer Canada and Bombardier billions of dollars in compensation. The stumbling block that arose, however, concerned the exact nature of the compensation. Canadian negotiators were keen to win Brazilian government contracts and achieve tariff reductions in export areas in which Canadian firms would benefit. They also wanted a bilateral mechanism to monitor all further regional jet sales. But this latter part was a controversial measure. It raised some concerns in the Export Development Corporation and Industry Canada because the mechanism might force Bombardier to reciprocate and share sensitive information. The Brazilians refused to negotiate such a mechanism, in part because of its implication that Canada did not trust Brazil, but also because the WTO did not call on Brazil to sign any extra bilateral pact. Though the WTO on 28 August provided Canada with some leverage during the negotiations by giving it permission to levy retaliatory trade sanctions worth $2.1 billion over six years, Canada did not receive the desired pay-off. On 29 November the talks between the two countries collapsed. December 2000 closed out with the WTO formally sanctioning Canadian economic countermeasures, but Ottawa had not yet decided upon the actual punitive components.

Finally, Canada recorded another 'win' in light of the 17 March WTO patent ruling on generic drugs. In short, though the WTO did not rule in Canada's favour regarding the stockpiling of generic drugs that could flood the marketplace when a particular patent expires, it did indicate that Canadian drug patent rules were legal such that generic drug companies could develop their 'copies' of patent drugs while the latter were still under patent protection. The EU and the United States had initially taken the case to the WTO given their concerns that Canada was not protecting patents for the required twenty-year period. An appeal made by these parties was also turned down by the WTO in September 2000.

Asia-Pacific

In addition to the troubles between Canada and China regarding illegal immigration and people-smuggling, other politically sensitive issues arose in 2000 in the context of Canada's relations with countries in the Asia-Pacific region, particularly those still under the banner of communism. On 27 April, Canada initiated diplomatic sanctions against Vietnam in condemnation of the 24 April execution by firing squad of a Torontonian, Nguyen Thi Hiep. The execution came four years after Ms Hiep, along with her mother, Tran Thi Cam, were charged with smuggling 5.45 kilograms of heroin out of the country, despite the fact that Canadian police investigations cast doubt on their guilt. Indeed, they might have been mere dupes. Following the execution, Ottawa recalled Canada's ambassador to Hanoi and withdrew Canada's offer to help prepare Vietnam's bid to enter the WTO. Foreign Affairs Minister Lloyd Axworthy also directed Canadian diplomatic staff to demand an explanation for the execution and a return of Ms Hiep's remains to Canada and to boycott celebrations marking the twenty-fifth anniversary of the end of the Vietnam War. Relations between the two countries eventually warmed again, but only after further worsening when the Vietnamese government released 12,000 prisoners on 28 April as part of its aforementioned anniversary celebrations. On 30 May relatives travelled to Hanoi to collect Ms Hiep's remains, and on 1 September Ms Cam was released from imprisonment as part of a countrywide amnesty.

In contrast, Canada's relations with North Korea improved markedly in 2000. In July, on the fiftieth anniversary of Canada committing troops to defend South Korea, Canada formally recognized North Korea as an independent state, making it only the third G8 member state to do so. This recognition came after Lloyd Axworthy met with his North Korean counterpart, Paek Nam-Sun, in Bangkok. Through Prime Minister Chrétien's rationale that 'isolation isn't good for anybody' (*Globe and Mail*, 27 July), Ottawa hoped the initiative would allow it to reward Pyongyang for its embrace of South Korean President Kim Daejung's 'Sunshine' policy and to press it on issues of concern: human rights, the development of nuclear weaponry, and the proliferation of missile technology. As for North Korea, official relations with Canada served as one more step towards emerging from international isolation and gaining a 'window on the United States' (*Globe and Mail*, 27 July). The actual decision on the nature of potential diplomatic relations (i.e., ambassadorial representation) was left for the coming year.

And lastly, the latest iteration of the Chrétien government's 'Team Canada' missions, this one to China and Hong Kong scheduled from 17 to 26 November, was cancelled due to the federal election call. The trip, involving approximately 300 businesspeople and all ten provincial premiers, was rescheduled for 9 to 18 February 2001.

Middle East

In April 2000 Jean Chrétien launched his first trip to the Middle East during his tenure as prime minister. In fact, Mr Chrétien was the first

Canadian prime minister ever to visit the region officially. The goals of the prime ministerial visit were threefold: to indicate Canadian support for the peace process and offer Canadian assistance, to enhance trade with the region, and to express Canadian concerns regarding human rights. This twelve-day trip, however, was fraught with controversy given Mr Chrétien's handling of highly sensitive issues pertaining to the region. On the first day of the trip, the Prime Minister laughed off complaints that he was ignoring the invitation by Falsal Husseini, a Palestinian leader, to visit him in East Jerusalem; 'I don't know if I am in West, South, North or East Jerusalem right now. I came here to meet with the Prime Minister [of Israel] and I'm here right now.' On the next day, he appeared to support a Palestinian threat of unilaterally declaring independence, an issue with clear implications both in the Middle East and in the domestic context with respect to Quebec: 'The solution is to keep it [a unilateral declaration of independence by Palestinians] as part of the negotiations because it puts pressure on both parties to come to a resolution.' On yet the next day, he asserted that Israel should maintain its access to the Sea of Galilee, the region's largest body of fresh water: 'It's quite evident that it is vitally important for the Israelis to keep this body of water. Lake Tiberias is under the control of the government and the people of Israel, and I find that they are right to want to keep it' (*Globe and Mail*, 21 April). This assertion was made despite the fact that the northeast shore of the sea was taken by Israel during the 1967 War and is one of the key points of contention for Syria in peace negotiations. Finally, though he had talked about the issue of Palestinian resettlement with Israeli Prime Minister Ehud Barak, Mr Chrétien had to contradict Israeli officials who suggested that Canada had offered to accept 15,000 Palestinian refugees as part of an ultimate peace deal: 'This statement that we made a formal agreement with anybody, it's not true' (*Globe and Mail*, 13 April). In light of the political sensitivity regarding the 3.5 million refugees in the region, Palestinian leader Yasser Arafat formally rejected any offer Canada might have made regarding resettlement. Though calls were made in the House of Commons for the Prime Minister to return home early in order to avoid any further embarrassment, Mr Chrétien asserted that his visit had not caused his Middle Eastern hosts any discomfort: 'Nobody has talked about these so-called problems that exist. Not once' (*Globe and Mail*, 20 April).

Later in the year, Canada's policy towards the Middle East was again criticized, this time for a seeming anti-Israeli bias. In October, Canada, along with thirteen other states sitting on the UN Security Council, supported a resolution that condemned Israel's 'excessive use of force' against the Palestinians. Though Prime Minister Chrétien argued that Canada's approval only signified Canada's support for regional peace, Opposition Leader Stockwell Day thought otherwise: 'I am not sure we will further the cause of peace if we as a nation join in the finger pointing, rather than working with both sides co-operatively' (*Globe and Mail*, 10 October).

Europe

Fallout stemming from NATO's attack against Serbia during the 1999 Kosovo crisis was prominent in Canada's relations with Europe in 2000. On 1 May, the Senate Foreign Affairs committee criticized the Chrétien government's decision to join fellow NATO member states in the Kosovo campaign because NATO lacked a UN mandate. The committee also questioned both the motives for the campaign and its ultimate effects. Similarly problematic for Canada were assertions made by Amnesty International in June that NATO air strikes caused undue civilian casualties that constituted war crimes. Amnesty International noted several instances in which air strikes harmed civilians and indicated that the resulting deaths 'could have been significantly reduced if NATO forces had fully adhered to the laws of war during Operation Allied Force' (*Globe and Mail*, 8 June). This charge came in contradistinction to arguments made by Carla Del Ponte, the chief prosecutor for the International Criminal Tribunal for the former Yugoslavia, to the UN Security Council in June that there was no basis upon which to charge NATO or the leaders of NATO member states with war crimes.

Equally troubling was Canada's relations with Serbia, the larger component of the remnants of Yugoslavia. On 1 August, Serb authorities arrested Canadians Shaun Going, owner of the Kosovo-based construction company Meridian Resources, and his nephew, Liam Hall, a student from the University of Victoria working with his uncle over the summer. The Serbs accused them of spying for NATO, conducting terrorist deeds, and training special police units in Montenegro, the other Yugoslav province at odds with Serbia. They similarly placed under arrest two Britons travelling with the Canadians who were instructors at the police academy of the Organization for Security and Cooperation in Europe, in Kosovo. The four were travelling back into Kosovo in Mr Going's vehicle after spending a holiday in Montenegro. The Serbs arrested the four individuals because they did not possess the appropriate visas and the Serbs found explosive equipment, required for Mr Going's construction work, in the trunk of his vehicle.

Canadian officials immediately doubted the veracity of the accusations, given that they seemed part of a propaganda campaign leading up to the Yugoslav elections on 24 September. Indeed, just a few days before the arrest of the Canadians and Britons, the Yugoslav Information Minister announced that four Dutch citizens had been arrested under allegations that they were assassins preparing to kill or kidnap Yugoslav President Slobodan Milosevic. In the eyes of Foreign Affairs Minister Lloyd Axworthy, the arrests of the Canadians were in keeping with President Milosevic's heavy-handed approach: '[I]t is simply another example of the kind of actions that Milosevic takes, where he uses the tactics of a thug to get his way' (*Globe and Mail*, 8 August). Canadian opposition parties were similarly calling for immediate action on the issue, especially Joe Clark and his Progressive Conservatives given that Mr Clark was a long-time friend of the Going family. In this regard, Mr Axworthy contacted Russia, a historic ally of Serbia, to see what Russian officials might do on behalf of the imprisoned Canadians. Mr Axworthy also asked the Serbian community in Canada to use any ties or influence it had in Belgrade to aid in the Canadians' release. In, addition Mr Axworthy ensured that the issue was raised at the UN Security Council given that Canada was a non-permanent member at the time.

Canada's diplomatic overtures, however, did not initially bear fruit. Canadians of Serb ancestry were incensed that Mr Axworthy had asked them to intervene because Ottawa took no note of their concerns during the bombing of Serbia in 1999. For Zana Vitrovich, the president of the Association of Serbian Women of Canada, '[w]e are very sorry about the arrests, but Axworthy is just being very arrogant and absurd' (*Globe and Mail*, 11 August). In response, Mr Axworthy toned down his language with respect to President Milosevic's thuggish nature. Another complicating factor was two British Labour MPs who had broken with their government in 1999 regarding the bombing of Serbia by NATO. They accused Mr Going of business dealings with the Kosovo Liberation Army (KLA), which, in turn, threatened the lives of the imprisoned Britons: 'The fact that the two British citizens ... have been detained in the company of someone who is linked with KLA terrorists and has taken part in dubious activities in Kosovo, places them in a precarious and compromising position' (*Globe and Mail*, 11 August). One success Canadian diplomacy did achieve, however, was on the UN Security Council, which called upon Belgrade to allow the detainees to have access to consular assistance as required under international law.

The two Canadians and two Britons eventually saw their release from Serb custody in October, shortly after President Milosevic, in the wake of the fraudulent elections on 24 September, was forced from power by massive street demonstrations. As surmised by Liam Hall, 'It couldn't have been a coincidence that we were released the day after the changing of the guard' (*Globe and Mail*, 9 October). Likely helping in addressing the plight of the Canadians was Prime Minister Chrétien's offer made to new President Vojislav Kostunica to lift sanctions that had been directed at the old regime.

Despite the trade disputes in 2000 between Canada and the EU mentioned earlier, Canadian diplomatic endeavours found synergy with some EU activities. On 26 June, Lisbon was host to a Canada-EU Summit, attended by Canada's Prime Minister, foreign affairs minister, and international trade minister, and, on the European side, by Portuguese Prime Minister Antonio Guterres, EU Commission President Romano Prodi, External Relations Commissioner Chris Patten, and Trade Commissioner Pascal Lamy. Among the issues discussed were several important to Canadian diplomacy, such as the promotion of human security, the advancement of trade liberalization, and the strengthening of multilateral rules. With respect to defence, Prime Minister Chrétien indicated that Canada would be willing to join EU peacekeeping missions should NATO or the UN choose not to respond to a particular crisis.

Also in 2000, Canada, like the EU, levelled sanctions in February against the newly elected coalition government in Austria that included the extreme right-wing Freedom Party, led by Joerg Haider. Despite the resignation of Mr Haider as leader of the Freedom Party on 29 February, Canada, the EU, and other concerned states did not drop their sanctions. It was only in September that the EU and Canada lifted sanctions unconditionally against Austria. This action came in response to reaffirmations made by the Austrian government towards its commitment to democratic values and to the introduction of constitutional amendments meant to protect ethnic minorities.

International summitry and the developing world

In 2000, as a member of a variety of organizations, Canada participated in, and in some cases also hosted, international summits. Two matters dominated the three-day meeting of the Organization of American States (OAS) held in Windsor in early June. First, outside the meetings, anti-globalization protestors, largely from Ontario and Quebec, attempted to disrupt the proceedings. The protestors were concerned about any discussions the OAS members would be conducting regarding trade liberalization and corporate power. At the very least, the OAS paid lip service to the protestors' issues, given comments made by Argentine Foreign Minister Adalberto Rodriguez: 'We got a strong message; more participation, more attention to sensitive issues' (*Globe and Mail*, 6 June). In this regard, Foreign Affairs Minister Lloyd Axworthy, the summit's host, praised OAS member states that endorsed resolutions regarding the promotion of human rights and the development of anti-corruption mechanisms for public and private businesses in the Western Hemisphere.

Second, the OAS discussions themselves were dominated by concerns over Peru's national elections, which had culminated in the 28 May run-off vote that elected President Alberto Fujimori to a third five-year term. These elections were marked by controversy. OAS observers left Peru before the May election, claiming that the conditions for a free and fair vote were non-existent. President Fujimori's challenger, Alejandro Toledo, withdrew his candidacy in light of perceived fraud committed by the government. Even before this, President Fujimori had orchestrated the removal of three judges who had deemed his candidacy to be unconstitutional. In response to this crisis, the OAS voted to send Foreign Affairs Minister Lloyd Axworthy to Peru to press President Fujimori for human-rights and election reforms. However, because of intra-OAS sensitivities, the OAS restricted Mr Axworthy's mandate to one of advocating future change, not of recasting the 28 May vote. Several member states feared that a more expansive mandate might open the door to unwanted OAS investigations into their own electoral processes and cause internal unrest in Peru.

The resulting three-day diplomatic mission occurred at the end of June and featured direct talks between President Fujimori, Mr Axworthy, and the OAS Secretary General Cesar Gaviria. Although, as decided in Windsor, Mr Axworthy and Mr Gaviria did not call for new elections in Peru, they did assert that President Fujimori should make a number of reforms to Peru's electoral structure and governmental institutions: promotion of free speech and a free media, development of an independent judiciary, augmentation of the power of the Congress vis-à-vis the presidency, limitations imposed upon the activities of Peru's military-intelligence agency, and the creation of an independent elections commission. The OAS mission pressed President Fujimori to make these necessary changes before the 2002 municipal elections. Opposition members and public protestors in Peru, however, felt that the OAS mission would likely not be a success. If anything, for them the OAS diplomatic mission only helped to affirm the legitimacy of Mr Fujimori's presidency. In fact, one Peruvian newspaper depicted Mr Axworthy as Tom Cruise, given that both were involved in a *Mission Impossible*.

With the U.S. national election coming in November 2000, the G8 Summit in Okinawa, Japan, marked President Clinton's last G8 appearance and the ascendancy of Prime Minister Chrétien as the group's elder statesman. The communiqué from the three-day event revealed that the world leaders discussed a wide variety of issues, many of them directed towards the developing world: expanding investment and sustainable development in the developing world, overcoming the North-South digital divide, reducing the spread of HIV/AIDS, achieving universal primary education by 2015, employing the WTO to deal with concerns expressed by developing world states, urging the implementation of the Kyoto Protocol, creating a plan to dispose of weapons-grade plutonium, and promoting debt forgiveness worth at least U.S.$15 billion for highly indebted countries. The developing-world focus was not surprising given the lack of pressing issues facing the G8 leaders and the relative strength of their countries' respective economies. Further emphasis was placed on the plight of the developing world given that immediately before the summit many G8 leaders met in Japan with the leaders of South Africa, Nigeria, Thailand, and Algeria, who pressed for developing-world issues to remain at the top of the G8 agenda. Certainly, Prime Minister Chrétien was open to this approach: 'As we meet all of the countries are growing, and so it allows us ... to look more closely at the problems of Africa and the developing countries' (*Globe and Mail*, 21 July).

Assessment of the Okinawan summit vis-à-vis issues pertaining to the developing world was, however, mixed. The G8 leaders turned down Japan's idea to create a G8 fund to fight infectious disease, and they decided not to open their markets to farm goods from the developing world in the near future. Canada's call for a collective boost in development aid was turned down, as was British Prime Minister Tony Blair's call to accelerate the debt-relief plan called for in the 1999 G8 Summit in Cologne, Germany. In fact, even though developing-world issues had been discussed at length during the previous three G8 summits, Prime Minister Chrétien was at least pleased that he had put forth in Okinawa the initiative regarding development assistance: 'I'm happy that I made the proposition, because if there was not an agreement on a specific number, there was an agreement that something has to be done, that the time has come to reinvest more money in that' (*Globe and Mail*, 24 July).

Following the G8 Summit Canada did act unilaterally on some developing-world issues, with greater effect in some instances than in others. In August Ottawa took steps to eliminate tariffs on most imported products from least-developed countries, a decision made in response to the G8 deliberations and the WTO's call for more equitable North–South relations. Though Canada did not put textiles on the list of tariff-free goods, an issue of particular salience in the developing world, it did, as of 1 September, increase the number of product categories awarded duty-free status from 82 to 90 per cent for exports from the world's forty-six poorest countries. In the end, however, the changes were not substantial; they entailed that Ottawa would forgo only $500,000 annually in tariffs.

On other fronts, however, Canadian moves were bolder in terms of policy towards the developing world. On 24–25 October, Finance Minister Paul Martin hosted in Montreal the second-ever gathering of finance ministers and bank governors of the G20, a group whose membership includes the IMF, the World Bank, the G8 countries, and countries with major emerging markets or with economies substantial enough that their downturn would cause a major international economic crisis.* Objectives included dealing with some of the aforementioned issues discussed by the G8 in Okinawa (overcoming the digital divide, AIDS prevention, etc.), but the major goal was to develop mechanisms to allow for the 'inclusive' benefits of globalization to spread and to prevent financial crises with considerable spillover effects, such as the 1998 crisis in Asia. Mr Martin summarized the rationale for these goals as follows: '[T]he fact is, that globalization, if its benefits are limited only to a privileged few, is not going to work. It is not fair' (*Globe and Mail*, 25 October). The outcome of the meeting, the 'Montreal Consensus' massaged by Mr Martin, was an attempt to link economic problems to social problems and to tie economic globalization with development: 'The Montreal consensus will help ensure that globalization brings the benefits of the greatest boom in decades to the greatest number of people, that its benefits are spread fairly to all people in all parts of the world' (*Globe and Mail*, 26 October). This

* The G20 includes Argentina, Australia, Brazil, Britain, Canada, China, France, Germany, India, Indonesia, Italy, Japan, Mexico, Russia, Saudi Arabia, South Africa, South Korea, Turkey, the United States, and the EU.

consensus featured the G20 committing to a variety of tasks: promoting social safety nets in the developing world, supporting research on disease, agriculture, and environmental issues, bringing debtor countries into the global economy, increasing the transparency of international financial institutions, countering corruption, and advancing the agenda of the WTO.

With respect to the crippling issue of debt reduction, a further meeting of finance ministers and central bankers, the September IMF / World Bank meetings in Prague, featured another Canadian initiative. Much to the chagrin of other countries, such as the United States that were not consulted beforehand, Mr Martin requested that there be an immediate moratorium on debt payments for the world's poorest countries. He also contended that this would be but the first step; creditor countries should also lighten the conditions for debt relief and consider even cancelling some debt. Mr Martin made his thinking on the matter plain: 'At a time of unprecedented prosperity in many industrialized economies, it is unacceptable that the promised debt relief has not been delivered' (*Globe and Mail*, 25 September). For Mr Martin, indebted countries would be eligible for relief as long as they developed the appropriate poverty-reduction and social policies. Though the Canadian initiative was not fully embraced in Prague, Ottawa did follow through on its rhetoric. On 19 December, Mr Martin announced a moratorium of debt payments to Canada, effective 1 January 2001, for indebted countries with sufficient social and human-rights records that collectively held $1 billion in bilateral debts to Canada: Benin, Bolivia, Cameroon, Ethiopia, Ghana, Guyana, Honduras, Madagascar, Senegal, Tanzania, and Zambia. This decision came on the heels of the British government's 1 December decision to institute a moratorium on debt payments from forty-one of the world's poorest countries. On the one hand, the decision by these two governments was not costly given that these countries could not afford to service their bilateral debts any way. On the other hand, this collective decision by Canada and the United Kingdom also served as a gesture towards reducing the considerable debt burden confronting the developing world.

United Nations and human security

The year 2000 marked the end of Canada's two-year stint as a non-permanent member on the UN Security Council. The objectives during Canada's tenure on the council were threefold: to promote human security, to reassert the effectiveness and leadership of the council, and to strive to make the council's undertakings more transparent, open, and responsive. Many of the endeavours Canadian diplomats undertook in 2000 at the UN in New York concerned the promotion of the human-security agenda: protecting civilians in armed conflicts, making UN sanctions more targeted and effective, clamping down on the trade in conflict diamonds, dealing with the thorny issue of state sovereignty when humanitarian catastrophe looms, reflecting upon the UN's inactivity in Rwanda in the midst of the genocide, addressing the humanitarian implications of conflict in Afghanistan, and restructuring the UN's peacekeeping apparatus to make it more efficient and effective. Taken together, these measures helped to promote a move away from state-centric thinking vis-à-vis security. In the words of Foreign Affairs Minister Lloyd Axworthy: 'Our goals are to foster a recognition that threats to people are just as important as threats to states, and to mobilize Council action on behalf of civilians who are increasingly targeted in today's conflicts' (*DFAIT News Release*, no. 64, 6 April).

Much of this activity was advanced in April, the month that Canada held the rotating presidency of the council. For instance, with respect to sanctions, Mr Axworthy presented to the council a Canadian-commissioned study prepared by the International Peace Academy (IPA) entitled *The Sanctions Decade*. The IPA found, in its analysis of UN sanctions over the 1990s, that the UN needed to make further efforts to make sanctions 'smarter' in terms of better targeting governments and avoiding the negative humanitarian consequences civilians often had to suffer. For Mr Axworthy, this first-ever open debate on improving the effectiveness of UN sanctions was overdue: 'The risk is real that the legitimacy, credibility, and utility of this important tool of the Security Council action will be increasingly questioned in the eyes of the international community' (*Hamilton Spectator*, 18 April). The 'openness' of the debate on the council following the release of the study allowed other aggrieved states to raise their concerns. Iraq, Cuba, and Libya called for sanctions to be lifted against them and cited U.S. manipulation of the sanctions regimen. As well, Bulgaria and Macedonia, two countries affected adversely by the UN sanctions directed against the former Yugoslavia, warned that the council needed to take into account the spillover effects of sanctions. The debate closed with Mr Axworthy announcing the creation of a working group to improve UN sanctions.

Also in April, Canada dealt with the specific issue of sanctions against the rebel movement UNITA operating in Angola. At the start of its tenure on the council, Canada had inherited the position of chair of the Angola Sanctions Committee. In order to improve the effectiveness of the sanctions regime, Canada had commissioned an expert-panel report on the issue, which was released in March 2000. This report and its thirty-nine recommendations upset many because it made accusations and actually named names, something that was not done in polite diplomatic circles. Several African leaders were targeted for their active participation in the trade of conflict diamonds that supported UNITA. France did not like the mention of many of its former colonies. European governments were accused of negligence in sanctions enforcement. Also, the report found that countries like Ukraine and Bulgaria were selling weapons to Southern Africa with no questions asked. Despite, or perhaps because of, this unprecedented aggressiveness, the Canadian initiatives paid dividends; the council passed a resolution outlining a seven-month process to tighten sanctions against UNITA with respect to diamonds, diplomatic ties, gasoline, and the travel of UNITA officials. Moreover, Mr Axworthy indicated that Canada would sponsor an international conference pertaining to the trade in conflict diamonds: '[The conference] would help devise a system of controls that would allow for increased transparency and accountability in the flow of diamonds from the source of origin to the world's diamond bourses' (*Cambridge Reporter*, 19 April).

Later, in the wake of the UN's Millennium Summit in September, Canada announced the creation of the International Commission on Intervention and State Sovereignty (ICISS) in response to the challenge to member states laid out by UN Secretary General Kofi Annan in his Millennium Report, *We the Peoples*. For Mr Annan, even though state sovereignty was no longer sacrosanct, the violation of it, for the sake of humanitarian endeavour, by an organization designed to protect states was still a sensitive matter because of the lack of agreed-upon criteria and mechanisms for effective operations. Such sensitivities, for instance, are evident in comments made by Chinese President Jiang Zemin: 'Willful use of force and interference in the internal affairs of other countries in the name of "humanitarianism" not only run counter to the purposes and principles of the UN Charter, but also will cause severe negative consequences' (Halifax *Chronicle-Herald*, 8 September). In light of this challenge, Prime Minister Chrétien announced the ICISS initiative in his 7 September speech to the UN General Assembly. Foreign Affairs Minister Axworthy followed up with the details of the commission a week later. With financial assistance supplied by the Carnegie, MacArthur, and Rockefeller Foundations, along with support from Canada, the ICISS was to 'build a broader understanding of the issues and to foster global political consensus on how to move them forward' (*DFAIT News Release*, no. 233, 14 September). To facilitate this understanding, the ICISS was granted a one-year mandate and was to be made up of state officials, academics, NGO members, former statesmen, and individuals of high international standing. For Canada, this inclusive and exhaustive approach appeared to be the best way to meet the challenge put forth by the Secretary General.

Not all the news was positive, however, for Canada's promotion of human security in 2000. Because of Canada's aggressive stance on the Angolan issue, activists targeted Ottawa for its seeming hypocrisy in letting the operations of a Canadian oil firm, Talisman Energy, in civil war–torn Sudan go unchecked. At the time, Talisman Energy owned a 25 per cent, CDN$800 million stake in oil concessions in Sudan's Upper Nile oil project. Though a report commissioned by the Department of Foreign Affairs, produced by John Hawker, found that Talisman Energy was fuelling the war and thus harming the country's civilians, and the U.S. State Department was highly critical of Talisman Energy's presence in Sudan, Mr Axworthy was unable to affect the firm's partnership with Malaysia, China, and Sudan. The reasons for Mr Axworthy's missing assertiveness on this file are many: he lacked the appropriate legislative tools, key cabinet members were not supportive of sanctioning Talisman Energy, and such sanctioning would have been both a threat to independent Canadian oil-production capacities and a problem for the Liberal Party in the Canadian oil patch in an election year. For activists such as Roger Winter, the executive director of the U.S. Committee for Refugees, Canada's stance seemingly put into question Canada's embrace of the human security agenda: '[T]he failure of Canada to impose sanctions on Talisman Energy reveals a dismaying inability to sustain a foreign policy independent from forces of narrowly conceived political and economic self-interest. It is a sad episode for a country that has been a beacon of humane concern on so many other occasions' (*Globe and Mail*, 23 March).

Perhaps to compensate for the Talisman issue and restore the shine to Canada's beacon, Mr Axworthy hosted in September a conference in Winnipeg with both a human security and a Sudan-oriented focus: the International Conference on War-Affected Children. This week-long global conference featured the attendance of government officials and ministers from fifty countries and of activists and war-affected children from 120 countries. While the dual goals of the conference, the seeking of solutions for children and war-torn societies and the development of child-centred reconciliation efforts, were in line with Canada's human security agenda, the conference was not without controversy. In particular, one speaker, Stephen Lewis, the former Ontario New Democratic Party leader and UNICEF deputy director, was highly critical of both Talisman's activities in Sudan and Canada's decision to invite to the conference Sudan's foreign minister, Mustafa Osman Ismail. For Mr Lewis, the issue of concern was Sudan's blithe support of the Lord's Resistance Army (LRA) battling the government of Uganda, an organization employing child soldiers: 'In my entire adult life, I have never encountered such a venal mask of innocence in the face of such a wanton destruction of children' (*Globe and Mail*, 14 September). In the face of this criticism, Foreign Minister Ismail only agreed to attend the conference at the last minute. Despite this controversy, some positive developments did occur of both a general and Sudan-specific nature. The conference featured over CDN$30 million worth of aid announcements and a drive to obtain one hundred signatures and fifty ratifications for the UN's treaty on child soldiers. In addition, a deal was reached between Canada and Sudan for the release of sixteen children abducted by the LRA. The deal also called for Canada, Libya, and Egypt to help to secure the release of over 6,000 children believed by UNICEF to be in the LRA's ranks.

Defence Policy

National missile defence

The year 2000 marked the renewed security and political importance of National Missile Defence (NMD), the successor to the Reagan-era Strategic Defense Initiative or Star Wars program. On the security side, Pentagon officials increasingly suggested that in light of the conventional military superiority of the United States, potential adversaries would likely turn to asymmetric measures, including attacks involving weapons of mass destruction and missile launches from so-called rogue states. In this vein, a congressional committee determined in 1998 that rogue states like Iran, Iraq, and North Korea did indeed possess the ability to develop the necessary technologies. Similarly, the National Intelligence Committee, in a report sponsored by the CIA, determined that 'the probability that a missile armed with [weapons of mass destruction] would be used against the U.S. forces or interests is higher today than during most of the Cold War and will continue to grow' (*Globe and Mail*, 27 December). Such a crucial finding did not go unnoticed by the two major political parties in the United States. In 1999, facing a Republican-dominated Congress, President Clinton issued a mandate for the United States to field an NMD defence as soon as technically feasible. President-elect George Bush made it clear, both during and after the election campaign, that his administration would develop NMD capabilities sooner rather than later.

For Canada, the NMD issue affected its relations with the United States in a variety of ways. Any operating NMD system would likely be managed through NORAD. However, a lack of Canadian participation might terminate NORAD and thus deprive Canada of vital information needed to protect its sovereignty. NMD would also likely involve Canada, through either the provision of infrastructure and technology or the sheer fact that the debris from destroyed incoming missiles might shower Canadian territory. A successful NMD system would also negate the 1972 Anti-Ballistic Missile Treaty, one of the cornerstones of Cold War–era stability and a device championed by Canada for limiting the nuclear arms race between the United States and the Soviet Union. For President Vladimir Putin of Russia, one of the Soviet Union's successor states, 'the cure of missile defence is worse than the disease' (*Globe and Mail*, 21 July). Moreover, NMD would make the smaller nuclear arsenal of China strategically irrelevant vis-à-vis the United States. As such, it could spark an upsurge in the nuclear arms race as China developed more weaponry to overwhelm U.S. NMD capabilities and, in turn, raise concern among other nuclear armed states such as India. In the same way, a limited NMD system, of perhaps twenty missile interceptors based in Alaska, might redouble the 'atomic' efforts of rogue states.

The year 2000 ended, however, without Canada developing a definitive stance on the issue. Some cabinet members, like Foreign Affairs Minister Axworthy, were hostile to NMD, whereas others, like National Defence Minister Eggleton, were more sympathetic to the U.S. initiative. Prime Minister Chrétien did have two opportunities to discuss the implications of NMD with Russian President Putin, first during bilateral meetings taking place at the G8 Summit in Okinawa and later, in December, during a three-day state visit by President Putin to Canada. While President Putin wished Canada to take the possible role of mediator, Mr Chrétien's approach was based more upon investigating the implications of NMD: 'Our preoccupation is to make sure the stability that exists at this moment is not undermined by this plan that has been put forth by the Americans' (*Globe and Mail*, 19 December). Though George Bush's transition team did not comment specifically on the Chrétien-Putin meeting, the U.S. Secretary of State nominee, Colin Powell, indicated that NMD would nevertheless go ahead and that the incoming Bush administration would enter into negotiations 'with those countries that don't yet understand our thinking' with respect to NMD (*Globe and Mail*, 27 December).

Reform and personnel management

In February 2000, the Defence Minister's Monitoring Committee on Change praised the Canadian Forces for its ongoing efforts to reform itself in the wake of the 1993 Somalia Affair and the subsequent public inquiry. The objective of the committee, formed in 1997, was to monitor the implementation of the 339 recommendations made by various boards and committees during the 1990s. By 2000 the military could claim that 90 per cent of these recommendations had been implemented. John Fraser, the committee chairman, contended that enough reform had occurred that a Somalia-type incident could never happen again. Though the committee indicated that more efforts were needed in the areas of military education and the management of the reserves, the committee's 'report card' revealed that much had been done to change the ethos and the culture of the military organization.* A list of the key changes included the following: improvements in the military justice system, the creation of a Military Police Complaints Commission (MPCC) and an ombudsman's office, and the development of anti-racism training, as well as training and orientation for troops bound for overseas operations.

Some events in 2000, however, revealed both how difficult things were in the early 1990s and that change and better management was needed in other areas of the military services. In 1999, the army admitted that some 3,000 of its troops might have been exposed to harmful PCBs while filling sandbags during overseas duty in Croatia from 1992 to 1995. Indeed, 10 per cent of these soldiers had complained of significant health problems since their return to Canada. The subsequent military investigation, the findings for which were presented to the department in January 2000, determined that though arsenic was found in the soil, there was not enough to cause harm. As summed up by

* With respect to the reserves, a report released on 6 June contended that they were understaffed to the degree that the whole system was at risk of collapse. With fewer than 12,000 reserve soldiers in Canada's ranks, the report asserted that these numbers needed to be doubled. Subsequently, Minister Eggleton announced on 6 October that the federal government would put $42 million over two years into reinforcing the army reserves. This money was part of a five-year restructuring plan to modernize the reserves and increase their effectiveness.

Colonel Joe Sharpe, the lead military investigator, 'The board has concluded that there is no scientific proof that the soil in Croatia, specifically in sector south, contained persistent contaminants in sufficient quantities to cause any serious health hazard to Canadian forces who served there' (CBC News Online, 26 January). Instead, the investigators hypothesized that the health problems were possibly caused by stress given the horrific environment in which the soldiers served. The report's finding left the affected soldiers frustrated, given that they were inconclusive about what was making them ill.

Also stemming from Canadian operations in Croatia were scandals regarding Delta Company, a mixed unit of reservists and full-time military personnel. In May, RCMP investigators revealed that up to twelve soldiers were involved in the poisoning of Warrant Officer Matt Stopford in order to sideline him from duty and that more superiors may have been targeted as well. In Mr Stopford's case, the soldiers, in 1992, added antifreeze, eye drops, and boot blackener to his coffee. Mr Stopford, since retired from the military due to illness, initially believed that his sickness was caused by the aforementioned PCB contamination and that the military was attempting to cover up this fact.

The case became even more intriguing when the military indicated that because a three-year statute of limitations had run out in 1995, the soldiers could not be charged. It also was revealed that though reports of Mr Stopford's poisoning dated back to 1993, military police were only alerted in the summer of 1999. Then it became clear that the alleged offending soldiers could indeed be prosecuted because the military's National Investigation Service had presented only a limited array of legal options to General Maurice Baril, the Chief of Defence Staff. General Baril then indicated that the case would be handed over to Ontario Crown prosecutors. This, in turn, sparked the military's top police officer, the Provost Marshal, Brigadier-General Patricia Samson, to request in June that the MPCC investigate her own staff in terms of its handling of the Stopford case. From June until November, the MPCC conducted its investigations, but its final report was not released before the end of 2000.

In another health-related matter, on 5 May the military's top judge, Colonel Guy Brais, stayed charges of insubordination against Sergeant Mike Kipling, a former air force officer, for refusing a dose of anthrax vaccine while stationed in Kuwait in 1998. Though Mr Kipling had received an earlier dose of anthrax vaccine while participating in the 1990 Persian Gulf War, he balked at receiving a second dose due to the negative effects it might have on his health. Even though military witnesses testified that Canada's Charter of Rights and Freedoms had to be interpreted narrowly in the military context given the need to maintain discipline, Colonel Brais concluded that the Charter did protect soldiers from being forced to take drugs: '[T]he government ... could never be justified to impose inoculation of soldiers with an unsafe and dangerous vaccine' (*Globe and Mail*, 6 May). As recognized by Jay Prober, Mr Kipling's civilian lawyer, such a decision was truly precedent-setting in terms of how the Charter impacts upon the military: 'It's a huge step forward for human rights in the military. The chief military judge has told the military that in the future, consider the Charter of Rights' (*Globe and Mail*, 6 May). Because of the case's setting of a precedent, the military's director of prosecutions, Colonel Kim Carter, filed a notice of appeal for the Kipling case with the Court Martial Appeal Court of Canada. Mr Kipling's fate remained unresolved at the close of 2000.

Defence budget and procurement

As a result of the 2000 federal budget, an additional $1.7 billion was allotted to DND/CF over three years. The budget provided $400 million, $500 million, and $600 million in new funding for fiscal years 2000–1, 2001–2, and 2002–3 respectively. In addition, in order to help defray the costs associated with CF operations in East Timor and Kosovo, DND/CF received a further $146 million in fiscal year 2000–1. These increases marked the second consecutive budget of augmented defence spending after a decade of cuts that saw the defence budget shrink by 23 per cent. Thus, the main estimates for fiscal year 2000–1 stood at $11.2 billion. At the time of the budget's release in 2000, Defence Minister Eggleton indicated that the additional monies would go towards Canadian overseas operations, quality-of-life improvements for personnel, and the purchase of maritime helicopters. Money would also be directed, said Mr Eggleton, towards ongoing procurement plans: 'A lot of it is going to be for things that we already have in the stream, such as new submarines or armoured personnel carriers. We'll just pay them off faster, just like paying a credit card off faster. We'll pay the debt off faster and we'll have more capacity for future purchases' (CBC Newsworld, 28 February). This stress on procurement was meant to help realize the government's plan to increase the capital portion of the defence budget to at least 23 per cent over five years. In 2000, the budget distribution stood at 45 per cent for personnel costs, 31 per cent for operations and maintenance, 5 per cent for transfer payments, and only 19 per cent for capital investment.

True to his word, Defence Minister Eggleton announced on 17 August that Canada would begin the procurement process to replace the forty-year-old Sea King helicopters. Upon attaining power in 1993, the Liberal government terminated the Conservative government's plan to replace the Sea Kings with the EH-101 helicopter. The Liberal procurement plans, valued at $2.9 billion, called for twenty-eight helicopters. In defence of the seven-year delay, Mr Eggleton indicated that the government's plan would save Canadian taxpayers as much as $1.5 billion, even after taking into account the cancellation costs for the EH-101 contract and the necessary upgrades to keep the Sea Kings flying during the estimated five-year procurement process. This decision, however, did not come without controversy. Opposition parties noted that the drawn-out process meant further delays that would continue to risk the lives of service personnel. In addition, E.H. Industries, the producers of the EH-101 and one of the competitors in the 2000 bidding process, requested in October that the Canadian International Trade Tribunal protect it from discrimination in light of the political saliency of the issue. E.H. Industries officials charged that the government had designed the procurement process so that it would lose: 'The procedures ... have been designed by the government to avoid political embarrassment by ensuring that the Cormorant [an E.H. Industries product] is not selected' (*Globe and Mail*, 13 October).

The year 2000 also featured the reinvigoration of Canada's submarine service with the October arrival in Canadian waters of HMCS *Victoria*, the first of four submarines meant to replace Canada's Oberan-class submarines as part of the Submarine Capability Life Extension project. HMCS *Victoria*, the former Upholder-class submarine HMS *Unseen*, arrived in Halifax following two years of refits and sea trials by Canadian naval personnel in the United Kingdom. The three additional submarines of the newly christened Victoria class were to arrive in Canada from the United Kingdom in six-month intervals over the following two years.

Finally, in July, Canada launched a joint public-private initiative to train, at Moose Jaw and Cold Lake, Canadian pilots, NATO pilots, and select pilots from other allied countries. Given that the capacity at Sheppard Air Force Base in Texas, a major NATO training centre, was limited, Canada hoped to cash in on the demand. Ottawa selected Bombardier to be the holder of the twenty-year contract. During that time, Bombardier is to provide simulators, aircraft, training materials, and ground support for the Canadian and foreign pilots training in Saskatchewan and Alberta.

CF operations of note

In light of the overextension the CF faced at the start of the new century, Ottawa announced in January the withdrawal of the 650 CF personnel performing Operation Toucan, Canada's contribution to the Australian-led International Force in East Timor (INTERFET). The CF had mounted this mission in September 1999 following the East Timorese vote to secede from Indonesia. By the end of January, Canada's air component, two Hercules transport aircraft, had returned. The naval component, HMCS *Protecteur*, returned in February and the land contingent arrived back in Canada in March. After INTERFET was replaced by the UN Transitional Administration in East Timor (UNTAET) in early 2000, three CF personnel served in staff positions at the UNTAET headquarters.

Force rationalization was also apparent in the CF's presence in the Balkans in 2000. In June 2000, the CF ceased Operation Kinetic, its battle group operation that formed the Canadian contingent in NATO's KFOR operations in Kosovo. Ottawa sent the 1,400-personnel contingent to Kosovo in June 1999 following NATO's air campaign against Serbia in the spring of 1999. Similarly, Canada also terminated Operation Echo, its air component for the NATO operations in Kosovo. At the height of the Kosovo campaign in 1999, eighteen CF-18 aircraft participated in NATO missions. Ottawa withdrew the final six aircraft from their base in Aviano, Italy, in December 2000. This left Operation Palladium, the 1,600-personnel force under UN mandate to help keep the peace in Bosnia-Herzegovina. To further reduce the strain on these personnel, DND introduced civilian contractors to provide logistical and communications support. The government hoped that through this Contractor Support Project, the introduction of these contracted personnel, supplied by ATCO Frontec of Edmonton, would reduce the force requirement by 150 uniformed personnel.

This retrenchment from some parts of the world, however, did not mean that Canada shied away entirely from foreign ventures elsewhere in 2000. In particular, in December 2000, Canada deployed a 450-strong infantry command group to monitor the disputed border and ceasefire between Ethiopia and Eritrea as part of Operation Eclipse. The Canadian contribution, alongside a military contribution from the Netherlands, was part of the first deployment of the Stand-by High Readiness Brigade and formed a major component of the UN Mission in Ethiopia and Eritrea.

Not all of the military's operations in 2000 were contemporary in orientation. Operation Memoria was directed at commemorating Canadian service personnel who had sacrificed their lives in earlier conflicts. On 25 May the remains of an unknown Canadian soldier, a casualty of the First World War buried at Vimy, France, were retuned to Canada under military escort. CF personnel participated in the laying-in-state on Parliament Hill and the operation culminated with the remains being interred at the National War Memorial in Ottawa on 28 May.

Perhaps the most unusual CF operation in 2000 was August's Operation Megaphone meant to recover Canadian military equipment returning from KFOR operations on the privately owned ship GTS *Katie*. The 36,000-tonne Soviet-built ship was to have been in port 16 July. The *Katie*'s owner, Third Ocean Marine Navigation Company of Annapolis, Maryland, had been subcontracted by the Canadian firm SDV Logistics, which in turn had been subcontracted by Andromeda Navigation Company of Montreal, the company initially tasked by the military to return roughly 10 per cent of the army's equipment. Third Ocean Marine was withholding the CF's equipment due to a payment dispute with its Canadian contractor. The Chrétien government ordered CF personnel to take hold of the vessel and regain the equipment to fulfil other national security tasks at home and abroad. The operation, culminating on 3 August, involved HMCS *Athabaskan*, HMCS *Montreal*, two Sea King helicopters, a Labrador helicopter, and an Aurora long-range patrol aircraft. A fourteen-sailor team boarded the ship by helicopter in international waters off Newfoundland. After seizing control of the ship, the navy brought the ship into Canadian waters and eventually to Bécancour, Quebec, on the St Lawrence River. Defence Minister Eggleton rationalized the government's decision to board the ship as follows: 'No responsible government can allow interference with its important military capability ... We had to take action' (*Globe and Mail*, 4 August). In addition to the general embarrassment regarding Canada's lack of military sealift capability, something Mr Eggleton vowed to change, another embarrassing revelation regarding Operation Megaphone was that only one Sea King helicopter participated in the boarding because the other helicopter had a malfunctioning rotor head. This increased the length of time for the boarding and potentially put at risk the boarding party.

Other than the final stages of Operation Abacus, 2000 did not require the major application of military resources for domestic operations other than for standard search and rescue and sovereignty patrol operations. During previous years in the 1990s, the CF was often requested to assist in the wake of environmental catastrophes such as ice storms and floods. The forces did, however, at the request of the Province of Alberta, provide both regular and reserve personnel to search for survivors and the dead and to provide relief assistance in the aftermath of the 14 July tornado that struck the Green Acres campground on Pine Lake, 40 kilometres southeast of Red Deer. The tornado, the fourth deadliest in Canadian history, claimed the lives of ten people and sent a further 130 to hospital.

EMMANUEL BRUNET-JAILLY AND
WARREN MAGNUSSON

Municipal affairs

Urban politics and local government

In the last quarter of the twentieth century, the neo-liberal model of governance came to predominate in almost every part of the world, including Canada. This model re-legitimized a role that municipal leaders here and elsewhere have often preferred: to be promoters of private investment rather than agents of a powerful state. In the Keynesian-liberal state of the post-war era, municipalities and other local authorities were enlisted in efforts to regulate the economy, stimulate economic development, redistribute income in favour of the poor, provide a wide range of social services, and control the physical development of cities. Municipal leaders often chaffed at the role they were assigned: they wanted to put their emphasis on attracting outside capital and stimulating local business. Social pressures for better and more uniform services and facilities led the provinces to take over more and more responsibilities from the municipalities in the 1950s and 1960s, but as neo-liberal ideas began to take hold in the 1970s there was a reaction against any further extension of state activity. There were demands for lower taxes, less bureaucracy, greater responsiveness to consumer preferences, decreased public spending, and greater reliance on private enterprise to provide what had formerly been regarded as public services. This meant selling off public enterprises that provided marketable goods, contracting out services to private suppliers, eliminating many regulations on businesses, and reducing the scope of state activity. The idea was that social goods would be more plentiful and of higher quality if private business were encouraged to enter the former public sector and compete for consumer favour in appropriately organized markets. The state as such would be reduced to its 'core' functions. It would not need such extensive resources, and so the money that had once gone to taxes would be freed up for other purposes. In this neo-liberal model of governance, municipalities, like the higher state authorities, would have a different role: part entrepreneurial, part facilitative, and in only a limited degree directive, regulatory, or immediately productive. This was in line with what many municipal leaders had always preferred.

The neo-liberal model is supposed to involve a shift in the locus of public authority: upward (to new trans-national bodies like the WTO or NAFTA), outward (to private contractors and non-governmental organizations), and downward (to local authorities). The first two of these movements have been quite noticeable, but the last has not been so apparent. In Canada, the local authorities had already lost a great deal of ground to the provinces by the mid-1970s. This was perhaps most evident in the fields of health, education, and welfare. If anything, the trend toward tighter provincial control in these fields was amplified in the last quarter of the century. For various reasons, local school boards and health boards have not been especially sympathetic to neo-liberal ideas. Provincial governments have used their powers to develop new arrangements that bring the private sector into service provision and management. On the other hand, municipalities have always operated in a way that is closer to the neo-liberal model, when permitted to do so. (One might say, in fact, that neo-liberalism is really the generalization of the 'municipal' model of governance.) Municipalities make deals with developers to get parks and other services paid for; they enter into partnerships with private businesses for the development of civic facilities; they work with an array of non-governmental organizations to provide social, cultural, and recreational services; and they see themselves less as 'governments' than as 'community promoters.' The disposition of municipalities to work on the neo-liberal model is partly an effect of the fiscal squeeze that puts them at a severe disadvantage (in relation to the federal and provincial governments) in the business of raising revenues by taxation. Municipal leaders, whatever their ideological bent, have usually found that they have had to work closely with local business in order to get things done. On the other hand, the unwanted effect of the neo-liberal revolution at other levels of government has been to shift responsibilities downward without providing matching resources, thus making the transfer of authority more apparent than real. Municipal politicians of all stripes have complained about this trend. Some of the provinces have tried to solve the problem by consolidating local authorities into larger units that can (supposedly) deal with the challenges more effectively.

By 2000, there were signs that municipal government was entering a new era. There was widespread recognition that the Canadian urban infrastructure had begun to deteriorate. Too little money had been invested in the renewal of roads and sewers. There had been few improvements in urban transit. The legendary cleanliness and hominess of Canadian cities seemed to be disappearing in face of an upsurge of homelessness, drug abuse, gang violence, and un-swept litter. Commentators suggested that Canadian downtowns were deteriorating, just at the time when their American counterparts were beginning to improve. Urban Canada was becoming more concentrated: half of all Canadians lived in just four mega-metropolitan areas: Toronto, Montreal, Vancouver, and Edmonton-Calgary. At the same time, the bigger cities were becoming more and more diverse, as immigrants from Asia, Africa, Latin America, and the Caribbean arrived by the hundreds of thousands every year. The strain on housing and social services (including education and health care) was apparent, and was exacerbated by the fact that people who could not find work or did not fit into rural or suburban life tended to drift toward the inner cities. This had always been the pattern, but the diversity of the new urban population posed particular challenges. What is more, the unpacking of the inner cities, which had been going on since the 1940s, had led to the dispersal of low-income housing to the suburbs. The result was that conditions associated with 'the inner city' emerged in pockets in the suburbs and in smaller towns. In greater or lesser degree, the crisis of Canadian urbanism was felt everywhere. It was by no means clear that the neo-liberal revolution had given the municipalities the means to deal with the challenges they faced.

In the year 2000 'Walkerton' came to symbolize the problems associated with the new model of governance. Walkerton is a small town in southwestern Ontario. In mid-May, it became clear that the local water supply had been polluted with a dangerous form of E. coli. More than one thousand people became ill, and seven died. This was a great shock to Canadians generally, because most of them had come to take clean municipal water for granted. As the media turned its attention on the issue, it became apparent that the regulatory systems that had been designed to protect the quality of water were generally not as good as they should be, in Ontario or elsewhere. Much attention was paid to the fact that the Province of Ontario had reduced staff in its Ministry of the Environment, loosened regulations, downloaded responsibility to the municipalities, and privatized testing facilities. These measures were all in line with neo-liberal ideas, but, in Walkerton at least, the results were disastrous. Had the province gone too far in reducing its own regulatory capacity? Was it relying too heavily on private contractors or industry self-policing? Was it expecting too much of small municipalities? For some, the lesson of Walkerton was that the neo-liberal revolution had gone too far, and that steps had to be taken to restore the wasted strength of the state. Others thought that this confirmed that municipalities had to be bigger and more professional than they had been in the past – in rural as well as urban areas. Still others thought that the principles of the recent reforms had been correct, and that critics were mistaking an issue of individual malfeasance for a structural problem. Whatever the case, 'Walkerton' highlighted the issues that had gradually come to the fore in the 1990s: the renewal of the urban infrastructure; the effects of downloading, privatization, and market-based regulatory regimes; questions of municipal fiscal and administrative capacity; and the looming crisis of the cities.

In this and subsequent annual reviews, we will be focusing our attention on the problems and prospects of government at the municipal level. Is yet another new model of governance emerging, or can we expect the neo-liberal model developed in the 1970s, 1980s, and 1990s to continue? Will the municipalities succeed in establishing themselves as a third order of government, comparable to the federal and provincial? Will the federal government come to their aid, as it did in the 1940s, 1950s, and 1960s? Will the trend toward larger units of municipal government continue? Will Canadian municipal politics continue to be predominantly non-partisan? Will new Canadians change the tenor, tone, and disposition of municipal government? Will the municipalities assume new functions or reinterpret old responsibilities, in light of new challenges? Will there be massive reinvestment in the Canadian urban infrastructure? Will the crises in health care and education lead to the development of new institutions at the local level? Will these institutions be democratic? If so, in what way? Will ordinary Canadians become more involved with municipal and other local institutions, or will they continue to focus on their private lives? What are the consequences of any of these things for Canadians?

This is the first time that the *Canadian Annual Review* has attempted to survey developments at the municipal level. Perhaps this first appearance is itself a sign of change. Our task is an unusually complicated one, because there are literally thousands of municipalities and other local authorities in Canada. At best, we can point to a few trends and developments that have caught our attention. We will be organizing our remarks year by year under five headings: Cities in the Marketplace, the Cultures of Cities, Regional Governance, Local Democracy, and Cities in Confederation. People have come to recognize that states are not really outside the marketplace: they are embedded within it. This is even truer for municipalities, which have always been constituted as public corporations whose business it is to promote local interests in a competitive market. As we know, that market is now global and not just national, regional, or local. Thus, the way cities respond to the market is crucial. Equally crucial is the fact that cities are the venues in which contemporary cultures meet, change, and re-form themselves. New modes of urban life emerge daily. So, the cultures of cities are constantly changing, throwing up new governmental problems and creating new political possibilities. Yet cities are embedded in a system of multilevel governance, a system that demands both vertical and horizontal coordination. Thus, the pattern of intergovernmental relations at the regional level is crucial, not least in the way that it affects municipal boundaries, functions, and resources. Municipalities are supposed to provide the basis for local democracy – the form of democracy that is, for many people, the most genuine. Local democracy has never been as vibrant as it might be; so, we are well advised to keep a watch on its character and quality. We also have to watch what place cities will have in Confederation: to date, they have been denied the role that might be expected of them, given their size and importance.

Cities in the marketplace

In the 1990s, everyone became aware of the globalization of markets. In that decade, the notion of a 'global city' – a headquarters centre in the global marketplace – entered into common consciousness and thus into the thinking of municipal leaders. Heightened recognition of the competitive context was reflected in various surveys that ranked cities nationally and internationally according to investment and quality-of-life criteria. By international standards, Canadian cities were relatively cheap places to do business, thanks to the low value of the Canadian dollar. Moreover, Canadian cities were still thought to provide a high quality of life – at least for business executives and other high-paid professionals. Some cities were thought to be especially friendly to business: the *Report on Business* had singled out Montreal, Vancouver, Edmonton, Winnipeg, and Moncton in this regard early in the decade. As always, the rate of growth varied from city to city. Calgary had been leading the pack for a number of years, but uncertainties in 2000 about oil and gas prices were putting a brake on new investment. In its annual survey *Metropolitan Outlook*, the Conference Board of Canada predicted that local GDP would increase in Edmonton by 4.1 per cent, Ottawa-Hull 3.9 per cent, Toronto 3.5 per cent, Montreal 3.3 per cent, Calgary only 2.8 per cent, Regina 2.8 per cent, Vancouver 2.5 per cent, Winnipeg 2.5 per cent, and Victoria 2.4 per cent. Problems on the west coast were connected to difficulties across the Pacific in Asia, whereas the central Canadian and Albertan cities continued to profit from the ongoing expansion of the U.S. economy. Although the traditional resource industries were still important, it was becoming apparent that Canada's future economic success would depend on its capacity to develop internationally competitive businesses in the 'knowledge-based' industries, industries that were inevitably centred in cities that had the appropriate urban infrastructure.

Canada has long been a highly urbanized nation, and it became more so during the 1990s. From 1995 to 2000, the urban population of Canada – defined as the population living in communities of over 10,000 – increased by over 5 per cent, whereas the rural population actually declined. By 2000, four of every five Canadians lived in urban areas. No less than 64 per cent lived in metropolitan areas with a population of over 100,000, and the great majority of these people were in agglomerations of more than a million: namely, the extended 'Golden Horseshoe' around Toronto (6.7 million by 2001), the greater Montreal area (3.7 million), the Lower Mainland of British Columbia and southern Vancouver Island (2.7 million), the Edmonton-Calgary 'corridor' (2.1 million), and the greater Ottawa area (1.1 million). Whatever its economic and social significance, however, this urban reality was little reflected in the structure of Canadian federalism. The Toronto, Montreal, and Vancouver regions dwarfed most of the provinces, and it would not be long before the Ottawa, Calgary, and Edmonton regions were all more populous than Manitoba, Saskatchewan, or Nova Scotia (let alone the three smaller Atlantic provinces). Although the fourth, fifth, and sixth biggest Canadian metropolitan regions would each be twice as big as Newfoundland, none would be represented at the federal-provincial conference tables. Ontario has long complained about being the 'milch cow' of Confederation, but Toronto accounts for 44 per cent of the province's GDP and makes a net annual contribution of $5.5 billion to the federal coffers. Vancouver accounts for 53 per cent of British Columbia's GDP, Montreal for 49 per cent of Quebec's, Winnipeg for 67 per cent of Manitoba's, and Calgary and Edmonton together for 64 per cent of Alberta's. However, the importance of these cities is rarely reflected in the policy attention that they get from the federal and provincial governments.

The attention they do get is not always welcome. Perhaps the most dramatic urban-related measure of the late 1990s was the amalgamation of the City of Toronto with the other five cities in the Municipality of Metropolitan Toronto. The Ontario provincial government forced this through against much political opposition, not least from the municipal councils concerned. The measure was supposed to improve the competitive position of Canada's largest city by eliminating administrative confusion and raising its international profile. However, preliminary assessments of amalgamation's effects were neither clear nor positive. In one report, economist Enid Slack underlined the complexity of the changes. The new mega-city had a population of 2.4 million, an operating budget of $6 billion, 26,000 staff, and an additional 18,000 staff working for about 214 local agencies, boards, and commissions. It had additional obligations as a result of the recent downloading of responsibilities for social housing and public health. It also had to cope with the effects of a major reorganization of the tax system, since the provincial government was now insisting that all properties be assessed at current market value for purposes of municipal taxation. Whatever the intrinsic merits of these changes, they posed an enormous challenge for municipal officials and politicians. Transition costs had been originally estimated at $153 million, but the new City of Toronto needed $56 million just to cover the cost of staff redundancy and needed a grant and two interest-free loans from the province (a total of $163 million) to help with additional transitional costs. City officials claimed that the preliminary cost-saving goal of 10 per cent of $1.5 billion of gross expenditure had been achieved and that staff and program rationalization had saved money. However, 62 new firefighters and 21 city planners had to be hired – too many had been let go in 1998 – and the new staff collective agreement and the new downloading were likely to affect the budget in future years. The city also faced increasing poverty, deteriorating infrastructures, and ongoing difficulties with its garbage disposal. The projected increase in net debt load from 2000 to 2004 is $1.2 billion.

Other municipalities in Ontario had also been amalgamated, for similar reasons. In 2000, an in-depth survey of fifteen municipalities revealed how complicated those amalgamations had been. The survey found that the municipalities' most important concerns were (1) the preservation of their values and community traditions, (2) getting stakeholders to agree on the process of change, (3) public cynicism about the restructuring, (4) animosity between council and communities, and (5) animosity between the communities involved in restructuring. Overall, the restructuring seemed to have had three outcomes:

- the new municipalities were able to either improve service delivery or at least maintain the same level and quality of services;
- most new municipalities had undertaken to equate taxes within their boundaries: in other words, taxes had gone up and down, depending on the communities;
- municipal staff members were under high levels of stress to adapt to new jobs, new functions, and uncertainties regarding their employment.

In non-metropolitan areas, enlarged municipalities have an additional problem in dealing with an urban-rural divide, now internalized within their own boundaries. The Ontario government's decision to restrict the scale of the Toronto mega-city, so that only about half the population of the Greater Toronto Area is included within its boundaries, has spared the city that problem, although it has raised serious issues about coordination within the larger area. Whether any of the measures related to municipal reform will make Toronto or other cities more competitive within the global arena remains to be seen.

In 2000, two connected issues relating to municipal competitiveness drew particular attention nationally: the apparent deterioration of the urban infrastructure and the fiscal incapacity of the municipal governments responsible for repairing and upgrading the facilities at issue. From 1995 to 2000, total local government revenues increased by only 6 per cent, while federal government revenues increased by 21 per cent and those of provincial governments by 13 per cent. This was during a period when the federal government was downloading responsibilities onto the provinces, and the provinces in turn were downloading them onto the municipalities. The latter process had been most marked in the largest province, Ontario. However, it was not only in Ontario that the municipalities faced financial problems. A Canada West Foundation study of municipal finance in Vancouver, Edmonton, Calgary, Saskatoon, Regina, and Winnipeg showed that, over the last decade, these six western cities had experienced great financial stress. They were faced with reductions in their grants from senior governments, stagnant revenues from inflexible property taxes, and ongoing pressures for expenditure increases due to population expansion and economic growth. Their overall expenditure strategy had been to try to maintain per capita capital spending, while cutting per capita service expenditures. Some cities, such as Calgary, increased their reliance on user fees and service sales, while others, such as Edmonton, relied on increased revenues from their utilities, particularly telephone, water, and electricity. (Edmonton is unusual in having such a large presence in the utility sector.) Surprisingly, all six cities were able to reduce their overall net debt, but not without putting a crimp on traditional service expenditures.

The Federation of Canadian Municipalities had been lobbying for federal support for the renewal of the urban infrastructure, and the first fruit of that effort appeared in the form of a six-year, $2 billion infrastructure program in the 2000 federal budget. Ottawa claimed that the program would have two guiding principles: that all three levels of government would be equal partners, including large and small, rural and urban municipalities, and that municipalities would be the primary sponsors of the projects. The projects had to involve rehabilitation, upgrades, or new construction, rather than maintenance projects. Critics complained that the ad hoc nature of the program was at odds with the need for long-term planning. Moreover, the focus of the program was on water and waste-water infrastructure: in a way not unwelcome, in light of the Walkerton experience, but nonetheless an approach neglectful of other aspects of municipal infrastructure, which account for 80 per cent of expenditures. Roads and bridges are a particular problem: municipalities are faced with a $10 billion rehabilitation or upgrade backlog. Critics also noted that the program did nothing to encourage more compact forms of development or alternative forms of transport that might have reduced pressure on urban roads. Relative to the municipal need, the federal commitment remained very limited.

In the 1990s, municipalities had come to rely much more on local property taxes and much less on provincial grants as a revenue source. Surprisingly, the proportional usage of user fees remained stable. The neo-liberal view – promoted by the IMF and the World Bank, as well as by many domestic lobby groups and economic analysts – is that user fees are generally preferable, since they encourage people to be economical. Suppliers will not offer more than consumers are willing to pay for; consumers will not demand things under the illusion that public services are free. The social-democratic view is that true-cost pricing of essential services will have a deleterious effect on low-income people (and hence indirectly on the quality of urban life generally). In any case, many urban services like public transit or public recreational facilities have a social benefit – to the environment or to the upbringing of the next generation – that goes beyond any benefit to the immediate user. Hence, there are difficult questions about the appropriate levels and forms of municipal subsidy. In a way, the property tax has always been regarded as a type of user-fee for the benefits associated with the urban infrastructure. Thus, there is a long-held view that property tax revenues should be used only for certain things – not including expensive health, education, and social services. On the other hand, there has been stout resistance to the economists' view that a fair property tax is one that is geared to market-value assessment. Given the often-rapid escalation of real estate prices in urban areas, property taxpayers are often shocked by sudden rises in assessment that threaten to trigger major tax increases. This makes it difficult for municipal councils to take advantage of what might otherwise be major revenue windfalls.

In British Columbia, Alberta, and Saskatchewan, there were important efforts at the provincial level to revise the arrangements for municipal finance, but the changes proposed were by no means dramatic. Although there was continued talk about diversifying municipal revenue sources, the pressure to keep taxes down was sufficient to forestall major initiatives. Instead, municipalities were being encouraged to enter into more public-private partnerships and generally to seek innovative ways of doing more with less. British Columbia, for instance, had brought in legislation in 1999 to facilitate public-private partnerships at the municipal level. That this occurred in a province with an NDP government was a sign of the general shift in attitudes in favour of market-based solutions to public policy problems. On the other hand, there were signs that the municipalities were beginning to respond to the broader social responsibilities thrust upon them by ongoing demographic shifts and changes in senior policy.

The cultures of cities

Canadian cities are always in a state of flux. People move into them from rural areas and smaller towns, from other provinces, and from other countries. Calgary and Edmonton have been magnets for Canadians from other provinces, whereas Toronto and Vancouver have been particularly attractive to immigrants from foreign countries. About half the annual population increase in Canada is the result of immigration from other countries, and the majority of the immigrants are from Asia. Over 43 per cent of Toronto's residents are foreign-born – a much higher percentage than in New York (24 per cent) or Los Angeles (31 per cent). Vancouver, at over 37 per cent, has a proportionately larger foreign-born population than any American city but Miami (40 per cent). Clearly, the local authorities are faced with a significant challenge in dealing with new immigrants, especially those who have little knowledge of English or French. Nonetheless, it is a different sort of migrancy – one that has almost nothing to do with immigration from abroad – that has put the municipalities and other authorities into an especially knotty predicament. This is the problem of homelessness, a problem connected in some degree with migration from the rural areas of Canada, but much more obviously related to issues of unemployment and underemployment, rising housing costs, falling welfare rates, the de-institutionalization of the mentally ill, and ongoing problems of alcoholism and drug abuse. The new ethnic and cultural diversity of Canadian cities has been a source of strength in a globalizing economy, and inter-cultural tensions have been remarkably limited in scope and intensity. On the other hand, the appearance of large numbers of beggars on the streets and of visibly homeless people in parks and other public areas has shocked many Canadians into the recognition that a substantial minority of the population are not faring at all well and not finding the services and facilities they need to lead better lives.

In November 1998, the 'big city mayors' caucus' of the Federation of Canadian Municipalities (FCM) had declared homelessness a 'national disaster.' A subsequent call for action was presented at the June 1999 FCM meeting. It asked for 20,000 new or acquired housing units each year for ten years, the rehabilitation of 10,000 affordable housing units each year for ten years, and the provision of income or rental assistance to make units affordable for 40,000 households each year for ten years. Shelter and rent assistance initiatives were also on the agenda of the FCM National Housing Policy Option Team. Their recommendations were integrated into the Quality of Life Infrastructure Program Proposal that the FCM presented to Finance Minister Paul Martin in 1999. As a follow-up, Claude Beaudoin, mayor of Val Belair, Quebec, and chair of the FCM standing committee on infrastructures, called for a federal, provincial, and local infrastructure plan to address homelessness, affordable housing, environmental infrastructures, urban transit, and municipal roads. The federal government response included a $2 billion commitment for infrastructures and an acknowledgment that a municipal, provincial, and federal partnership framework was needed, as were clearly distinguished investments for transportation and housing. There was speculation that this proposal might well become an example of new multi-level government cooperation. In October 2000, an FCM position paper entitled 'A National Affordable Housing Strategy' was submitted to the federal and provincial governments, as well as to builders, developers, lenders, and nonprofit housing organizations across the country. Finally, in December 2000, the federal government announced that it would contribute $753 million toward homelessness for the next four years.

In 1999, the FCM initiated an annual 'Quality of Life' survey. The survey allows municipal governments to identify and promote awareness of issues affecting quality of life across Canadian communities, to better target policies and resources aimed at improving quality of life, to support collaborative efforts to improve quality of life, and to establish municipal governments as strong and legitimate partners in public-policy debates in Canada. The year 2000 survey revealed an increase in income disparities in Canada's urban centres. New variables on the environment and social infrastructures, as well as on homelessness and housing, were added to the survey the following year.

In 2000, the FCM's annual policy paper on social infrastructures articulated a clear stand on two issues. First, it asserted the need for consultation by other governments with municipal governments, arguing that they are consulted too rarely in advance of policy or program changes despite their knowledge of economic and social problems, their assessment capacity, and their strong desire to influence the policy process. Second, it stressed the exclusive importance of federal redistribution programs, which must both protect equalization programs (as stated in the Constitution) and meet the basic needs of all (as enshrined in the Universal Declaration of Human Rights) in order to protect equality and fairness among Canadian municipalities.

The FCM also succeeded in getting $125 million in federal support for a Green Municipal Enabling Fund and a Green Municipal Investment Fund. The FCM–federal government 'green infrastructure' partnership promoted audits and interest and loan guarantees toward environmentally efficient projects. Aware of the amount of greenhouse gas resulting from municipal infrastructure and energy use, sixty municipalities, representing 40 per cent of the Canadian population, became partners in a climate protection program, a joint initiative of the FCM and the International Council for Local Environmental Initiatives. Both of these actions highlighted the increased influence of the FCM, which, since the mid-1990s, has become the prominent voice of Canadian municipalities.

Municipal officials' inherent proximity to citizens puts them at the forefront of most urban social problems. Their ability to identify and define social and urban problems more quickly than officials at other levels of government allows them to participate productively in national policy discussions, be involved in the policy implementation process, or, at the very least, be able to assess federal and provincial programs effectively. Take, for example, the Harris government of Ontario's downloading of social housing to cities in 1998. Such downloading of social programs or of the administration of social policies has had the effect of strengthening the policy position of cities and increasing their evaluation capacity. In 2000, their concerns about housing and shelters were heard at the federal level in a short time, which may be a sign of the increasing political clout of better-organized and coordinated urban regions.

The Vancouver Agreement, signed in March 2000, sets an exemplary form of partnership between the municipality of Vancouver, the province of British Columbia, and the federal government. After the failure of the Vancouver city caucus of 1995, which had brought together the three levels of government, but did not result in any concrete actions, the Vancouver Agreement, by contrast, focuses on the policy. It is an initiative of the federal Department of Western Economic Diversification, and is the first of its kind in Canada that explicitly recognizes that an urban development agreement should include all levels of governments so as to allow actions to be taken in policy areas that are not formally the responsibility of the city in question. For example, the federal Secretary of State for Western Economic Diversification and the Secretary of State for Multiculturalism and the Status of Women, the provincial Ministry of Community Development, and the Mayor of Vancouver signed the agreement, engaging a dozen federal and provincial departments and agencies and the municipality. It is a complex and ambitious effort to address specifically problems associated with Downtown Eastside, and regarding housing, employment, and social and economic development strategies, as well as enforcement and security strategies.

The problems in Vancouver's Downtown Eastside are by no means unique. For instance, a study by the Canadian Council on Social Development revealed that 27.6 per cent of Torontonians were living in poverty, as compared with 12.9 per cent in the surrounding suburbs. A surprisingly wide range of commentators complained that the Ontario government was simply not dealing the problems of cities, and that Toronto especially needed a new constitutional deal. Mayor Lastman speculated publicly about the merits of separation from the province, and that helped stimulate a broader debate about constitutional reform. The so-called 'Charter' movement attracted support from across the political spectrum, and the Toronto council itself endorsed the idea of a separate municipal charter in a February resolution. Some other Canadian cities (such as Vancouver) already have their own charters, but the Toronto activists had something more robust in mind: a sort of charter of municipal independence. Many of the activists – influenced by the local urban theorist, Jane Jacobs – were of the view that the major cities were so different from the rest of the country that they needed political institutions that would enable them to break free from rural/ suburban domination.

Regional governance

Urban autonomy is only one of a number of issues involved in the problem of regional governance. In the mid-1990s, there was a revival of the idea that all municipalities (both urban and rural) had to be enlarged to be really efficient and effective. In the first three decades after the Second World War, the emphasis had been on creating authorities big enough to deliver the major services of the welfare state and to plan appropriately for the development of large urban regions. By the 1990s, the emphasis had shifted to cost-saving. In the latter part of the decade, the two largest cities in Nova Scotia (Halifax and Sydney) and a set of medium-sized Ontario cities (Belleville, Chatham, Kingston, Peterborough, and Trenton) were amalgamated with neighbouring rural areas. The Ontario government generally put enormous pressure on rural municipalities to amalgamate 'or else.' As a result, the number of municipalities in Ontario dropped from 815 in 1996 to 500 in November 2000, and the number of elected officials fell by 39 per cent to 2,804. As noted, Toronto and its immediate suburbs were amalgamated in 1998. The provincial government then turned its attention to the next largest cities in the province – Ottawa and Hamilton – and both those cities were amalgamated with their suburbs in 2000. There was a similar amalgamation in Sudbury. In a more rural area, two consolidated municipalities (Haldimand and Norfolk) were created. All of these bodies replaced two-tiered municipal authorities created in the 1970s.

By 2000, similar changes were under way in Quebec. The provincial government had indicated that it wanted to amalgamate most of the municipalities in the province's three largest urban regions: Montreal, Quebec, and the Outaouais (the Quebec side of the Ottawa-Hull region). Changes in the Montreal area were bound to be particularly controversial, because questions of suburban autonomy were mixed up with issues about anglophone rights: many of the West Island municipalities had anglophone majorities. From the beginning, Montreal mayor Pierre Bourque took the position that Montreal should become 'one island, one city.' At first, this view was rejected both by Premier Lucien Bouchard and by his Minister for Municipal Affairs, Louise Harel; however, in August 2000, a provincial proposal along these lines was leaked to the media. The idea was to enlarge the City of Montreal to encompass the whole Island, and to create twenty-seven 'boroughs' (nine for the old City and eighteen for the current suburbs) to provide for continuing local control over certain services. The new city would have one mayor and councillors elected at large and for each borough, but each borough would also have its own council and mayor. Functions would be distributed, with the city proper retaining control over the police and fire departments and the boroughs keeping snow removal, garbage collection, street and sidewalk maintenance, and other such frontline services. Mayor Bourque continued to argue for full unification, while most suburban leaders held out for continuing autonomy. Twenty-seven Montreal Island municipalities decided to organize referendums, which were held on 19 November. However, Montreal's Mayor Bourque refused to do so, stating that a referendum was unnecessary and that his city did not have the $4 million needed to organize one. The province stuck to its basic plan, and legislation providing for the new city was passed on 20 December.

Unification of the Island of Montreal did not affect the South Shore and North Shore suburbs; however, the provincial government also imposed amalgamation on the South Shore, creating an enlarged City of Longueuil. It did the same with Lévis, on the south shore opposite Quebec; as well, it enlarged the City of Quebec to encompass the neighbouring suburbs on the north side of the St Lawrence. A similar amalgamation occurred in Outaouais region near Ottawa.

The Ottawa region was affected by amalgamations on both sides of the provincial border. While the Quebec government negotiated the Outaouais amalgamations, the Ontario side of the region was led through its transition year by a specially created seven-member cabinet, chaired by former Ontario minister Claude Bennett. This cabinet had extensive powers to overrule councils, hire administrative personnel, establish the municipal organization, and negotiate with unions on behalf of the new government. It was also bound to organize local elections by the end of 2000. The goal was to save local taxpayers $75 million. The amalgamation costs, estimated at $103 to $175 million, were to be covered by a provincial government grant. During his tenure, Bennett had to ask for greater powers to deal with policy areas that had been forgotten in the restructuring act: the merger of libraries, the arrangement of insurance, and the negotiation of severance packages with thirty-six unions. At the end of the year, the transition cabinet unveiled a $1.9 billion draft budget that did not include any tax cuts, noting that in the first year amalgamation would result in $26.5 million in savings and $36.2 million in increased expenditures. In other words, there would be a $9.7 million deficit. Despite this prediction, Mr Bennett argued that there would be savings of $9 million in year two, $20 million in year three, and $22 million in year four, and that, overall, the amalgamated city would save rate-payers $79 million over a five-year period. He also predicted that 1,100 jobs would disappear because of overlap.

The Edmonton region was also the subject of amalgamation discussions in 2000, prompted in part by a study initiated by the province's Department of Municipal Affairs. The sixty-six members of the Alberta Association of Municipal Districts launched a public consultation. The mega-city idea was on the table again (as it had been in the 1970s), but Lou Hyndman, the provincial commissioner, suggested the amalgamation of water, sewage, and emergency services only. He did not recommend any change in municipal boundaries. Edmonton City Council rejected his scheme, because it would give the city only 50 per cent of the votes on the proposed regional body, although it had 72 per cent of the area's population. In response, Mr Hyndman withdrew his proposal. Unlike Quebec and Ontario – but like British Columbia – the province of Alberta is loath to impose restructuring against local wishes.

In British Columbia, the major development in regional governance was that the Greater Vancouver Regional District signed an agreement with the provincial government to create a new transportation authority called Translink, to take over functions that had previously been provincialized. The province agreed to transfer a portion of the gasoline tax and 7 per cent of parking revenues to Translink in exchange for the municipalities assuming a greater share of the debt of SkyTrain (the automated light rapid transit system) and taking over responsibility for urban transportation, including buses and roads. This agreement was supposed to allow the greater Vancouver municipalities to expand the regional transportation network. One proposed project was to extend the SkyTrain route from the commercial centre of Vancouver southwest towards the University of British Columbia, a measure that could cost up to $800 million. There were extensive consultations about the various options. During the summer and fall debates, the three suburban communities south of the Fraser Valley (Surrey, Delta, and Langley) became increasingly discontented. They argued that they would not benefit from proposed improvements to public transit, improvements that Translink proposed to finance by levying a special $75 tax on automobiles. There were threats of secession. In the end, Translink backed down on the proposed levy, but secessionist fervour was dampened in any case by calculations to the effect that it would cost Surrey, Delta, and Langley residents $2,200 per capita to disentangle themselves from existing regional arrangements.

It must be noted that the 'mega-city' reforms in Toronto, Montreal, Ottawa, Quebec, and Hamilton leave many issues of regional governance unresolved. In no case will there be a single transportation authority or land-use planning authority for the urban regions centred on these cities. There are still 'horizontal' divisions between Ottawa and Outaouais, Quebec and Lévis, Montreal, Longueil, and Laval, Toronto, Mississauga, and Markham, etc. Moreover, there are 'vertical' divisions between the municipal authorities and provincial or federal bodies like GO Transit and VIA Rail. Thus, multilateral, multilevel governance will remain the rule despite these recent changes.

Local democracy

On 9 May Toronto City Council asked its Chief Administrative Officer to develop a comprehensive strategy to deal with the issues that had been raised in the context of public debates about the need for a new 'charter' for the city. In a series of reports, the CAO set out a number of goals for the City to pursue:

- being recognized as an accountable order of government with rights and responsibilities to act on local matters (including a 'stand alone' piece of legislation that noted the specificities of Toronto, clearly identified spheres of power, with power to act independently within these spheres, and the capacity to incorporate non-profit and business enterprises)
- the right to grant special 'bonusing' incentives to attract and retain businesses
- the ability to raise money on specific assets or to enter into sales and leaseback agreements
- long-term financial commitments, such as the capacity to raise revenue on bonds and asset-backed securities, as well as a share of gasoline and retail taxes and vehicle registration fees
- the ability to participate directly in policy discussions with the federal government on matters of mutual interest, such as urban infrastructures, housing, and immigrant settlement, and to negotiate funding arrangements directly
- the right to participate in federal-provincial discussions on policy

> matters that affect the city, such as health, economic and labour markets, cultural policies, or even criminal justice

The burden of these reports was this: whether the city was to continue with initiatives on the neo-liberal model or whether it was to find some new direction, it needed to have powers commensurate with the responsibilities that had been thrust upon it. Moreover, the provincial government had to recognize that a city the size of Toronto was very different from a smaller city in its governmental needs.

There had been some moves in the 1990s – most notably in Alberta and British Columbia – to give municipalities more freedom of action. In Ontario, the government's emphasis was on more freedom to act in a business-like way, greater transparency in municipal activity, and closer accountability to the municipality's 'shareholders' (that is, its tax-paying voters). One measure, adopted by the provincial legislature in June 2000, was to provide for an ongoing 'municipal report card' covering nine service areas, including water supply, fire protection, and roads. The idea was to make it possible for voters to compare their own jurisdiction with other municipalities, ones that might have chosen a different mix of in-house provision and external contracting. A complementary measure was to facilitate municipal referenda. Other legislation authorized municipalities to enter into business partnerships with the private sector or to offer tax incentives to attract businesses. Meanwhile, the Social Housing Reform Act of 2000 transferred 84,000 units of public housing to municipal managers. This was in line with earlier measures to devolve social-service responsibilities upon the municipalities. The province still insisted on setting major policies in this and other areas, and indeed indicated that it would soon be introducing new province-wide standards on various matters. From a Toronto perspective, the province's attitude toward local autonomy was indicated by the sudden ultimatum the city had received in January to reduce the number of its wards from fifty-seven to forty-four, in time for the next municipal election. This measure had the effect of disrupting the community committees that had just been established in the context of amalgamation two years earlier. On the other hand, it was in line with the province's theme that there were just too many municipal politicians.

Ontario voters had an opportunity to express their support for municipal government in the November 2000 elections. The turn-out was poor, however. Overlap with the federal electoral campaign may have contributed to voter fatigue, but in any case only about 30 per cent of voters went to the polls. Toronto mayor Mel Lastman was re-elected with more than 80 per cent of the votes, despite considerable criticism of his conduct in office. The controversy over amalgamation, which had mobilized many people in 1997–8, played little part in the election. The main controversy was over Toronto's garbage problem: a vexed issue relating to the lack of suitable landfill sites. Elsewhere in Ontario, Walkerton's mayor David Thomson was re-elected, despite the problems with respect to water supply. Meanwhile, Robert Chiarelli, a fiscal conservative, was elected as the first mayor of the newly enlarged City of Ottawa, and Robert Wade (the former mayor of suburban Ancaster) became the mayor of the new City of Hamilton. The 1999 provincial elections had confirmed that amalgamation controversies were not a big enough issue to swing many votes against the party in power. The municipal elections in 2000 seemed to confirm that changes in municipal structures were accepted quite quickly.

In Saskatchewan, the Task Force on Municipal Improvements and Governance, chaired by Joseph Garcea, published *Options 2000*, its final report on renewal in the rural and urban municipal sectors and in the northern municipal sector. *Options 2000* was not presented as a blueprint but rather as a proposal resulting from the work of local public and elected officials and from broad consultations. It suggested further discussion was required on the need for and nature of municipal renewal. Key points were the need for renewed legislation emphasizing permissive provisions and for a clear legislative framework; these would give municipal governments an independent, accountable, and responsible status and establish a clear relationship between types of local government, their purpose, and their functions. The report also called for broader powers, greater autonomy, enhanced financial authority, and more accountability for local governments. The provincial government pledged to review the report and to start work on a blueprint for a new municipal act. In 1999 the Province of Alberta had passed Bill 14, a new streamlined municipal act, and initiated reviews of provincial and municipal roles and the property assessment system. It also launched Municipal 2000, a major program promoting innovation, inter-municipal cooperation, and excellence in local government through funding improvements in municipal governance, administration, services, and inter-municipal cooperation. The Province of British Columbia spent three years negotiating with the Union of BC Municipalities over a reform to the Municipal Act. The reform, Bill 31, proposed to increase municipal autonomy, provide local governments with greater power and flexibility, and recognize local governments as an 'independent and accountable and responsible order of government.'

The bill was also expected to include changes to the current legislation on regional districts, planning and land use, and counter-petitions with respect to development proposals. All of these reports and initiatives in the West were keyed into the idea that municipalities needed more autonomy if they were to fulfil their democratic mandate.

Cities in Confederation

Municipalities and other local authorities have usually been conceived as 'creatures of the provinces.' This is a dubious constitutional doctrine, but the Supreme Court of Canada has not seen fit to question it. During the debates and negotiations that led to the Constitution Act of 1982 and the abortive Charlottetown Accord of 1992, municipal leaders had attempted to get their issue on the agenda: recognition of municipalities as a 'third order of government' with protected status. They were not successful. On the other hand, the Canadian Federation of Municipalities (which traces its origins to a first meeting in 1901, but was established in roughly its present form in 1937) became an increasingly effective lobby group in the 1990s. The FCM is a federation of similar lobbying organizations at the provincial and territorial level. An important offshoot is the Big City Mayors' Caucus, which gives voice to distinctively urban concerns. As noted above, many important recent initiatives at the federal level can be attributed to the Mayors' Caucus and the FCM. There is every reason to expect the FCM and its off-shoots to play an increasing role in Canadian governance.

Although the year 2000 could not be called a 'triumph of the local authorities,' there were some signs that urban affairs was coming back on the federal policy agenda and that municipal leaders were having more impact within broader policy communities. There were also some moves at the provincial level to give the municipalities more freedom of action. In central Canada, the provincial governments pressed ahead with municipal restructuring, despite much opposition from local politicians. Whether the restructuring would strengthen local government as promised (or even lead to the promised administrative economies) was yet to be determined. Although municipal leaders may have protested against the downloading of service responsibilities, the reorganization of property assessment systems, and the forced amalgamation of many municipalities, these very changes did bring increased attention to municipal government and put municipal officials in the front line with respect to a wide range of crucial policy issues. Thus, the ground may have been laid for municipal resurgence later in the decade. Provincial leaders have talked much about strengthening local governments, assigning them more responsibility, and allowing them more autonomy. This talk was often accompanied by rough intervention in municipal affairs – no less in the neo-liberal era than in the preceding one. Now the question is whether municipal leaders will respond to the challenge with the necessary vigour. They may not do so, however, unless voters show more commitment to local institutions than they did in 2000.

CAREY HILL

British Columbia

Labour unrest was a common thread in British Columbia throughout the year, especially in the health and forest sectors. It was a year of strikes. Some strikes were for wages and benefits. There was also the striking of a new era with an Indo-Canadian being elected Premier for the first time in Canada. There were striking events like the passing of Pierre Trudeau, whose connection to British Columbia was familial – he found a love and lost a son in this province. For his part, Federal Environment Minister David Anderson offered a pre-emptive strike to those suggesting the moratorium on offshore drilling should be lifted: he said the federal government would not allow it, and that he had been there to advise the Prime Minister on the matter in the 1970s.

British Columbia got a new Premier and a new Balanced Budget Act in 2000. Nevertheless, some things remained constant. Glen Clark was still in the news as well as on the stand throughout the year. The NDP continued to lag in the polls, even though its new leader was popular in the province and admired across the country.

The province continued to lag behind the rest of the country in terms of its economy, even though it posted its highest growth since 1994 at between 2.5 and 2.7 per cent. Finances were central as the NDP geared up for an election the following year. Three major financial bills were introduced as well as an increase in the minimum wage. Some of the bills, such as the Balanced Budget Act, appeared contrary to NDP ideology, but others, such as the Income Tax Act changes and the minimum wage increase to the highest in Canada, were very much in line with party traditions.

Premier Dosanjh

The race for the Premier's office was not much of a contest. The leadership convention took place the weekend of 19 February, with 1,400 delegates attending. Leadership candidates included Attorney General

Ujjal Dosanjh, Agriculture Minister Corky Evans, Education Minister Gordon Wilson, and labour activist Len Werden. Ujjal Dosanjh was viewed as the front-runner throughout the course of the leadership race. A Global News poll taken just before the convention showed the NDP would receive 39 per cent of BC voters' support if the party was led by Mr Dosanjh.

In contrast, Len Werden was the longshot candidate and the only one not in the cabinet, let alone elected to government. He told the convention, 'Our government and our party are in trouble, big trouble ... Working people in British Columbia have lost their trust in us' (*National Post*, 19 February). While he began the contest with much energy, Mr Werden withdrew from the leadership race just before the vote at the convention.

Agriculture Minister Corky Evans was viewed by the media as the second choice of most delegates, but was far behind the leader until Mr Dosanjh's team suffered a scandal regarding members who did not know they had bought memberships. Mr Dosanjh's ability to sign up new party members was phenomenal. His team signed up over 10,000 new members during the leadership race, including a considerable number of Indo-Canadians. According to critics some of these memberships were bogus (*National Post*, 19 February).

Like Len Werden, Gordon Wilson withdrew from the leadership race before the vote. He claimed that his withdrawal from the race was necessary so he could throw his support behind Corky Evans. Mr Wilson said his delegates to the convention had recommended this course of action because they were concerned about the scandal surrounding the Dosanjh team's membership drive (*Gazette*, 21 February).

Nevertheless, Mr Dosanjh easily defeated Mr Evans on the first ballot with 769 votes to Mr Evans' 549 votes. One of the delegates from Surrey–Green Timbers, Balwant Singh Gill, said of the victory, 'We got the voting rights only in 1947, and now today Ujjal Dosanjh is the first Indo-Canadian Premier elected in the country' (*Gazette*, 21 February). BC Federation of Labour president Jim Sinclair was also very positive about Mr Dosanjh's victory: 'I think everybody is feeling good about having a new leader.' Liberal leader Gordon Campbell offered congratulations, but urged Mr Dosanjh to call an immediate election. In sharp contrast to the positive sentiments of other politicians and community members, William VanderZalm, leader of the provincial Reform Party, said of Mr Dosanjh's election: 'Let's face it. He did play the race card in order to get the votes and that's going to work against him when he gets out there among the populace' (*Gazette*, 21 February).

In the rest of the country, and, indeed, among the provincial populace, Mr Dosanjh proved to be a popular Premier, significantly more popular than his party. On 24 February, Ujjal Dosanjh was sworn in as the thirty-third Premier of British Columbia and the first Indo-Canadian Premier of any province. Mr Dosanjh took over from Dan Miller, who had continued in his post as interim premier for the first two months of the year. He had become caretaker premier after Glen Clark resigned amid controversy in August of 1999. Mr Dosanjh said of his swearing-in: 'When I started my journey on December thirty-first 1964, leaving India at the age of seventeen, little did I know, think or imagine that I would be standing before you today being called Premier Dosanjh' (CBC-TV, 24 February). A onetime mill worker, Mr Dosanjh's law career included fighting for the rights of immigrant farm workers he said were victims of racist policies, and serving as Attorney General under Glen Clark's leadership.

Mr Dosanjh's popularity was not limited to any one community or political party. A MarkTrend First opinion poll after he had been at the helm two months showed 63 per cent of respondents rating Mr Dosanjh's performance as Premier 'satisfactory' and only 19 per cent rating his performance 'poor.' While a majority of British Columbian respondents approved of his leadership, that approval did not extend to his party, which finished third in the poll, five points behind the BC Reform Party and forty-two points behind the BC Liberal Party. While Premier Dosanjh's popularity improved, his party's standing in the polls dropped eleven points after he took over the leadership from interim premier Dan Miller. Mr Dosanjh explained this discrepancy by noting, 'It's partly a function of all the matters before the courts. That's going to have an impact on the polls' (*National Post*, 22 April).

Mr Clark on trial

The matters before the courts that Premier Dosanjh referred to in his explanation were linked to the NDP via their association with its former leader and the former premier, Glen Clark. The former premier made the news several times during the year as he was sued, called to testify about his government's budget, and faced criminal allegations over his neighbour's casino licence. Mr Clark's fourteen-year political career was stalled in November as he left politics, saying he would return when the criminal charges against him were settled. Mr Clark had become Premier in 1996 and resigned in August 1999 while facing charges of breach of trust and fraud for allegedly receiving a benefit of home and cottage renovations in exchange for helping his neighbour get a conditional casino licence. Mr Clark explained his need for a brief exit: 'In politics, perception is reality and the media have done a pretty effective job of trying to convict me ... It's very difficult to escape that until I am exonerated. I expect I will be' (*National Post*, 18 November).

In addition to the criminal trial, Mr Clark took the stand in the balanced-budget trial and in the fast-ferries lawsuit. In the latter, Mr Clark was being sued by a marine engineer who alleged that Mr Clark attacked his reputation in order to discount criticisms of the fast-ferries project (*National Post*, 22 April). The balanced-budget trial went beyond the Premier to calling the whole government to account, with Mr Clark called to testify in light of his leadership role. The case was brought forward by David Stockell's organization, Help BC. Three citizens alleged they were defrauded of their votes because Mr Clark promised a balanced budget that his government failed to deliver two years in a row (*National Post*, 28 April). Help BC's argument was that the NDP violated Section 256 of the provincial Elections Act with false campaign claims. This section prohibits the use of 'fraudulent means' in persuading anyone how to vote. Help BC and the three citizens believed the election should be declared 'null and void.' NDP lawyers tried to have the case thrown out, but Justice Mary Humphries of the BC Supreme Court refused to do so, saying she 'want[ed] to hear all the evidence' (*National Post*, 24 April).

Mr Clark was not the only member of his government called to the stand. Former finance minister Elizabeth Cull was an obvious witness in the case as she tabled the so-called balanced budget. She told the court she was 'uncomfortable' tabling a balanced budget on the same day the election was called in 1996. She claimed that Mr Clark had told her that the budget shortfall, if applicable, could be made up by dipping into the Forest Renewal fund. The fund was set up in 1994 to assist logging-dependent communities in responding to environmental concerns and resource costs associated with Native land claims. Ms Cull's discomfort did not appear to overshadow her belief that the budget was simply a forecast. She explained: 'The only absolute thing you can say about a forecast is it won't be correct. It would be pure luck to get the exact number on a forecast eighteen months later' (*National Post*, 27 April).

Mr Campbell in question

While Glen Clark faced trial by judges, Gordon Campbell faced what could be referred to as a trial by a jury of his own party faithful, some of whom were unsure of his leadership. Gordon Campbell met some apprehension from Liberal Party members in the first quarter of the year when an opinion poll suggested that one in five Liberals thought Mr Dosanjh would make a better premier. Two polls were conducted: one suggested 42 per cent of respondents believed Mr Campbell would make a better premier than Mr Dosanjh, with 40 per cent saying Mr Dosanjh was the better candidate; the second poll had Mr Campbell trailing Mr Dosanjh by twelve points. A key concern for the Liberal leadership was that undecided voters also preferred Mr Dosanjh. In early March, Liberal Party leaders met behind closed doors to discuss whether or not Mr Campbell should lead the party into the next election (*National Post*, 11 March). As the year closed, Gordon Campbell remained at the helm of the official opposition.

Speech from the Throne

While Glen Clark's role as leader and Gordon Campbell's ability to lead were seemingly on trial, Premier Dosanjh's leadership began with a Speech from the Throne on 15 March. In keeping with tradition, Lieutenant-Governor Garde Gardom read the speech, which had a budget transparency law as its centrepiece, along with a tuition freeze, and innovations in health care and child care. Referring primarily to the budget transparency law, the speech stated, 'The aim of this act is to give British Columbians the facts, all the facts, and nothing but the facts' (*National Post*, 16 March).

The lieutenant-governor's role in the Throne Speech was certainly not out of the ordinary, but it came on the heels of a comment by him that caused consternation within the British Columbia Native community. On 2 March, when Premier Dosanjh's first cabinet was sworn in, the lieutenant-governor's opening remarks included praise of Captain George Vancouver, quoting him: 'The serenity of the climate, the innumerable pleasing landscapes and the abundant fertility that unassisted nature brings forth requires only to be enriched by man to render it the most lovely country that can be imagined.' Native leaders Chief Joe Matthias and Grand Chief Ed John took exception to Mr Gardom's comments, stating, 'We did not attend the swearing-in ceremonies in Victoria to be patronized and insulted' (*National Post*, 2 March).

Health

Just days after Ujjal Dosanh was sworn in as the new Premier, Justice Ronald Holmes of the BC Supreme Court ruled that a provincial law enacted by the NDP government to recover smoking-related health costs from tobacco companies was not constitutional. The judge declared that the legislation was extraterritorial and beyond the power granted to British Columbia as a province under the Constitution Act. The government's lawyer, Daniel Webster, said the government could either appeal the ruling or craft new legislation. A spokesperson for the tobacco industry, David Laundy of the Canadian Tobacco Manufacturers' Council, said the industry was 'gratified' and that the proposed law had been 'clearly an attempt on the part of the government to extract billions of dollars from the industry' (*National Post*, 22 February).

While the government suffered a setback on the tobacco-control front, physicians underwent considerable strife in multiple ways throughout the year as they were targeted, underpaid, and pushed into job action. In July a British Columbia obstetrician and gynecologist who performed abortions was ambushed and stabbed. Under police guard at Vancouver General Hospital, he was expected to recover. The assailant was unknown and had been last seen running away from the clinic. Dr Garson Romalis had been the victim of anti-abortion violence six years earlier as well, when he was shot by a sniper as he ate breakfast. In response to his stabbing, the BC government brought together doctors who perform abortions, nurses, health-care union representatives, and others in a health security summit (*National Post*, 15 July).

Besides being the target of protesters, and, in the case of Garson Romalis, potentially violent ones, physicians also became protesters in the year 2000. Their low pay and lack of services were key issues. Across British Columbia, rural physicians walked off the job in September. Physicians in Terrace, Quesnel, Cranbrook, Prince Rupert, Kitimat, and Smithers all resigned their hospital privileges or left their workplaces. Around rural BC, more than 200 doctors refused to work except for emergencies. They demanded money to attract new doctors and increased pay for on-call work (*Province*, 24 December). Other specialists threatened similar action if the government did not settle the dispute. An internal-medicine specialist in Terrace, Dr Michael Kenyon, explained: 'When I was working 100 hours a week five years ago, 95 of those was spent with patients. The bottom line is that now I am spending 25 of the 100 hours shuffling beds, finding drugs that we don't stock because they're too expensive, filling out triplicate forms for the government they've put up as an obstacle to a medication I know they're going to approve, anyway. None of this is remunerated, none of this is rewarding and some of this is quite demoralizing' (*National Post*, 12 September).

In response to the physicians' job actions, Premier Dosanjh recalled the Legislature to approve $40 million in funds that had already been announced for rural physicians as well as a $250 million larger health-care package (CBC-TV, 15 September; *National Post*, 18 September). Physicians who had walked off the job in September returned to work on 2 October when mediation began. A three-member panel of mediators led by lawyer Alan Hope called for the implementation of the $40 million offer the government had made to rural doctors in September. The report also stated that acceptance of these funds would not prejudice the bargaining position of the physicians in future negotiations (*Vancouver Sun*, 9 December). Contract talks between the province and all 8,000 physicians of the BC Medical Association were scheduled for 31 March 2001, with outstanding issues to go to binding arbitration.

Physicians were not the only casualties of the health-care system during the year. A probe into the death of a man in Victoria's Capital Health Region was begun as the year closed. Former wheelchair athlete Dwayne Gough, a paraplegic, died alone in his apartment sometime during the weekend of 16–17 September. The coroner concluded he had died of dehydration. A coalition of the BC Paraplegic Association and the Home Support Action Group, referring to themselves as the BC Coalition of People with Disabilities, said Mr Gough would still be alive if his home care had not been cut off. Mr Gough had been receiving home-care services since 1993.

Nurses joined doctors in questioning their remuneration and the state of the health system. The British Columbia Nurses Union (BCNU) provided some of its contract demands late in the year as a precursor to bargaining in March of 2001. Demands included changing the top hourly rate from $26.50 to $42, as well as changes in shift differentials and mileage rates (*Vancouver Sun*, 9 December). The head of the Health Employers Association of BC, Gary Moser, said in response that increased wages would not solve the labour supply problem with respect to nursing in the province.

Forests

Similarly to the health sector, the forest sector suffered considerable labour strife during the year. About 12,000 forest workers in seventy mills on the BC coast were on strike for nine days in late June and early July. Negotiations between Industrial, Wood, and Allied Workers of Canada (IWA-Canada) and Forest Industrial Relations broke down over disagreements regarding the pension fund and changes to holiday allocations. Dave Haggard, president of IWA-Canada explained: 'It's our pension plan, which is fully funded in two years. The industry wants to take money out of it. The other issue is a section of our collective agreement that's been in place since 1964 that would change how our holidays are taken' (*Toronto Star*, 29 June). Terry Lineker, president of Forest Industrial Relations, claimed the union's contentions were false. A three-year contract was finally reached on 7 July after two hours of negotiations. The agreement included wage increases of 2 per cent per year, plus improvements in long-term disability and health care, and a bolstering of the contentious pension plan. 'It's a good agreement for our membership,' said Dave Haggard (*Calgary Herald*, 7 July).

In other forest news, in October David Emerson, president of Canadian Forest Products Corp., told the Board of Trade that investors were 'tired of getting a minuscule return – an average of 2.9 per cent over the last decade' (*Times-Colonist*, 6 October). He compared this to the roughly $30 the government received in stumpage fees for every dollar investors received. He also condemned 'waterbedding,' a practice that predated the NDP government, which provides stumpage concessions to troubled companies. Two years prior, Mr Emerson claimed, the practice had been used by the NDP government to help Prince Rupert–based Skeena Cellulose.

Balanced-budget law

The NDP government once again promised a balanced budget – this time by putting its guarantee in writing. The Balanced Budget Act, Bill 28, passed on 6 July with thirty-seven in favour and thirty-four opposed.

Finance Minister Paul Ramsey encouraged MLAs to vote for the bill by noting that it fell in line with three priorities of British Columbians: (1) support for core social programs, (2) personal and business tax relief, and (3) ensuring the province's fiscal house was in order (*Hansard*, 4 July). The purpose of the bill was to hold the government accountable if it failed to balance the budget, and included penalties for cabinet ministers in that event. Twenty per cent of the annual pay of cabinet ministers would be deducted for failing to produce a balanced budget.

The Opposition's response to the government's bill focused on the government's fiscal record during the past nine years. Gary Farrell-Collins explained at the second reading of the bill, 'Unfortunately, this isn't the first year of the NDP mandate. This is the ninth year of the NDP mandate.' Moreover, members of the Opposition suggested that the bill was primarily the new Premier's project, and 'a surprise to everyone.' Mr Farrell-Collins continued: 'This side of the House has always supported balanced-budget legislation; we continue to support balanced-budget legislation. But if this Premier asks members of the opposition or anyone in this province to vote on the confidence of this government, the answer will be a resounding no.' The Opposition's concerns with the Balanced Budget Act centred on a lack of spending limits and an absent debt-management plan (*Hansard*, 4 July).

Bill 28 required a balanced budget beginning in the year 2004. The NDP government argued the bill was an integral aspect of its three-part strategy to regain the confidence of British Columbian voters in the face of its failure the previous two years to balance the budget as it had promised. The other two pieces of fiscal legislation in this strategy included changes to the Income Tax Act and a Budget Transparency and Accountability Act.

In February, Finance Minister Paul Ramsey announced his government would be changing BC's tax system from charging a percentage of the federal tax rate to levying a tax on personal income. This move enabled the provincial government to delink its personal income tax system from the federal system and to set its own tax brackets. The changes to the provincial tax system took effect during the year and, according to the NDP, gave the government 'more autonomy in targeting its tax breaks to low and middle-income earners, instead of being tied to federal tax rates.' Minister Ramsey explained, 'The only way I am going to adjust any category is down. I've no intention of raising any provincial tax rates.' Opposition Liberal leader Gordon Campbell suggested some British Columbians would end up paying more taxes as federal tax breaks would be redistributed (*National Post*, 25 February).

The Budget Transparency and Accountability Act, the final part of the three-pronged strategy to bring the government's fiscal house in order required British Columbia's budgets to be the 'most open and transparent in Canada' (*Hansard*, 4 July). The Act introduced a summary accounting approach in addition to its transparency. According to the government, this approach to accounting includes a bottom line that presents results for all ministries plus all Crown corporations. As Minister Ramsey explained, 'You don't have to look in the back of the book. Everything's there in black and white; all the facts are there' (*Hansard*, 4 July).

In addition to efforts to address the balanced-budget controversy, the NDP also introduced a bill more in line with their party's ideology: a minimum wage increase. The minimum wage was raised to $7.60 per hour in November – the highest rate in Canada. In the rest of the country it ranged from a low of $5.50 in Newfoundland to a high of $7.20 in the Yukon. In British Columbia, the increase affected roughly 68,000 workers who earn the minimum wage, or about 3 per cent of the workforce. Premier Dosanjh reasoned, 'It is time to give our lowest-paid workers a pay raise' (*National Post*, 30 August).

Natural resources

The provincial government's efforts to get the budget on track were positively affected by soaring natural gas prices. The energy sector also made the news when the water supply of a northeast BC region was threatened as a pipeline burst that dumped more than 10,000 barrels of oil into Pine River (*Gazette*, 4 August). The pipeline, owned by Calgary-based Pembina Pipeline Corporation, ran between Taylor and Prince George. The town of Chetwynd, located upstream from Pine River, was affected by an oily residue from the spill and had to shut off its water supply. Downstream in Taylor, the water supply was safe as the town had switched to well water earlier in the year (*Times-Colonist*, 5 August). Premier Dosanjh visited the spill site just days after the tragedy and determined that it was not necessary to declare a provincial state of emergency. The company that owned the pipeline said it had insurance to cover the costs of the spill.

In the face of this interior oil spill, a controversial debate ensued over ending a moratorium on offshore oil and gas exploration. The offshore reserves in question are estimated by the Geological Survey of Canada to include 9.8 billion barrels of oil and 25.9 trillion cubic feet of gas (*Times-Colonist*, 6 November). Dan Miller, who had served as interim premier when Mr Clark stepped down, led the debate. Prince Rupert was his hometown as well as the city that borders the prime coastal exploration zone. When Mr Miller was energy minister, he had launched a reconsideration of the federally and provincially imposed moratorium. Soaring energy prices resulted in new attention being drawn to the debate as the year closed. Premier Dosanjh emphasized the need to safeguard coastal waters, noting that no moratorium could be revisited until 'science is able to address the dangers' (*National Post*, 26 December). There was discord among other cabinet members over reconsidering the moratorium. Among them, Moe Sihota threatened to quit if the government removed the moratorium on offshore oil and gas exploration (*Times-Colonist*, 20 December).

Environmental groups also came out strongly against reconsidering the moratorium, and the federal Environment Minister, David Anderson, found himself in their company. The David Suzuki Foundation attacked the NDP government's release of a report stating that the issue 'warranted examination.' The Foundation said the government had taken a 'backward step.' The Sierra Legal Defence Fund also came out against removing the moratorium. Minister Anderson said that he would oppose a lifting of the ban (*Calgary Herald*, 18 August), explaining that he helped create the ban in the 1970s: 'Ultimately, I went to Trudeau directly and pointed out the absurdity of attempting to complain about tanker traffic on our coast while at the same time drilling on our coast' (*Province*, 6 August).

Wildlife

While Environment Minister Anderson was onside with environmentalists regarding his opposition to removing the moratorium, his endangered-species act remained controversial and suspect within the environmental community of his home province. Meanwhile, former premier Glen Clark moved to introduce a bill protecting the grizzly bear.

On 15 June Mr Clark introduced the Grizzly Bear Hunting Prohibition Act, stating,'This act prohibits the hunting, taking, trapping, wounding or killing of grizzly bears for sport. Grizzly bears are classed as vulnerable in British Columbia by the Committee on the Status of Endangered Wildlife in Canada' (*Hansard*, 15 June). He noted that grizzly bears are listed as threatened in the United States under its Endangered Species Act. The bill invokes penalties and fines for killing a grizzly bear equal to that for other threatened or endangered species. Deaths of grizzlies caused by accident or in self defence were not penalized under the bill (*Hansard*, 15 June).

Economy

While Mr Clark argued that bears were in danger and in need of protection, some viewed the British Columbia economy similarly. The NDP, for their part, introduced several measures to restore confidence, including the Balanced Budget Act. According to an Ipsos-Reid poll of 800 respondents released at the November BC Business Summit, British Columbians continued to feel that the economy was underperforming. Sixty-five per cent of respondents said the economy was on the wrong track (*Vancouver Sun*, 20 November). In contrast, just over a third of respondents (35 per cent) described the economy as 'good' or 'very good.'

Those who felt the economy was good could point to its best growth since 1994 at between 2.5 and 2.7 per cent. Similarly, those who believed the economy was on the wrong track could point out that this 'high rate' still lagged behind the rest of Canada for most of the decade (*Nanaimo Daily News*, 28 December).

The Royal Bank of Canada's deputy chief economist, Craig Wright, explained that the NDP government was not 'solely responsible' for the poor economic state of the province at a speech to the Board of Trade in November. He pointed to the 'slump in worldwide commodity prices' (*Times-Colonist*, 29 November). The Royal Bank forecast growth of 3 per cent for BC in 2001, still half a per cent behind the expected rate of growth for the nation as a whole.

The unemployment rate in the province averaged 7 per cent, but for the BC interior it was closer to 14 per cent. The high unemployment in the interior was connected to the poor performance of the traditional resource industries.

The outlook for the forest industry continued to be bleak as the year closed. The absence of a softwood lumber agreement left analysts concerned about the future of the industry. Estimates of American-imposed countervailing duties were as high as 15 per cent, which would entail a potential billion-dollar impact. Negotiations faltered as the Americans claimed BC forest policy involved a form of subsidy that allowed Canadian companies to produce lumber cheaper than their American competitors. Laurie Cater, publisher of *Madison's Canadian Lumber Reporter*, suggested three main issues would continue to plague BC lumber producers in 2001: (1) North America's oversupply of lumber, (2) a depressed Japanese market, and (3) European producers' inroads into U.S. and Japanese markets, which are BC's main lumber importers (*Vancouver Sun*, 29 December).

While resource industries suffered, the New Economy blossomed. Though small contributors to BC's overall economy, information technology and biotech industries demonstrated significant growth, posting double-digit figures. High-tech companies employed 52,000 people, up 10.1 per cent from the previous year. This performance was also mixed when compared with other jurisdictions. A report offering detailed comparisons showed that BC rated as either average or below average in most categories when compared with Alberta, Ontario, Quebec, Washington state, Oregon, and Massachusetts, which also have thriving high-tech sectors. British Columbia's wages, while in line with those of other provinces, were considerably lower than those of all three states.

Natural gas was another one of the primary economic drivers, providing considerable revenue generation for the government. Gas prices soared, resulting in additional gas exploration and development in the province's northeast. The royalties from natural gas meant a projected $1 billion surplus for the government.

While high gas prices helped some sectors, including the public sector, these high prices hurt others such as the BC hothouse industry, whose heating bill doubled during the year. Analysts suggested there might be a ripple effect on other industries as well as residential consumers.

As the year closed, the NDP proved that the best defence is a good offence as they took on the role of the Opposition, accusing the Liberals of 'going into campaign mode.' The NDP did their part to hold the government-in-waiting to account by noting that the income tax and corporate tax cuts of Gordon Campbell's Liberals would result in losses of $1.8 billion and $380 million, respectively. Premier Dosanjh explained, 'I want [Campbell] to tell the truth about what are his plans for the economy of British Columbia, for the education of British Columbians, for the health care of British Columbians.' The newly appointed caucus chair, Dan Miller, backed Premier Dosanjh, referring to Mr Campbell when stating, 'This is a man who could be Premier next year' (*Times-Colonist*, 17 November).

HAROLD JANSEN

Alberta

Alberta is not known for vigorous political debates over public policy. The province has a reputation for being politically monolithic, a status reinforced by the fact that in 2000 the Conservative government was approaching thirty years in power. Those criticisms of Alberta could not be levied against the province in 2000, however. Three policy areas – health care, tax policy, and electricity – preoccupied the government and the public. With a provincial election looming, the fact that the public was concerned over government handling of health care and electricity was significant. The result was that 2000 was a year unlike others. These policy concerns also raised questions about whether the Conservatives would face an easy re-election in 2001.

Bill 11

Without question, the public debate of the year occurred over a single piece of government legislation: Bill 11, the innocuously titled Health Care Protection Act. This debate saw Alberta politics unfold in a very un-Albertan way: large protests and petitions, overflowing and noisy galleries at the provincial legislature, and extensive mobilization by unions, health-care, and consumers' groups. In the previous decade, the Conservative government had restructured government significantly, cut or privatized many government programs and services, and terminated hundreds of government employees, but they never saw a reaction from the public that camc close to what happened in response to Bill 11. Although the government never wavered from its determination to see the bill become law – and it passed – the whole process left the government feeling shaken and the ramifications of the debate continued to be felt throughout the year in a variety of contexts.

Bill 11 was introduced in the Legislature at the beginning of March. The central feature of the legislation was a provision to allow regional health authorities to contract with private health-care providers to provide minor surgical procedures, even if they included overnight stays. The Alberta College of Physicians and Surgeons would decide what constituted a 'minor' surgical procedure. Payment for these services would come directly from the health authority, not from the patient. Any such contracting-out provisions would require the approval of the provincial health minister.

Critics of the bill argued that the legislation would allow for the expansion of private health-care provision in Alberta. Many suggested that it would be better for regional health authorities to pump more money into the public health-care system rather than to pay money to private providers. The government countered that Bill 11 in fact strengthened the public health-care system, pointing to its very first section, which outlawed private hospitals. This distinction between 'private hospitals' and privately owned and operated 'surgical facilities' was often difficult for many opponents to see, however. The government also pointed to the provisions of the bill that explicitly forbade private clinics from providing services that allowed for 'queue-jumping,' the practice of health-care clients bypassing the waiting lists for publicly provided services by using private clinics. These did little to mollify the bill's opponents, however, and they waged a well-organized and aggressive opposition campaign.

Part of the effectiveness of the campaign was that only the details of Bill 11 were a surprise. The government had introduced similar legislation in 1998, but backed down in the face of overwhelming public pressure. In late 1999 Premier Klein signalled his intention to introduce a new version of that legislation in the Spring of 2000. Even before the legislation was introduced, unions, seniors, and other health-care groups were busy mobilizing in opposition to the legislation. There were signs that the government was losing the public debate, chiefly in that it saw the need to counter opposition with an extensive, multipronged, taxpayer-funded public relations campaign that saw the government mail out copies of Bill 11 to every household, and a print, radio, and television advertising campaign. The Premier went so far as to create what he called 'truth squads' of government MLAs to counter what he saw as misinformation about the bill. Despite these government efforts, polls showed that a majority of Albertans harboured significant misgivings about the legislation and its intentions.

The mobilization by groups such as Friends of Medicare culminated in large public rallies across the province that attracted significant crowds and drew celebrities such as *This Hour Has 22 Minutes* star Mary Walsh and actor Kiefer Sutherland, whose grandfather, Tommy

Douglas, was widely hailed as the founder of Medicare in Canada. The demonstrations spilled into the Legislature as protestors began to attend debates over the bill, filling the rotunda and the public gallery with noisy crowds. Although the vociferous protests might have rattled the government a little, Premier Klein and his government did not waver from their determination to see the legislation pass. Ultimately, the Conservative government's sizeable majority in the provincial legislature ensured that the bill would pass. The government resorted to procedural tools to limit debate, including applying closure on the third and final reading of the bill in May.

Given the federal government's involvement in health-care, it was inevitable that it would be drawn into the debate. Indeed, it seemed that federal Health Minister Alan Rock almost relished the opportunity to chastise Alberta for the expansion of private-health-care services in the province. Shortly after the bill was introduced in the legislature, Mr Rock indicated his misgivings about the legislation. Later, he urged Premier Klein to withdraw the bill. Mr Klein reacted angrily to Mr Rock's interventions, wondering why Alberta was being singled out for legislation that he claimed was similar to that in other provinces. For his part, Prime Minister Chrétien took a more conciliatory approach in his dealings with Mr Klein and the legislation, calling for a few changes to address some of his concerns. In the end, Mr Rock conceded that Bill 11 did not violate the Canada Health Act, but warned that he would be monitoring the situation in Alberta very closely.

It is safe to say that the province had not been mobilized around a discussion of a particular piece of legislation in quite some time. Even some prominent former members of Conservative governments, such as former speaker Gerard Amerongen and former cabinet minister Dave King, opposed the bill publicly. Although the government ultimately prevailed, it expended a significant amount of its political capital in the process. The formal passage of the bill in May marked the end of the debate, but the fallout over Bill 11 continued to be felt throughout the year.

Energy and rebates: Power politics in action

The second issue that caused some difficulties for the government was energy. Although energy politics are never far from the heart of governing Alberta, the debates have usually not engaged voters directly. In 2000 the Alberta government faced a triple threat. First, consistently high oil prices caused a sharp increase in gasoline prices that consumers felt every time they filled up their vehicle. Second, increased demand for natural gas increased prices for homeowners, who saw their heating bills skyrocket as winter set in late in the year. For example, the Atco gas company applied for and received permission to increase their gas prices by 32 per cent. Third, the prospect of deregulated electrical prices in 2001 in a context of increased demand and low supplies of power raised concerns that Albertans would be feeling the pain in their electrical bills. This was a potent combination for a government that hoped to be facing the voters in the first part of 2001.

The first two problems were not unique to Alberta; higher gasoline and heating prices were felt all over Canada. In Alberta, though, these increased prices came with an added complication in the form of a major surge in government revenues, due to energy royalties. By September the government was projecting a surplus of almost $6 billion. That the provincial government was seemingly awash in money while average Albertans were struggling to heat their homes and fill their cars was politically difficult. The problem contained its own solution as the province decided to distribute some of the windfall to consumers in the form of energy rebates. In September the province announced that each person over sixteen who had filed a 1999 Alberta tax return would receive two $150 rebate cheques – one in November and one in April 2001. In December the province announced a rebate on natural gas bills. Home users would receive a $50 monthly rebate from January to April.

While consumers of gasoline and natural gas were easily mollified by rebates, the problems with the province's electricity market were more difficult for the government to shake off. In the case of gasoline and natural gas, the province could rightfully point to world markets as the cause. Arguably, the problems in electricity were of the government's own making. The province had been working for the past several years at deregulating the province's electricity markets. Since 1999, industrial users had faced market prices for power; starting in 2001, home consumers would face a deregulated environment. The rapid economic growth in the province had strained the province's electrical generation capacity. The higher demand was leading to price increases for all classes of customers.

The government's initial response was to hold firm and argue the merits of deregulation, which would allow electricity producers a stable environment for investment in new generating capacity that would eliminate the supply problems. In other words, the government argued that deregulation would be short-term pain for long-term gain. Unfortunately for the Premier, many consumers (voters) could not get past the short-term pain part of the equation. Nor, with an election looming, was the government inclined to wait for the long-term gain. The government announced a $20 a month rebate on electrical bills for 2001, but even that did not completely satisfy critics. The clamour over deregulation grew steadily. By November, the government appeared to be making energy policy on the fly, announcing a ten-point plan to provide new sources of electricity early in the month, then promising to review all rake hikes to make sure they were justified in the middle of the month. Finally, at the end of November, the Premier announced a decision to shelve all residential rate increases for 2001. This about-face angered the electricity industry in the province, which had been counting on increased consumer prices in the deregulated environment. The industry called for the province to make up the shortfall. Just before Christmas, Premier Klein appeared to reverse his position on electricity again, announcing that he was raising the level of the cap on electricity rates. At the same time, the government announced that it would be doubling the electricity rebate to $40 a month.

The government's handling of the energy issue in 2000 did not stand out as one of the prouder moments in the Klein government's history. The government's solution to problems appeared to be to throw money at them in the hope that they would vanish. The move struck many as a thinly veiled attempt to ease the minds (and fatten the wallets) of voters before the next provincial election. The government's shaky treatment of the electricity deregulation file was in stark contrast with the confident determination shown about health care in the Bill 11 debate. Deregulation was shaping up as a prime election issue.

The flat tax becomes reality

The third issue that preoccupied Alberta was the implementation of the province's flat tax. In 1999, the government had announced that it would scrap its progressive taxation system and implement a flat tax of 11 per cent. This tax would be levied directly on income rather than be calculated as a percentage of federal tax as in the current system. Furthermore, the province announced a plan to increase the basic personal and spousal exemptions, which would have the effect of dropping thousands of low-income earners off of provincial tax rolls entirely.

Compared with the thorny terrain of health care and spiking energy prices, this would seem to have been the easy part of the government's policy agenda. The flat tax would see the tax bills of all taxpayers drop to some extent and, as such, was a popular move. This seemingly simple plan was derailed by developments beyond the province's control. The most significant challenge was the federal tax cuts announced by Paul Martin. The combination of the changes to the federal personal exemptions and the drop in the tax rate for middle income earners meant that Albertans from middle income families with two incomes (a significant proportion of the population) would actually be better off with the existing system than with the proposed flat tax. This was because of Alberta's decision to levy taxes directly on income and not on the proportion of federal tax. Under the existing system any federal tax reductions would automatically affect the levels of provincial taxation.

Stockwell Day went ahead and introduced the flat tax legislation anyway, even though he admitted that the bill would need to be amended to ensure that Albertans would benefit fully from the federal tax cuts. The contrast between the federal and the provincial tax cuts pointed out the biggest vulnerability of the Conservatives' flat tax plan. Critics pointed out that high income earners were the ones who received the proportionately biggest tax cut, while middle income earners received relatively little. The federal cuts, by contrast, were concentrated on those very earners. The provincial government felt further pressure when Ontario announced a sweeping set of tax cuts, putting Alberta's status as the least taxed jurisdiction in Canada in doubt.

The government's response was to tweak the flat tax proposal. In May, it introduced amendments to the bill that would lower the tax rate to 10.5 per cent and increase personal exemptions. The government invoked closure to pass the bill before the Legislature adjourned for the summer, and the issue seemed to be dealt with. The federal government's fall mini-budget reopened the debate. The tax cuts announced in October would once again not trickle down to Albertans. The provincial government promised to consider dropping the flat tax rate to 10 per cent to compensate for this. None of this tinkering satisfied critics, who pointed out that this adjustment did little to change the fundamental problem with the flat tax – that the benefits would accrue primarily to the most wealthy.

The Legislature

These three issues dominated the Alberta legislature in 2000 and made it a much more interesting and exciting place than is usually the case. The Legislature sat for its traditional two sittings in 2000: a relatively lengthy spring sitting and a brief fall sitting. Health care and taxation dominated the spring sitting, while soaring energy prices dominated the fall sitting. These hot-button issues generated the most headlines and were the focus of Opposition attacks during Question Period, essentially overshadowing everything else the Legislature did in 2000.

In February, provincial treasurer Stockwell Day introduced what could only be described as a 'good news' budget, which featured the adoption of the flat tax as its centrepiece. The budget also saw a number of user fees slashed, in compliance with a Supreme Court of Canada ruling that excessive provincial user fees were illegal taxes. In a demonstration of the health of the province's finances, Mr Day managed to deliver tax cuts and a surplus budget while increasing spending by $1.6 billion. The bulk of the spending increases were directed towards health care and education, and were earmarked to hire front-line health-care workers and teachers. The spending increases continued to feed the grumbling of the province's fiscal conservatives, coming as they did on the heels of a similar spending increase in 1999.

Besides Bill 11 and the flat tax proposal, one of the most controversial pieces of legislation was the Statute Revision Act (Bill 3), a housekeeping bill that would consolidate the province's statutes. This seemingly inoffensive bill became controversial because it empowered bureaucrats to identify inconsistencies in the law and make minor changes accordingly. The provincial Liberals objected strenuously that this power was open to abuse. Justice Minister Dave Hancock agreed to introduce changes that would satisfy the Liberals' concerns.

The Legislature also passed Red Deer MLA Victor Doerksen's private member's bill that would restrict marriage to heterosexuals and commit the provincial legislature to invoking the notwithstanding clause in the Charter of Rights and Freedoms to maintain that limitation. Seven Conservatives voted against the bill, including Justice Minister Hancock, who dismissed the bill as essentially irrelevant, given that marriage is a federal responsibility. Neither Premier Klein nor opposition leader Nancy MacBeth were present in the Legislature for the vote.

Another piece of legislation was controversial, even though it never made it to the Legislature floor. In the 1999 session, the government had withdrawn the Natural Heritage Act, which was designed to provide various levels of protection for wild lands in Alberta, and promised to reintroduce it in 2000. The bill was stalled in government committees because of the government's inability to craft a compromise over the balance between resource development and environmental protection.

Stockwell Day goes national

For a change, Ralph Klein was not the Alberta politician with the highest profile in 2000. The year saw the transformation of Stockwell Day from provincial cabinet minister to national party leader. Mr Day had always been warmly received in Reform Party circles and in the party's discussions to create a so-called 'united alternative' to the Liberal Party. Mr Day's name began to be seriously circulated as a potential leader of the new movement shortly after the Reform Party decided to reshape itself into a new movement. Initially, Mr Day did not publicly express any interest in the position. Shortly before the Reform Party's final referendum on transforming itself into the Canadian Alliance Party, Mr Day officially announced his intention to seek the leadership of the new party, a move seemingly designed to encourage ambivalent Reform Party members to support the formation of the new party.

The leadership contest for the new party was of obvious interest to Alberta, as it pitted two prominent Albertans – Preston Manning and Stockwell Day – against each other. In many ways, the two men were similar politicians in basic beliefs, but Mr Day benefited from being a fresh face and a feeling that Mr Manning had taken the party as far as it could go. One effect of Mr Day's entry into the race was that it drew many provincial Conservatives who had been ambivalent about Reform into the orbit of the new party. Chief among these was Ralph Klein. Besides publicly endorsing Stockwell Day, Premier Klein took out an Alliance membership, something he had not done with the Reform Party. A more profound link between the provincial Conservatives and Mr Day's campaign was the decision of Rod Love – Mr Klein's former chief of staff – to sign up with the Day camp as a senior campaign strategist. After Mr Day won the leadership, Mr Love became his chief of staff.

Stockwell Day's decision to enter national politics necessitated some adjustments in Alberta. During the leadership campaign, Mr Day took a leave of absence from his position as provincial treasurer. Even before the contest was done, Premier Klein shuffled his cabinet, dropping Mr Day. Steve West moved from resource development into Mr Day's old job, Mike Cardinal was brought back into the cabinet to replace Mr West, Health and Wellness Minister Halvar Johnson traded positions with Environment Minister Gary Mar. After winning the leadership, Mr Day resigned his Red Deer North seat in the Alberta legislature, which he had held for fourteen years. The Conservatives easily held onto the seat in the ensuing by-election.

Although Alberta's Conservative government moved on from Stockwell Day quickly, the former treasurer's Alberta past continued to cast shadows over his national leadership. The federal Liberals took every opportunity to point to Mr Day's statements and actions in Alberta politics as ammunition. With the public's anxiety over health care figuring as the major issue in the federal election, it was not surprising that the Bill 11 debate would find its way into federal politics. During the federal election, Mr Day often seemed to be put in the position of defending Alberta's controversial policy, while allowing the Liberals to cast themselves as the defenders of public health care.

Stockwell Day's attempt to make a clean move into federal politics was also complicated by a defamation lawsuit that had been filed against him in 1999 by Lorne Goddard, a Red Deer lawyer and public school trustee. Mr Day had written a letter to the *Red Deer Advocate* criticizing Mr Goddard for acting as legal counsel for an accused pedophile. Mr Goddard retaliated with a $600,000 defamation lawsuit. Early in 2000, a trial date of 6 November was set for the case. The federal election call necessitated a delay of the actual trial until January 2001, but Mr Day lost a number of pre-trial motions in November, including one that would have allowed a defence based on an expanded definition of free speech that protected political discussions. Just before Christmas, Mr Day settled the lawsuit with Mr Goddard, but neither party would reveal or discuss the terms of the agreement. This incensed many Albertans because taxpayers would directly pay the first $1 million of any settlement through the government's risk-management fund. The controversy over the settlement was still raging as the year drew to a close.

The federal election in Alberta

The transformation of the Reform Party into the Canadian Alliance and Stockwell Day's ascension into the leadership of the new party generated some significant interest in the federal election in Alberta, the bastion of support for the Alliance/Reform. Many in the province saw the re-making of the party as an opportunity for genuine change in federal politics. As the rumours of a fall federal election became more frequent and more intense, there was a sense of genuine anticipation in Alberta.

Going into the election, some Alliance supporters had mused about sweeping all twenty-six of Alberta's seats in Parliament. The Alliance targeted two sitting Liberal MPs: David Kilgour in Edmonton Southeast and Justice Minister Anne McLellan in Edmonton West. Ms

McLellan was the most attractive target for the Alliance; not only was she the highest-profile federal Liberal in Alberta, but as justice minister she was overseeing two policy areas near and dear to the hearts of most Alliance members: crime and punishment and gun control. Her slim margins of victory in previous elections also made her a tempting target. Alliance candidate Betty Unger closed the gap to 1.5 per cent, but Ms McLellan held the seat. For his part, Mr Kilgour held his seat easily, winning over half the vote.

Mr Kilgour and Ms McLellan's victories were indicative of a general trend in the province that saw incumbent MPs re-elected. There were only two exceptions. In Crowfoot, Alliance candidate Kevin Sorenson defeated former Reform Party MP Jack Ramsay, who had been expelled from the party because of a conviction for attempted rape in an incident that happened thirty years earlier. The most high-profile race was in Calgary Centre, where Conservative Party leader Joe Clark defeated Alliance MP Eric Lowther. Mr Clark's decision to seek election in Calgary Centre struck many as foolhardy, since Calgary was the centre of the Alliance's strength (although Calgary Centre was the weakest constituency for the party in the city). Mr Clark appears to have benefited from a coalescing of support; the Liberal and NDP shares of the vote were down significantly from what they had been in 1997. Mr Clark's gamble paid off: he earned the party its twelfth seat in the Alliance's backyard, allowing the Conservatives to maintain official party status in Parliament and enabling the party to live to fight another day.

One sign of the interest in the election in the province was the voter turnout: 60.2 per cent of Alberta's registered voters cast ballots on election day. Although this was not a particularly high percentage, it marked an increase from the 1997 election. Most other provinces saw sharp declines in voter turnout in 2000. Although the transformation of the Reform Party into the Canadian Alliance did not produce the desired breakthrough for the party in Ontario, it did manage to solidify the party's already tight grip on the province's parliamentary representation, as the Alliance's vote share was 58.9 per cent, up from the 54.6 per cent the Reform Party took in 1997. The Liberals experienced a corresponding decrease in the popular vote from 24 per cent in 1997 to 20.9 per cent in 2000.

The aftermath of the election saw the expression of a certain amount of frustration in the province. Although the 2000 election result was, in many ways, a repeat of the 1997 election, many Albertans went into the 2000 election with the sense that this time it would be different. In

1993 and 1997 Albertans seemed to be self-consciously supporting an opposition party. This time, expectations were higher. The combination of higher turnout and increased support for the Alliance suggested that many Albertans believed that they had a chance to change governments. The failure of significant numbers of Ontarians to embrace 'their' party, even though it had reshaped itself significantly, led many to question whether Albertans could meaningfully influence federal politics. There was even discussion of renewed interest in Alberta separatism, although the strength of such a sentiment was difficult to determine. One thing was clear, however, and that was that the uneasy relationship between Albertans and their federal government would continue.

The parties

The three major provincial political parties were all preparing for the upcoming provincial election. There were rumblings that the governing Conservatives might jump the gun and call a fall election, but the surprise federal election put a quick end to that speculation. Premier Klein told an October Conservative Party convention that the election would in fact be in spring of 2001. Throughout the year, the parties were heavily involved in the process of choosing candidates in preparation.

Although the smallest party in the provincial legislature, the New Democrats did a good job of generating headlines in 2000. The year's focus on health care played into a traditional policy strength for the party, something they exploited to full advantage. Some of the headlines the party gained were not for good reasons, however. In early February, leader Pam Barrett suddenly and dramatically announced her resignation from politics after suffering a severe allergic reaction to a local anaesthetic during a trip to the dentist. Ms Barrett said that the near-death experience made her re-evaluate her life and led her to search for a new direction. Ms Barrett's resignation was a blow to the party; besides the loss of a popular and effective leader, the party lost half of its caucus just before joining the debate over Bill 11. Raj Pannu, the only other NDP MLA, took over as interim party leader, and was acclaimed as full leader at a party convention in November.

The resulting by-election in Edmonton Highlands attracted a lot of attention, but the result was almost pre-determined when popular Edmonton city councillor Brian Mason announced his intention to seek the NDP nomination. Mr Mason took an impressive 59 per cent of the vote in the 12 June by-election. Most telling was the Conservatives' third-place finish (just behind the Liberals). The fall-out from Bill 11 appeared to have been a factor in the disappointing showing for the Conservatives. Even former Highlands Conservative MLA David King backed Mr Mason.

The Liberals' poor showing in the by-election was symptomatic of the challenge faced by the party. Bill 11 and the government's uncertainty on electricity deregulation created opportunities for the party to make some gains. As the year went on, however, there was no clear sign that the Liberals were translating their opposition to government policy into votes. The Liberals had to share the spotlight on opposing Bill 11 with the New Democrats and the party had difficulty articulating an alternative to the complex issue of deregulation. The party did receive a bit of good news in the fall when Kevin Taft announced that he would be seeking a Liberal nomination. Mr Taft, a former government bureaucrat, was a prominent critic of government fiscal, health, and energy policy. The challenge for the year ahead was how to harness the discontent with government policy in the upcoming provincial election.

The Conservatives had their hands full in 2000, as they tried to maintain control of three complicated and large policy areas. That they managed to do this without serious division was significant. The battles over Bill 11 did take their toll, however. Ralph Klein and the party looked and sounded less sure of themselves by the end of the year than they had at the beginning. This change hit home at the party's fall policy convention, where the Premier's speech was much less aggressive than usual. Its theme was public consultation and listening to constructive criticism. The party adopted a number of non-binding policy resolutions, including the elimination of health-care premiums and the eventual elimination of provincial income taxes.

The economy

Towards the end of 1999, a booming oil and gas sector jump-started Alberta's economy and the province continued to ride the wave throughout 2000. Oil prices averaged over U.S. $30 a barrel in 2000 and over the course of the year the price of natural gas doubled. These sustained high energy prices led to an expansion of the province's energy industry. Investment in the industry was up, as was oil- and gas-well drilling. In fact, this drilling was up 61 per cent over the previous year.

The prosperity of the energy industry was not matched uniformly by the agricultural sector. The livestock industry in the province enjoyed a productive year, with continued high cattle prices and increasing hog prices leading the way. This impressive performance was not seen on the crop side. Wheat prices did not recover from the decline in 1999, and increased revenue from the province's barley production was offset by decreased revenue from canola. Overall, Alberta's crop revenues were down by over 4 per cent; livestock revenue was up by 11.5 per cent.

The traditional economic engines of agriculture and energy production were joined by strong growth in other sectors of the economy. The province's manufacturing sector showed growth and the prosperity in the province was reflected in an 8.9 per cent increase in retail sales in 2000. The bottom line was a phenomenal 6.1 per cent increase in economic growth and an inflation rate that had declined to 4.8 per cent by December 2000, a full point lower than it had been in 1999. The rapid economic growth and improving job market raised concern about possible skill shortages in some economic sectors. Not surprisingly, the robust economic growth led to an increase in interprovincial migration to Alberta; almost 22,000 people moved to the province in 2000.

Miscellaneous

The trials of Wiebo Ludwig and Richard Boonstra occurred from February to April. The two men were tried on several charges related to a series of explosions at oil and gas wells in northern Alberta in the previous couple of years. Mr Ludwig and Mr Boonstra had been charged in 1999 and elected to face trial before a judge. The Crown's case against Mr Ludwig and Mr Boonstra raised questions about the tactics used by the Royal Canadian Mounted Police. Over the course of the trial, it was revealed that the RCMP had gone to great lengths in its attempt to gather evidence against Mr Ludwig, whom they suspected was responsible for the oil-patch vandalism. The testimony of an informant was crucial to the Crown's case, and much of the trial focused on this witness's credibility and the evidence he provided. In order to help the informant gain Mr Ludwig's confidence, it was revealed, in the course of the investigation the RCMP blew up a shack at one well site. This revelation raised some eyebrows because this explosion had heightened community fears over the vandalism spree. Furthermore, it was revealed that Alberta oil companies, frustrated at the lack of progress by the RCMP in halting the vandalism and at the spiralling costs of providing security, donated money to a local crime-prevention group. This money eventually found its way to the RCMP, financing a greater police presence in the area. Despite these lingering questions over the investigation, the judge found Mr Ludwig guilty on five of the fourteen charges he faced. Mr Boonstra was found guilty on two charges. Taking into account time already served and house arrest, the judge sentenced Mr Ludwig to twenty-eight months in prison and Mr Boonstra to twenty-one days. Mr Ludwig was up for parole late in the year, but the parole board decided that he would stay incarcerated until late in 2001. The sentence was greeted with relief in the Beaverlodge area, near the Ludwig farm, but the lingering question of who was responsible for the death of Karman Willis cast a shadow over the verdict. Ms Willis was shot and killed on Mr Ludwig's farm while on a late-night joy ride with a group of friends in 1999. The police continued to investigate her murder, but as of the end of 2000, no charges had yet been laid in connection with the case.

Edmonton area garden expert Lois Hole was sworn in as the province's new lieutenant-governor in February. Ms Hole had to attend the ceremony in a wheelchair because of a broken ankle. Her appointment was poplar, but her term in office got off to shaky start when she publicly indicated that she had concerns over Bill 11, which she wished to discuss with the Premier. Ms Hole quickly clarified that she would not block the legislation.

Senate appointments are always a touchy subject in Alberta, given the province's long-standing support of Senate reform. The debate was joined once again when prominent Alberta Conservative Ron Ghitter resigned from the Senate. Prime Minister Chrétien angered many Senate reform supporters when he once again passed over the so-called 'senators in waiting,' elected by Albertans in 1998. Instead, Mr Chrétien appointed Edmonton band leader Tommy Banks, an appointment that surprised even the self-described apolitical musician.

JOSEPH GARCEA

Saskatchewan

On 1 January 2000 Saskatchewanians awoke from their post–millennium celebration slumber to realize that, although they were now living in a new century and a new millennium, very little had changed from the day before. Neither their best hopes nor their worst fears for their province had been realized. Economically, politically, and technologically things remained much as they had been in the recent past. To the chagrin of some and the happiness of others no magical millennial mystery or muse emerged that would change their objective conditions or reality. Notwithstanding the lack of radical change, the remainder of the year would produce a series of interesting, and in some instances even important, public affairs.

Elections

The new millennium afforded voters the opportunity to influence the course of the future through the electoral process. There were three sets of elections in the province of Saskatchewan: a provincial by-election, the federal election, and municipal elections.

Provincial by-election

One of the most interesting developments on the provincial electoral scene was the resolution of the protracted political machinations on the issue of which party would represent the constituency of Wood River. This particular constituency was tied at 3,162 votes for each of the top two candidates in the general election of 1999. The Liberal candidate, Glen McPherson, was declared the winner when the returning officer cast the deciding ballot in his favour. Shortly thereafter an automatic judicial recount was held that confirmed the one-vote victory. However, the Court of Queen's Bench justice who conducted the recount indicated that there had been something irregular, though not necessarily intentional or illegal, in the handling of the ballots. Shortly after the Saskatchewan Party candidate, D.F. (Yogi) Huyghebaert, announced that he would be challenging the results of the by-election in court, the incumbent MLA decided to resign his seat in the Legislature and not run in the resulting by-election. Although the election regulations permitted NDP Premier Romanow to postpone holding a by-election until as late as November of 2000, he decided that politically it was best to hold it as soon as possible even though he realized that the chances of either his own party's candidate or a Liberal candidate winning would be very difficult. This was due to the disenchantment that had emerged both with the creation of the NDP-Liberal coalition government after the 1999 election and with what some deemed to be the mistreatment of the incumbent by the leadership of the coalition. In the by-election held on 26 June, approximately ten months after the 1999 general provincial election, the SaskParty candidate, D.F. Huyghebaert, was declared the winner. The results of the by-election were remarkably different from the general election's. Whereas in the general election support for the parties was 20.5 per cent for the NDP, 39.8 per cent for the SaskParty, and 39.8 per cent for the Liberal Party, support for the parties in the by-election was 17 per cent for the NDP, 65 per cent for the SaskParty, 11.6 per cent for the Liberal Party, and 6.4 per cent for the Green Party. The by-election results constituted bad news for the ruling coalition government. First, it lost some important ground in its battle with the SaskParty for legislative seats (NDP 29, SaskParty 26, and Liberal Party 3), and second, both the Liberals and the NDP lost substantial popular support. The gains made by the SaskParty at the expense of both the NDP and Liberal Party revealed a dangerous trend for both of them in the eventuality that a general election was called in the near future either of the government's own accord or as a result of a loss of a vote of confidence in the Legislature.

The coalition government's commitment to stay together and to avoid an election in the near future was undoubtedly heavily influenced by a poll conducted in the spring of 2000 indicating that if an election were held at the time the Saskatchewan Party would have received 31 per cent support, compared with 17 per cent for the NDP and only 7 per cent for the Liberal Party. Given its low level of support, the Liberal Party ran the greatest risk of losing all of its seats if an election were called. Despite that risk, a substantial number of Liberal Party members wanted their caucus members to withdraw from the coalition government for fear that the longer they stayed the greater the prospects of losing electoral support because of their close working relationship with the NDP.

Federal election

The federal election was interesting and, at least for the NDP, quite important. In one of the most ironic twists on the political landscape, the province with the most profound socialist roots in Canada and North America had now become a stronghold for the neo-conservative Alliance Party. In the 2000 federal election the Alliance Party won ten of the fourteen seats, the Liberal Party won two, and the NDP two. It was a big loss for the NDP, losing two seats to the Alliance Party and one to the Liberals (the seat held by Rick Laliberte, who defected from the NDP to the Liberals just before the election). The biggest loser of all in the federal election, however, was the Progressive Conservative Party, which, as in the previous election, was unable to make any gains. Indeed, even David Orchard, who had run against Joe Clark for the party leadership, was unable to win his seat. To understand the magnitude of the problems of the Progressive Conservative Party in Saskatchewan one merely has to note that its popular vote in 2000 was only 4.8 per cent compared to 42 per cent in 1984. By contrast, the popular vote for the Reform/Alliance jumped from 1 per cent in 1988 to 47.7 per cent in 2000. Clearly, the Alliance had supplanted the Progressive Conservative Party in the province.

The most interesting outcome of the election was that the vote count for some constituencies was so close that recounts were sought in four ridings. In all four cases, however, the election results stood. This included the two recounts granted by the courts to defeated NDP candidates Dennis Gruending in Saskatoon, who lost by sixty-four votes, and John Solomon in Regina, who lost by approximately three hundred votes. Before, during, and after the federal election campaign there was a growing realization that the Alliance Party's success was based on the vote splitting that was occurring for the centre-left vote by the NDP and the Liberals and the gravitational pull that favoured the Alliance Party on divisive issues such as gun control, farm subsidies, and tax cuts, as well as the general antipathy toward a federal Liberal government and a provincial NDP government. The 2000 election confirmed that until the other two parties found a way to alter the electoral dynamics created by the gravitational pulls of such cleavage issues, they would not find it easy to recapture the ground they had lost to the Alliance Party in the province. The other remarkable aspect of the election was the low voter turnout, which reflected a continuous downward trend for five successive elections: 77.9 per cent in 1984, 77.8 per cent in 1988, 69.4 per cent in 1993, 65.3 in 1997, and 64.6 per cent in 2000.

Municipal elections

The year 2000 was an election year in all urban municipalities and in the even-numbered wards of rural municipalities. There was nothing extraordinary about the election campaigns in either urban or rural municipalities. Despite the fact that the Task Force on Municipal Legislative Renewal had released its final report, neither the contents of the report nor the broader issue of reforming the municipal system was a major or significant issue in the campaigns, debates, or results of the elections. Two municipal elections of some note were those that produced a change in mayor's office in the province's two largest cities – Regina and Saskatoon. Saskatoon's mayor, Henry Dayday, who had run and lost as a Liberal candidate in a federal by-election held a year earlier, lost the mayoralty race to a former police officer whose main plank in his election platform was achieving better relations with civic unions and improvements in policing. Regina's incumbent mayor, Doug Archer, lost to Pat Fiacco, a former amateur boxer, whose platform was based largely on the promise that he was better equipped than his opponents to boost the profile and economic development of the city.

Provincial political parties

This was a dramatic year for both of the provincial parties involved in the coalition government. A combination of the election results and their decision to establish a coalition government the previous year created some internal machinations that produced substantial change for both of them. Both the New Democratic Party and the Liberal Party were engaged in major struggles related to their leadership.

New Democratic Party

For the New Democratic Party this was unquestionably one of the most dramatic years since it formed the government nearly a decade earlier. The drama began in July when Deputy Premier Dwayne Lingenfelter announced his resignation, and intensified considerably in September when Premier Romanow announced his intention to resign both as Premier and as a member of the legislature after his successor was chosen. Although the leadership convention was set for the last week in January 2001, the leadership race was in full swing within two weeks of Mr Romanow's announcement. The contenders included four sitting MLAs, Chris Axworthy, Buckley Belanger, Joanne Crofford, and Maynard Sonntag; a former MLA and cabinet minister, Lorne Calvert; a former president of the National Farmers Union, Nettie Wiebe; and long-standing party activist and executive officer Scott Banda. One of the most interesting aspects of the leadership race was the fact that some high-profile cabinet ministers decided not to run. The most notable of these were former deputy premier Dwayne Lingenfelter, former minister of finance and then Minister of Economic Development Janice Mackinnon, Minister of Health Pat Atkinson, and Minister of Finance Eric Cline.

As the year drew to a close the candidates engaged in a series of debates around the province in their efforts to convince individual party members to support them. The NDP was experimenting with a system that gave every member a direct vote in choosing the leader. That proved to be a controversial issue between those who favoured the traditional delegate selection process and those who favoured a direct vote by every party member either before or during the convention. The candidates' efforts to garner support for their respective campaigns contributed to a substantial increase in the membership list of the NDP, which grew by 4,000 between the start of the leadership race and the deadline for purchasing memberships at the end of the year. That was little consolation for those who realized that between 1991 and 2000 the NDP membership had dropped by 30,000. The major issues in the leadership debates were financial support for the farm economy, reforms in health care, reforms in the Crown corporations sector, and the best strategy for economic development. The platforms of the various leadership candidates were generally not very critical of the former government's policies and programs, save for the position taken by Chris Axworthy to scrap the health boards, and Nettie Wiebe's commitment to provide substantial increases in financial support for farmers.

The NDP had to wait until the new year to see who would be its new leader in the first leadership selection process since 1971, when Allen Blakeney defeated Roy Romanow. Mr Romanow had been at the helm since he was acclaimed leader in 1987. As it moved toward the leadership convention, the NDP had to deal with a $600,000 debt load from the provincial election in 1999 that constrained it to lay-off thirteen employees. En route to the leadership convention the NDP had its policy convention, for which six committees produced discussion papers on policy issues such as aboriginal and northern affairs, fiscal policy, agricultural policy, education and employment, and agriculture and land usage. The ensuing discussions and debates did not help either the party or the government much in charting a course through the complicated political rapids they were navigating.

Liberal Party

Without a doubt, 2000 was one of the most difficult years in recent times for the Liberal Party of Saskatchewan. The involvement of the small Liberal caucus in the coalition government with the NDP created major internal problems for the party, and particularly for its leader, Jim Melenchuk. He was strongly criticized both for leading the caucus into a coalition government with the NDP and for not leading them out of it when it became clear that many party members were expressing strong opposition to it. The loss of the Wood River constituency in the June by-election resulting from the resignation of one of the party's own members compounded the problems and complaints. The internal dissension within the party reached a critical point in the fall of 2000, when the Liberal party held its annual convention in Prince Albert. At the convention the majority of members voted in a secret ballot for a leadership review despite the efforts of Mr Melenchuk to encourage members not to hold such a review.

As the convention approached, one of the three members of the Liberal caucus, Jack Hillson, began to distance himself from both Mr Melenchuk and the coalition agreement. By the end of the year it became clear that he wanted to seek the leadership of the Liberal Party. The Romanow government had as much at stake in the party's leadership contest as did Jim Melenchuk, because the future of the coalition government hinged in part on what happened. As anticipated, the coalition agreement became a central issue in the leadership review, especially in light of the pending change in the leadership of the NDP when Roy Romanow announced his resignation.

Saskatchewan Party

The Saskatchewan Party spent most of 2000 waiting for the wheels to fall off the coalition government, necessitating either a general election or possibly a Saskatchewan Party/Liberal Party coalition. Recognizing that an election could be called at any time, the Saskatchewan Party was very careful to avoid taking strong ideological stances that could harm its image and credibility, as had happened shortly after the party was formed. The party was particularly careful in this respect during its annual convention, where its leader Elwin Hermanson's substantial ability to manage both the caucus and the party was clearly in evidence.

Conservative Party

Even in its state of official 'hibernation' the provincial Progressive Conservative Party continued to suffer from the aftermath of the financial scandals that had plagued it for nearly a decade as yet another trial for misuse of funds was taking place. In this particular case, former Progressive Conservative Party MLA Ralph Katzman was being tried for allegedly diverting $450,000 from the caucus account and using it for personal and non-sanctioned purposes. The party also suffered additional embarrassment from a sex scandal involving another of its former MLAs, Jack Goohsen, who had resigned his seat in the Legislature in the spring of 1999 due to the scandal. The Court of Appeal upheld Mr Goohsen's 1997 conviction for buying sex from a fourteen-year-old girl. All this occurred at approximately the same time that former Progressive Conservative Party member and deputy premier Senator Eric Berntson was seeking bail pending the appeal of his fraud conviction to the Supreme Court of Canada.

Aboriginal parties

The only other activities of political parties of some note were those of two emerging parties in the aboriginal community. One of these was the First Nations Party. The attempt to establish the First Nations Party at the provincial level produced more shenanigans than support. Its founder, Brendan Cross, was unable to establish sufficient credibility either at the personal or party level to produce the requisite support to become a force or even a factor in provincial politics. The other was the New Metis Party established by John Melenchuk, whose main platform was to increase accountability within the Metis governance and management circles.

Federal political parties

The provincial wings of the national parties were very active in 2000 as they prepared themselves for the federal election to be held in the fall.

Liberal Party

The first major development of some note for the federal parties in

Saskatchewan in 2000 resulted in the pre-election gain of one seat by the Liberal Party at the expense of the NDP. This occurred when the MP for the northern constituency of Churchill River, Rick Laliberte, crossed the floor of the House of Commons near the end of September. The crossing of the floor by Mr Laliberte effectively ended any speculation that the Liberals and NDP would collaborate in the federal election later in the year to enhance their respective chances of winning some of the seats held by the Alliance Party.

New Democratic Party

This was not a good year for the federal wing of the NDP in Saskatchewan. The defection by Rick Laliberte to the Liberal Party, in what had to that point been considered a relatively safe seat for the NDP, and the inability to recapture that seat in the federal election after the defection, was the first major setback. The second major setback was the loss of two other seats held by incumbents John Solomon and Dennis Gruending. During the election Alexa McDonough visited the province on a few occasions in an effort to play up the party-that-cares-for-medicare theme, but in the end it did not generate much enthusiasm or many votes for her party.

Alliance Party

The Alliance Party, like its precursor, continued to struggle in its efforts to enhance its credibility in the aboriginal sector. When the new Alliance Party leader, Stockwell Day, tried to court Saskatchewan voters, he received a rough reception from the leader of the newly formed First Nations Party of Saskatchewan, Brendan Cross, who burned a copy of the Alliance policy book that dealt with aboriginals. What made Mr Cross's action particularly poignant was that he had been a card-carrying member of the Canadian Alliance who explained that he had turned away from the party when he realized that he would not be able to change its policies related to aboriginals.

The Alliance Party's credibility problems were compounded immensely by the insatiable penchant of one of its highest-profile MPs in Saskatchewan, Jim Pankiw, to criticize various aboriginal rights as well as any accommodation or compensation for aboriginals. Although it is not clear how much support he had for his views among the general public, support from his constituents and members of his own party's executive, and his re-election in the 2000 federal election as an Alliance MP, suggests that it was not insignificant.

Progressive Conservative Party

The most disappointed of all federal parties in Saskatchewan had to be the Progressive Conservative Party. Fielding candidates was hard and encouraging people to vote for those candidates was even harder. David Orchard, the high-profile candidate who had come in second for the party leadership won by Joe Clark in 1998, was unable to secure the requisite votes to win the constituency that had sent John Diefenbaker to Parliament.

The Legislature and government

The executive

There were three major developments in Saskatchewan's executive branch of government of some note in 2000. The first of these was Lynda Haverstock's appointment as Lieutenant-Governor to replace Jack Wiebe, who was appointed to the Senate. The notable aspect of Ms Haverstock's appointment is that she was the former leader of the provincial Liberal Party during the 1991 and 1995 provincial elections. During her term as party leader she had managed to develop a policy platform based on fundamental principles of good governance and good public management that resonated with the electorate and garnered considerable respect, if not always electoral support. Unfortunately for her, and possibly for her party, she had a substantial number of detractors within her own party who mobilized members to replace her in a leadership review in November 1995. Ms Haverstock decided not to run in the resulting leadership convention. Instead, she opted to sit as an independent member of the Legislature until her resignation just before the 1999 election. The irony of her appointment as Lieutenant-Governor at the same time that some of the very people who had forced her to resign as Liberal Party leader were occupying cabinet posts and seats on both sides of the house in the Legislature was not lost on those who observed and commented on politics in the province. Within the first few months in her new post she performed two major functions – she read the Throne Speech and hosted the Governor General, Adrienne Clarkson, on her visit to Saskatchewan.

The second major development of note was the changing configuration of the provincial cabinet. The changes were additions and deletions resulting from resignations of Liberal Party and high-profile NDP members. Two of the three members of the Liberal Party who agreed to participate in the coalition government were assigned cabinet posts and the other was appointed Speaker of the Legislature. The cabinet posts were Minister of Health and Minister of Intergovernmental Relations, and eventually Minister of Municipal Affairs, Culture, and Housing.

The only member of the Liberal Party who did not receive a prominent position in either the cabinet or the Legislature was Glen McPherson. This proved to be a contentious issue as he waited to find out whether he would be declared the representative for his constituency following the ballot recount and any judgments from the court. Some confusion and a debate emerged regarding whether Mr McPherson had been offered a cabinet post. Whereas he indicated that he had, Premier Romanow stated that for his part he had never made such an offer and did not intend to do so at that time. This difference between the two men on this issue undoubtedly contributed to Mr McPherson's decision to resign his seat and force a by-election. Premier Romanow's reticence to include Mr McPherson in his cabinet was based on the fact that the latter had defected from the NDP to the Liberal Party approximately seven years earlier in protest of the NDP government's decision to close some rural hospitals, and also because his hold on his seat was tenuous. Undoubtedly, Mr McPherson's decision to resign his seat in the spring of 2000 was based on a desire to send a 'plague on both your houses' message to the NDP and Liberal members of the coalition government.

By far the two most significant changes to the cabinet were the resignations of the Deputy Premier and Premier within three months. The first to resign was Deputy Premier Dwayne Lingenfelter, who had served in several senior cabinet posts in the Romanow government. His resignation caught most political pundits by surprise because he was seen as the heir apparent who had worked persistently to build a personal base of support for a run at the party leadership. Although his stated purpose for leaving politics was that he had found a position in the private sector, rumours circulated that several other factors weighed heavily in his decision, including the erosion of support for the NDP, disenchantment with the creation of the coalition government, the internal differences within the NDP cabinet and caucus regarding the current and future directions in governance, and the likelihood that he had become tired of waiting for Premier Roy Romanow to decide when he would step down as party leader. While some saw this move by Mr Lingenfelter as a complete and final break from provincial politics, others wondered whether it was a clever move on his part to distance himself from the negative sentiments toward the governing coalition with the aim of coming back after Roy Romanow resigned as Premier and party leader.

The second major surprise for political pundits in 2000 was the decision by Premier Roy Romanow to resign. What was particularly surprising was that his announcement came after nearly three months of denials that he had any intention of doing so. Notwithstanding his repeated denials, however, the first tangible sign that perhaps he was on his way out came with the resignation of his deputy premier.

The Legislature

The legislative session, which officially began in December 1999 with an emergency debate on agriculture, was as much about posturing as it was about policy. As anticipated, the Saskatchewan Party headed into the spring sitting with the intent of breaking up and toppling the coalition government. In addition to criticizing the coalition government for operating without a mandate and against the will of the majority of voters, the Saskatchewan Party devoted considerable effort to raising wedge issues that could potentially lead to the end of the coalition. For their part, the NDP and Liberal coalition partners remained vigilant on matters regarding attendance by their members to ensure that they were not at risk of losing any votes of confidence. The coalition government did survive the session and was still in place at the end of the year.

Accusations and counter-accusations between the parties regarding each other's integrity, hidden agendas, and finances punctuated the legislative session. On the matter of party finances, the various parties were keen to highlight the types of donors that were supporting the other parties as a way of suggesting that, based on the source of those contributions, they were likely vulnerable to bias and possibly even conflict of interest.

During the legislative session, which lasted seventy-one days, eighty-one pieces of legislation were passed. The major policy issues of note included the perennial farm crisis, the condition of the highway and road systems in the province, the future governance and management of health care in the province, the restructuring of the municipal sector, the problems of financial management with the Saskatchewan Indian Gaming Authority, the investment practices and problems of some Crown corporations and the utility rates being charged by others, the expanded application of the provincial sales taxes to various goods and services that were not previously covered, and the regulations regarding unionization of contractors' 'spinoff' companies established before 1992. Although all of these were difficult issues for the provincial government, three of the most difficult were those affecting the rural areas of the province: the farm crisis, which generated some concern for the Premier's safety at public rallies; the level of commitment to improving the highway and road system in the province, which raised serious issues of safety and liability and led some communities to establish volunteer work bees to fill potholes; and the debate over the restructuring of the municipal sector.

The budget

In Saskatchewan as in other provinces the budget exercise continues to be in part a function of the federal budget. In 2000 this included both an annual budget, presented in the spring, and a mini-budget, presented in the fall. The provincial government's response to the annual budget in the first quarter of the year was quite predictable, notwithstanding the fact that there were now provincial Liberals in the coalition government. The response from the Premier was that the amount of money that would be transferred to Saskatchewan for health care, education, and infrastructure was inadequate to accomplish any major programmatic goals. In defence of the federal government's level of transfers, the lone federal minister from Saskatchewan, Ralph Goodale, noted that the Premier conveniently forgot to mention that the provincial government had received some tax points from the federal government for health and education that would provide Saskatchewan with an average of approximately $1 billion annually over the next four years.

The response to the federal mini-budget in the fall of 2000 was surprisingly warm from both the provincial government and the official opposition: in the case of the former because the budget adopted the government's own philosophy of devoting any surplus more or less proportionately to spending, debt financing, and tax reduction, and in the case of the latter for the planned tax reductions. For its part the official opposition took the opportunity of the federal mini-budget to argue that the provincial government should follow the federal example and adopt the practice of producing mini-budgets and holding a fall sitting of the Legislature.

The provincial government's own budget continued to be designed according to the long-standing practice of balancing the principles of economic rationality with those of political rationality. That balancing effort produced a budget with a projected increase in revenues of approximately $800 million and a decrease in expenditures of approximately $200 million. The key provisions in the provincial budget include the following:

- a projected budget surplus of $9.4 million
- a projected accumulated debt of $11.3 billion
- a delinking of provincial tax rates from federal tax rates
- a new income-tax rate regime of 11 per cent for the first $35,000 in earnings, 13 per cent for $35,000 to $100,000, and 15 per cent for anything over $100,000
- a sales tax credit for families earning up to $35,000
- application of the sales tax for status Indians making purchases off-reserve
- an additional $63 million increase in funding for health
- an additional $52 million increase in funding for school boards
- a $350 income-tax benefit for graduates who take a job in Saskatchewan
- a $25 million two-year rebate program on property taxes on the school portion of the property tax bill
- the elimination of the farm fuel tax, and a reduction in the capital gains tax for farmers to 11 per cent

In what was viewed as a deceptive strategy for a budget presentation, not all the details of how the revenues would be raised were released on budget day. Approximately one week later the Minister of Finance revealed that the provincial government would be introducing some increases in taxes and fees, including an expanded provincial sales tax on such items as legal fees, architectural and real estate fees, used cars, and bedding plants; an increase in fishing, hunting, and camping fees; and one of the most politically sensitive and controversial budget measures of all, a substantial increase in the monthly fees for long-term care. The government was hounded for the rest of the year by complaints over that particular increase. The pressure led the government to promise a review and possibly a revision of the proposed changes to those fees.

The provincial budget received mixed reviews. Positive reviews focused on two key matters. The first was the two-year program that provided farmers with a rebate on the education component of their property tax for the agricultural portion of their property, which was seen as a positive first step to either a long-term rebate or possibly the elimination of the education property tax for agricultural lands. This was a long-standing issue in the agricultural sector that had fuelled the emergence of some fledgling protest groups in the province. The second was the fact that the budget provided Saskatchewan taxpayers with the largest tax break in the province's history, something that from a comparative standpoint would place 70 per cent of taxpayers in the same income tax circumstances as their Alberta counterparts within four years. This was a goal favoured not only by the provincial taxation committee headed by Jack Vicq in 1999, but also by the official opposition. Indeed, this particular budget measure served the coalition government well in its efforts to take one potential plank out of the Saskatchewan Party's policy platform. However, the Saskatchewan Party continued to up the ante on the tax-cutting front as it responded by calling for even deeper tax cuts.

Negative reviews of the budget focused on the expanded PST, the increased taxes and fees, as well as some hidden cuts. The sentiments in such reviews were echoed by respondents to polls conducted by the Saskatchewan government, and another by the Hollinger newspaper publishing company. Although the expansion of the PST was roundly criticized by the general public, the extension of the PST to purchases by aboriginals off-reserve was not. Support for that particular budget measure was led by both the Saskatchewan branch of the Canadian Taxpayers Federation, which submitted a 29,000-signature petition to the provincial government on the matter, and the Saskatchewan Party. They did so despite the fact that they acknowledged that currently the government was actually getting more in fuel and tobacco taxes on-reserve than it was losing from PST exemptions on purchases by status Indians off-reserve. Evidently the government took this initiative because it recognized that it would not be able to collect tax for fuel and tobacco sales made on-reserve.

Criticism of that measure came from the aboriginal sector. Indeed, a few days after it was announced a court challenge was launched by the Federation of Saskatchewan Indian Nations, who maintained that it abrogated a treaty right. The suit was launched despite the fact that a 1998 Supreme Court decision regarding such taxation in New Brunswick upheld the right of a provincial government to impose a sales tax on off-reserve purchases by status Indians. The FSIN hoped that the court would rule in its favour by arguing that in determining whether status Indians were exempt, the focus should be on the individual treaties, as was the case in a court case in Alberta, rather than on the Indian Act, as was the case in the New Brunswick court decision.

The economy

At the turn of the millennium a substantial portion of opinion leaders, and to some extent the general public, became increasingly cognizant that the economic future of the province would be tied much less to the performance of agricultural and non-aboriginal entrepreneurs and workers than in the past. Increasingly important would be the technological and biotechnological sectors and aboriginal entrepreneurs and workers. Not surprisingly, therefore, those looking for the silver lining in the cloudy forecasts of the province's economy pointed to initiatives such as the Canadian Light Source synchrotron whose advocates suggested was destined to be a windfall not only for the University of Saskatchewan and the city of Saskatoon, but ultimately also for the province as a whole. Others pointed to the increase in size, improving education, and growing entrepreneurialism of the aboriginal population in the province. Those emphasizing the growing importance of the aboriginal sector pointed to the study commissioned by the Federation of Saskatchewan Indian Nations which indicated that by 2045 one-third of the province's population of approximately 1.33 million people would be of aboriginal ancestry. Those advocating progressive agendas for ensuring that the aboriginal population is fully engaged in the economy pointed to the importance of aboriginal workers for ensuring that there is an appropriate ratio in the future between the total number of workers and the total population in the province.

The provincial government attempted to put a positive face on what looked like grim economic prospects for the province as reflected in part on job growth rates for the first quarter of the year. Although the Premier noted that more people were working than ever before in the history of Saskatchewan, he did not note that during the previous year Saskatchewan shared the lowest job growth rate for the country. Shortly after the Premier made his optimistic remarks regarding the future economic performance of the province, the short-term economic prospects became increasingly grim as stock markets started to tumble downward around the world. The bad news from the markets sent a shockwave through various sectors of the provincial economy, including the Crown corporations, where an optimistic target for projected revenues of $152 million was likely to be adversely affected by the markets to a point where this sector would be generating less than half of what it had generated just two years earlier.

By the end of the year, politicians and at least a majority of

Saskatchewan's residents alike were happy that the provincial economy was still not experiencing any devastating effects from the new problems in the markets and the perennial problems of the farm economy. Saskatchewan was holding its own, even though it remained unclear how long it could do so with the siren call of Alberta next door ringing in many people's ears, in particular the youth of the province. Toward that end the Minister of Economic Development released a document titled *Partnership for Prosperity*, which projected the need to create at least 30,000 jobs, especially for youth and aboriginal persons, and reduce income taxes by 25 per cent by 2005.

Intergovernmental affairs

Federal–provincial relations

The major issues in federal–provincial relations continued to be federal financial transfers for equalization payments, agriculture, and health. Increases to equalization payments were advocated by Saskatchewan as well as by the ministers of finance of the other 'have not' provinces.

Increases in financial transfers for agriculture and health were the top issues at the Western Premiers' Conference, at the national Premiers' conference, and in the federal election. As the agricultural sector continued to struggle with adverse weather and market conditions, provincial politicians pressed the federal government for increased financial transfers targeted at farmers. They sought substantial improvements in transfers for roads and in various farm safety nets for the agricultural sector. As well they wanted some trade issues resolved with the United States that were adversely affecting sales and profits. The farm crisis engendered considerable controversy all year long, and featured a series of negotiations, protests that included a sit-in at the provincial legislature, and federal commitments for additional funds. Various financial-aid promises and packages were received, with mixed reactions.

An equally contentious issue was the level of federal financial transfers for health care, which was the most prominent issue at the Western Premiers' Conference. Premier Romanow led the Premiers' charge against the federal government to increase funding. He encouraged the federal government to establish a royal commission on health care and a new reporting mechanism to measure the health outcomes from the medical system. In addition, he pressured the federal government to develop its long-promised national child-care program as a means to improve health as well as social outcomes. Health care remained high on the public agenda throughout the year, and as the federal election approached, Premier Romanow found substantial support for his position not only among his fellow premiers, but also with the leaders of the federal opposition parties.

Aboriginal affairs

The issue of political leadership came to the forefront with the elections for Chief and Vice-chiefs of the Federation of Saskatchewan Indian Nations. Chief Perry Bellegarde was able to ward off the challenge and criticism of his two principal opponents, Morley Watson and Terry Sanderson, to retain his position for a second term. A third opponent, Terrence Lavallee, did not make it onto the ballot because his nominator left the leadership convention just before the official oral nominations. Three key issues prevailed in this election. The first was financial accountability throughout the First Nation sector, including within the Saskatchewan Indian Gaming Authority (SIGA), which, as explained in greater detail below, was subjected to a detailed forensic audit. In a post-election interview, Chief Bellegarde promised that the SIGA issue would be addressed in November both by the FSIN economic development commission and by a special chiefs' assembly. The second issue was the wisdom of the agreement between FSIN and the provincial government on the elimination of the PST exemption for Indians on purchases off-reserve. The third major issue was the nature of the election process itself. Some criticized the existing process, in which approximately six to seven hundred band representatives were involved in the elections of the FSIN executive, and advocated a new system in which all bona fide First Nations people would have a vote.

Another notable development in the aboriginal sector in 2000 was the electoral reform introduced by the federal government at the band level. An amendment to the Indian Act designed to conform to a 1998 Supreme Court decision provided members of Indian bands living off-reserve with the right to vote in band elections. Shortly after that amendment was enacted, First Nations leaders in Saskatchewan began preparing to participate in the Herculean project of overhauling what most viewed as an anachronistic and paternalistic Indian Act. The official announcement that such an overhaul would be undertaken was made later in the year by the Minister of Indian Affairs.

Of continuing significance in 2000 was the ongoing work of the RCMP task force on the tragic and disturbing deaths of several aboriginal men in Saskatoon. Although the task force was initially established to investigate the deaths of two men, the scope was widened when two other men died under suspicious circumstances. Questions regarding police treatment of individuals of aboriginal ancestry prevailed inside and outside the city for months. At issue was whether either negligence or criminal intent on the part of police officers had contributed to any or all of the deaths. For its part the Saskatoon Police Service was conducting its own internal review. Collectively, these events gave Saskatchewan a public relations black eye. The *National Post* ran a series that depicted the province as 'Mississippi North.' Despite the outrage at such a depiction expressed in the legislature, all parties recognized that the affair was a public relations disaster.

The issue of spending by the Saskatchewan Indian Gaming Authority, which was established to operate four casinos on behalf of the Federation of Saskatchewan Indian Nations, came to the fore this year. SIGA was subjected to intense scrutiny and two investigations, one in the form of a forensic audit conducted by the Saskatchewan Liquor and Gaming Authority. The other was undertaken later in the year by the Provincial Auditor, as a result of which the provincial government ordered that SIGA's CEO and chairman, E. (Dutch) Lerat, be fired. SIGA refused to do so until it was satisfied there was some wrongdoing. Eventually, however, SIGA acceded to the order when the Liquor and Gaming Authority threatened to close its four casinos. Subsequently, SIGA tightened its conflict-of-interest regulations, and the provincial government imposed even tighter regulations and audit requirements pursuant to several recommendations made in the Provincial Auditor's report. At the same time that the SIGA financial-management issue was being addressed, the FSIN was negotiating the purchase of an existing casino in Saskatoon to be added to SIGA's gaming establishments.

Within the educational sphere, it was announced that construction would begin on a new facility for the Saskatchewan Indian Federated College (SIFC) on a parcel of land at the University of Regina campus. The $29.6 million facility would be funded in part by a $10 million grant from the federal government.

Another positive development in this sector were the agreements signed between aboriginal governments and various other levels of government. The most notable are the following three. The first was a self-governance framework agreement between the Federation of Saskatchewan Indian Nations and the federal and provincial governments that provided the principles and parameters for FSIN to negotiate self-governance on specific matters. The agreement contained an understanding that the first matters likely to be the subject of such negotiations were jurisdiction and authority in education, and child and family services, to be followed by negotiations on issues related to justice, lands and resources management, hunting, fishing, trapping and gathering, health, and housing. The other major negotiations would concern financial arrangements related to taxation and revenue sources, for which a target date of January 2002 was set. The projected total price tag from the start to the completion of the self-government negotiations was approximately $25 million.

The second major agreement provided five First Nation reserves with the right to replace RCMP officers with their own police officers for their reserves with full authority to enforce the federal Criminal Code, provincial laws, and band bylaws. Although they were prepared to sign the self-policing agreement, the provincial and federal governments were not yet ready to endorse an FSIN proposal for the creation of a parallel system of courts for First Nations in the province.

The third agreement provided compensation for aboriginal land claims to rural municipalities and school boards. The agreement signed in March 2000 provided compensation in a one-time lump-sum payment worth approximately fifteen times the amount of taxes that would have otherwise been collected had the land not been transferred to First Nation governments in response to specific land claims. Pursuant to this agreement, the federal government gave the Saskatchewan Association of Rural Municipalities $2.8 million and the Saskatchewan School Trustees Association $1.2 million for up to 300,000 acres of rural land and provincial Crown land purchased and converted to reserve status.

The federal and provincial governments also signed a partnership agreement to work with industry in promoting First Nations economic development within the forestry and tourism sectors, as well as providing training and financial support through the Northern Development Fund.

Another agreement involved the provincial government and various aboriginal governments or governing authorities. Designed to facilitate the participation of aboriginal persons in the province's Aboriginal Employment Development Program, the agreement was signed by the FSIN, the Saskatchewan Metis Nation, and the Congress of Aboriginal Peoples (CAP), which represented persons of Metis ancestry as well as Indians and non-status Indians living off-reserve.

Concluding observations

In reflecting on public affairs in Saskatchewan in 2000, one is struck by the fact that it was a relatively eventful year. One is also struck by the fact that whatever changes occur in the protagonists, the politics, and the policies in this province, there is a continuity of something that is quintessentially Saskatchewanian in nature. Those who have lived here for any length of time know its character and its flavour and value it. Nevertheless even in the heady days of the new millennium, many of the province's residents, both young and old, continued to leave it for other parts of Canada.

GEOFFREY LAMBERT

Manitoba

The final year of the twentieth century in Manitoba was one of low-profile, unobtrusive government from the NDP. The party's election platform the year before had been extraordinarily prudent. Their behaviour in government suggested they had been in earnest in promising progressive but not radical government.

The former premier, Progressive Conservative Gary Filmon (Tuxedo), gave up his seat, and his party found a new leader. The economy was on the whole healthy, though the plight of some of Manitoba's farmers was bleak. Moreover, the optimism of the last several years seemed to be on the point of fading somewhat.

The legislative session

The Legislature resumed in April, and sat until July. Later, in keeping with recent Manitoba practice, there was a short session in December, when a new Throne Speech was read.

Greg Selinger (St Boniface), the Finance Minister, brought down a budget on 10 May. It was a sound effort, reflecting the NDP's promise to maintain the balanced-budget legislation introduced by the Tories. A financial surplus enabled the government to avoid new taxation, and to introduce a few goodies of their own. Thus, tuition at Manitoba universities was to be frozen, and the government would provide a 10 per cent tuition rebate for students. (No provision was made for the shortfall in university revenues this brought about, but as Mr Caldwell, the vocal Minister of Education, pointed out, the universities had big budgets and ought to be able to cope.) Further, a Manitoba Families Tax Credit program was to be introduced.

A key feature in the New Democrats' successful campaign the previous year had been a promise to fix the health-care system, to do away with 'hallway medicine,' as Premier Doer (Concordia) repeatedly put it. It is unlikely that any government anywhere in Canada is, or will be, able to adequately cope with the demands likely to be placed on the health-care system as the population ages, and as the famed baby-boomers begin to experience intimations of mortality. Still, the NDP was prepared to give it a try. Thus, expenditure on the health-care system would rise to $2.4 billion in the new fiscal year, an increase of $135 million (or about 6 per cent) over the previous year. The amount of support for the Pharmacare drug coverage program was also increased. The NDP was still enjoying a honeymoon period, and could safely continue to blame their Tory predecessors for defects in the system, as well as pour hot coals on the heads of the federal Liberals for their cuts to transfer payments during the 1990s.

In other policy areas, the NDP opened the public purse to a relatively modest degree. What they sought to prove with this budget was that they were fiscally responsible, and nothing like the free-spending NDP governments of the past. To that extent, they pleased the broad generality of the population, while displeasing some in the public sector by their frugality, and earning the predictable disgust of the free-enterprise community because they promised no massive reductions in taxation rates.

Perhaps the most noteworthy legislation introduced during the spring session involved the government's amendments to the labour code, and its new plans for controlling political financing. The labour code changes, among other elements, changed the procedures for certifying a union. Whereas previously a vote of all potential members was required, now all that was necessary was that the union sell a certain number of union cards, specifically, up to 60 per cent of the workforce. This bill, supported by the unions, was a red flag to the business community. It seemed to remind them vividly of the belief that the unions were the New Democrats' 'paymasters' who called all the shots. It was one of the relatively few moments in the political life of the province in 2000 when 'class politics' seemed to have much of a hold in Manitoba.

The campaign-finances legislation essentially forbade corporate donations, a definition that of course included organized labour. The legislation was intended as a means of providing the so-called level playing field. It tended to bolster the New Democrats, who derived much less of their income from corporate sources than did the Tories. The law was not to come into effect until 1 January 2001, giving the parties a few months to 'clean up their acts,' as some observers put it.

The Doer cabinet kept a low profile, with a few exceptions. The Premier himself did not seek centre stage any more than was absolutely necessary. Greg Selinger, by virtue of his position as Finance Minister attracted some attention, but Jean Friesen (Wolseley), Deputy Premier and Minister for Municipalities was, in contrast, seldom heard from. Steve Ashton (Thompson), Highways, and the Reverend Tim Sale (Fort Rouge), Family Services, previously outspoken left-wingers, seldom said either boo or peep.

But, as stated, there were exceptions. Drew Caldwell (Brandon East), the Education Minister who had previously been a substitute teacher in Brandon, was frequently in the news offering his views (solicited or not) on a wide range of educational and associated matters. The pressures of the portfolio are immense; there are many interest groups involved, and it consumes a large portion of the provincial budget. Mr Caldwell gained attention when the government froze tuition fees at Manitoba universities and implemented a rebate scheme for students. Later in the year, the government split the education portfolio into two components. Dr Diane McGifford (Lord Roberts), holder of a doctorate in English, and Minister for Culture, Heritage and Recreation, became Minister for Post-secondary Education, a newly created department. Mr Caldwell retained the schools portfolio, an area of work where he seemed more comfortable.

Mr Oscar Lathlin (The Pas), a First Nations cabinet member, and Minister for the Environment, attracted some attention for the wrong reasons. His private finances were such as Mr Micawber would recognize. Namely, they were frequently in the hole. There were some demands for his resignation, on the usual grounds (if he can't keep his bank balance straight, how can he ...), but nothing came of them.

Becky Barrett (Inkster), the Minister of Labour, whose subsidiary functions included responsibility for the Manitoba Public Insurance Corporation (MPIC, though better known to the public as Autopac), got herself into hot water when she consented to a scheme whereby the MPIC would give its surplus of about $10 million to the universities for capital projects. The universities liked the idea, but most others thought it was a peculiar way of doing business, and suggested that the money be given back to downtrodden insurance payers of the province. The universities grant idea was abandoned, and the money went into general revenue.

Finally, Mr Gordon Mackintosh (St Johns), by virtue of his post as Attorney General, was frequently in the news. Nothing, not the slightest misdemeanour seemed to escape his sober, Cromwellian attention.

When the Legislature resumed on 5 December, the Throne Speech was delivered by Mr Peter Liba, who had relatively recently been appointed Lieutenant-Governor. Ebullient and engaging, he had been an executive of CanWest Global, the company owned by the Asper family, which had featured prominently in the headlines when it acquired most of Hollinger Corporation, becoming the largest media empire in the country.

In keeping with its general approach, the government seemed, one inferred from the Throne Speech, to aim at low-cost but nonetheless useful changes. Thus, for example, maternity leaves were extended from seventeen to thirty-seven weeks. There was to be a commitment of $31 million to Red River College to enable it to develop a downtown site, and hence expand its programming and its clientele: the NDP had, during the campaign, made much of the fact that the rate of participation in post-secondary education in Manitoba is among the lowest in Canada. The University of Manitoba, with millions of dollars' worth of structural repairs to be done, was to be given $50 million towards that purpose. The amount fell far below what was needed, but it was gratefully received nonetheless.

Elsewhere in the Speech the government reiterated its commitment to improving health care by better funding and by a vigorous program of attracting new nurses. This commitment, of course, would prove no easy matter. Also, the government promised action on several fronts to preserve and enhance the environment, and vowed to take up as a matter of priority the question of the future faced by aboriginal youth. This commitment, besides being politically astute in light of the strong support given the NDP by the province's aboriginal population, was of major necessity. The First Nations population of Manitoba is in excess of 10 per cent of the total, and the figure exceeds 12 per cent in Winnipeg. The higher birth rate among aboriginals means that these proportions will continue to grow.

The injustices suffered by the Native people in Manitoba and Canada in general have been widely documented, and need no restatement here. But in a year when the more radical Matthew Coon Come defeated Winnipeg's own, more moderate, Phil Fontaine for the leadership of the Assembly of First Nations, and when confrontations over fishing rights on the East Coast had turned ugly, it showed common sense for a government to treat the issue of the future of aboriginal people with something approaching a sense of urgency. The Throne Speech was not especially specific, but it was clear that the government would at least try to implement the recommendations of the Aboriginal Justice Inquiry, which had reported to the former PC government a decade before. The failure to act on the Inquiry report had symbolized to many Native people just how unimportant they were considered to be. In addition, the government promised to put together an economic package designed to stimulate employment opportunities for young aboriginals.

The government was also obviously concerned about the farmers, whose incomes had fallen, and many of whom were threatened by flooding. The Manitoba NDP made a strong commitment to help, and recruited other provinces to the cause of the Western farmer.

The Throne Speech was full of the usual clichés and generalities that mark such documents. But as an indicator of the government's working style and ideological range, it was priceless. Much like the Blair government in the United Kingdom, the New Democrats were in no hurry to strip away the good things their Tory predecessors had done. They seemed instead to have their back turned to anything too doctrinaire, and promised what Disraeli once called 'reform with a light touch.' Indeed, some observers were tempted to refer to the Doer government as the 'best conservative government we've got.'

There was a cabinet shuffle at the end of the year. Some ministers with a heavy workload off-loaded some responsibilities. Basically, it was a game of musical chairs, though some new blood was brought into the cabinet. Mr Scott Smith (Brandon West) was appointed to the Consumer Affairs portfolio, carrying as well responsibility for the Liquor Control Commission. Mr Ron Lemieux (La Verendrye) became Minister for Culture, Heritage and Recreation.

Politics and political parties

According to polls published during the year, the New Democrats held a comfortable lead over the Tories. The NDP appeared to be hanging on to about the share of the vote it had received in the 1999 election (namely, about 45 per cent), while the PCs seemed to be losing ground to the Liberals. This may have reflected a turning against the Tories in the wake of their defeat. And bad memories were rekindled as a result of allegations regarding improper conduct by a Tory organizer in the Interlake constituency during the late election. The Chief Electoral Officer for Manitoba had not, however, reached a conclusion in the matter by the end of the year.

The Progressive Conservatives elected a new leader in 2000. Gary Filmon had won the leadership in 1983, and served as Premier from April 1988 to October 1999. Only three men had served as Premier for longer periods. It was, therefore, a strange feeling to contemplate life without Mr Filmon. He had been an effective Premier, avoiding the society-rending slash and burn approach of Mike Harris in Ontario and

Ralph Klein in Alberta. He had been a somewhat authoritarian party leader, and had drawn around him many people who exuded an excess of self-esteem. Never high profile in national-provincial matters, he nonetheless deserves credit for his attempts to modernize and diversify the province's economy. He had every reason to be optimistic about his place in Manitoba history.

Mr Filmon's successor was to be Stuart Murray, the president of Domo Gas, who had married the boss's daughter. A former road manager for a rock group, Mr Murray had considerable political finesse. To many, however, he seemed too nice a guy to be leading the provincial party. While his decision to run surprised many, his only opponent was Darren Praznik, the former health minister, who represented Lac du Bonnet, east of Winnipeg, in the Legislature. Mr Praznik was not able to match Mr Murray's financial support, nor his impressive array of support. Unfortunately, although the PCs had planned on a November convention, the leadership was settled by the end of the summer. Thus, the PCs robbed themselves of the publicity always generated by an exciting leadership convention.

In November, by-elections were held in the ridings previously represented by Mr Filmon (Tuxedo) and former finance minister Eric Stefanson (Kirkfield Park). The PCs retained both ridings. Mr Murray chose to contest Kirkfield Park, while the former premier's seat was won handily by Heather Stefanson, the spouse of an Eric Stefanson nephew.

The provincial Tories split into two camps federally, with the bulk of the caucus and much of the ordinary membership backing the Alliance – clearly a recipe for discord later on. In the federal election on 27 November, Manitoba achieved a unique status as the only province to elect members from four different parties. The Liberals lost one seat to the Alliance, falling to five members, all from Winnipeg. There were four Alliance members, all elected from rural Manitoba, and four New Democrats (three from the city plus the Churchill riding). Mr Rick Borotsik, PC, won Brandon-Souris. The Alliance candidate for Winnipeg South Centre, Betty Grainger, a Winnipeg school trustee, quit the campaign a week before polling day as a result of negative reaction to a remark she had made about an 'Asian Invasion' on the West Coast.

The economy and economic developments

The provincial economy continued to grow, albeit slowly. In common with the rest of the country, the economic pace of the preceding few years began to lose momentum in Manitoba. The rural sector was clearly going through a crisis, if a less severe one than in other parts of the Prairies. Inflation was about 2 per cent (using the CPI for Winnipeg as the indicator), eating away most of the gains achieved in personal income. Housing construction declined compared to the year before, and consumers were more cautious than they had been in 1999. The Christmas trade, for example, did not lift the boat as high as had been hoped. Yet, population grew (to 1.149 million) and unemployment levels remained low, at 5 per cent, by national standards. In any case, some slowing down was perhaps to be expected after so many years of strong growth.

Several companies announced plans to expand in the near future. Air Canada, secure in its near-monopoly position, talked of bringing hundreds of new jobs to the province. There was to be expansion at Motor Coach Industries. Loewen was to set up an operation in Steinbach. And Schneider's said it planned to build a substantial meat-processing plant in St Boniface, near the stockyards. This was seen as a mixed blessing. Meat-processing plants smell, badly. And the expansion of hog farming in the wake of expanding meat processing was not universally greeted with enthusiasm. Eventually, Schneider changed its corporate mind.

A great deal of attention in 2000 was focused on opportunities for the city of Winnipeg and for the province in general. For most of the twentieth century, Winnipeg has been something of a backwater, its image negative. No amount of promoting the Royal Winnipeg Ballet, the Fringe Festival, and so on could shake the city's image as a rather dreary place.

Obviously, this situation was not going to improve quickly. As with so many other cities, the downtown core had declined as population and the retail trade had moved, big boxes and all, to the suburbs. Exacerbating this had been a pro-development outlook held by generations of city councillors that had permitted a rather willy-nilly pattern of growth.

One of Winnipeg's assets, however, is a large stock of heritage buildings, located downtown. This has proved beneficial in attracting movie-makers to the city, though no doubt the province's generous tax credits played a not unimportant role here. Yet the city had been slow to adapt to the residential potential of living downtown, in spite of the availability of lofts, attics, and like space.

One development possibility was the relocation of a significant portion of the operations of the province's largest community college, Red River College, from its site near the airport to some disused turn-of-the century buildings close to City Hall. The province was encouraging, but preferred to see the college use land behind the University of Winnipeg, a relatively short distance to the west of its main site. However, the costs of expropriating the property close to the university site were prohibitive enough to override any academic benefits that might have accrued from locating the college buildings there. The Princess Street site, therefore, was to be the home of Red River College students.

The further development of The Forks (the intersection of the Red and Assiniboine rivers) is always a conversation when the rejuvenation of downtown Winnipeg is discussed. A favourite place for Winnipegers and for those visiting the city, it has been suggested as a site for a new arena (said to be essential, even though the Winnipeg Jets have long fled the city), for further commercial development, or for either seniors or 'upscale' residential properties. However, it is unclear whether development of The Forks could be expected to give downtown Winnipeg the boost it is said to require. After all, other buildings, such as the Centennial Concert Hall and Portage Place, had in their day been hailed as the cure to centre-city blight. They had not proved to be the answer.

There remained on Portage Avenue a nostalgic reminder of past glories, namely, the Eaton's store. Nearly a century old, it had been a landmark in the city. The statue of Timothy Eaton at the store had been a favourite rendezvous for generations of people. Now, the symbol of the Eaton family's long and pathetic fall from grace, it stood empty. Again, its use for alternative purposes (residential, commercial, social-service agency) was much discussed. And, once again, the possibility of a new arena was canvassed.

The old arena, at Polo Park, had been built in the 1950s. Still serviceable, it nonetheless lacked most of the modern amenities that state-of-the-art arenas are said to absolutely require. Its principal tenant was the Manitoba Moose of the International Hockey League, who used it on forty-one occasions a year, plus whatever playoff games they could earn. The arena also played host to a number of concerts, the occasional trade show, and so forth. The Moose averaged 6,000 or 7,000 people a game. The argument was that building a new arena would (in addition to its allegedly transformative effect on the downtown area) increase the city's attractiveness, pulling in more prestigious concerts and the like. But at the end of 2000, Eaton's stood silent and vacant, and no new arena was on the horizon.

Winnipeg and Manitoba have always enjoyed a relatively stable economy, with unemployment rates below the national figure. This is because it possesses a diverse economy, insulating it from the traumas of single-sector-based economies in times of recession. Yet the province and its people still have a 'have not' mentality. Many of its young people depart for the purportedly greener pastures of Calgary, Vancouver, or Toronto. Thus, the search goes on for an economic stimulant, which some have looked for in the development of more high-technology jobs, an area where Winnipeg has been lacking. For years, too, many had talked of Winnipeg as being a transport hub.

There was, therefore, considerable excitement when CanWest Global vastly expanded its media empire with acquisitions from the Hollinger Group. CanWest is one of only a handful of companies with its headquarters in Winnipeg, a product of the commitment of its ruling family, the Aspers, to the city. It was therefore speculated that Winnipeg might become the 'media capital' of Canada. At least, perhaps a few jobs would move there. However, Mr Leonard Asper, the son of Izzy Asper and CEO of the company, was quoted as saying that it would be hard to persuade high-flying executives to relocate, given the city's image and the poverty of its civic thinking.

The rest of the province, often accusing Winnipegers of 'perimeteritis,' coped in its own way. Some of the real success stories in Manitoba came from smaller towns not far from the capital. Morden, Altona, and Steinbach, all bulwarks of the province's Mennonite population, personified thrift and initiative, and a number of small companies located there. The labour situation there was stable, taxes not too outrageous, and the cultural amenities of Winnipeg not far away.

KEN COATES AND GREG POELZER

The Territories

The new millennium marks a new era for the Territorial Norths of Canada. At a time of declining national interest in the North generally, with territorial issues rarely attracting federal attention or interest in the southern media, the three northern territories attempted to revitalize stalled economies and provide a measure of hope for the increasingly disconsolate residents of the Far North. The territories struggled through difficulties of economic stagnation, uncertain government finances, resource busts (and one boom), and the added challenges of adapting to new realities of territorial self-government. In the shift toward greater regional autonomy and self-management, all three territories found the focus shifting from the role and responsibilities of the federal government to the actions and policies of territorial administrations. The year 2000 found the Territorial Norths in the midst of crucial transitions from the status of colonies to self-administered jurisdictions, with all of the attending challenges, mistakes, and accomplishments.

On a general scale, the Yukon, Northwest Territories, and Nunavut experienced continued success in attracting tourists to the region, and the small communities of the North placed increased emphasis on catering to this expanding, but volatile market. The two stable resource sectors of the past, mining and oil and gas development, retained their prominence, but with relatively few positive movements in the region. High rates of unemployment, particularly in the smaller centres and among aboriginals, dominated government agendas, as did stalled land-claims negotiations in several quarters and the socio-cultural difficulties that continued to transform indigenous communities. The territories, almost uniquely in Canada, struggled with the implications of the 'politics of smallness,' the structural, personal, and institutional difficulties of running territorial political systems among very small populations. This latter challenge, almost universally overlooked by media commentators, profoundly influenced the manner and nature of political life in the region, resulting in what outside observers might find to be odd and unanticipated election results and government initiatives.

Territorial issues continued to be significantly offset from national priorities throughout 2000, reflecting the unique demographic, social, and economic challenges of the Canadian North. The Northern leaders, Piers McDonald of the Yukon, Paul Okalik of Nunavut, and Stephen Kakfwi of the Northwest Territories, found much common ground during the Northern Leaders Forum (which followed up on the Northern Cooperation Accord of 1999), particularly on issues of economic diversification and federal support for the North. As Mr Okalik noted, 'We are challenged by a small population spread over an enormous geography. Northern realities require an approach to funding that is flexible and based on these realities, rather than population' (Canada News Wire, 6 March). The leaders identified a series of uniquely northern issues, including federal funding for economic diversification, postal rates, climate change, airline service, and federal funding of aboriginal programs. During a March 2000 Premiers' conference, for example, representatives from the Yukon, Northwest Territories, and Nunavut argued aggressively for attention to the Kyoto protocols on global warming, finding themselves at odds with the Premiers of Ontario, British Columbia, and Alberta on the issue.

Perhaps the dominant regional issue in 2000 continued to be the matter of an oil and gas pipeline. Two different proposals vied for government and corporate support: the construction of a pipeline through the Mackenzie Valley, with an 'over the top' branch line to carry natural gas from Alaska's North Slope, or the development of the Alaska Highway route through Alaska and the Yukon. In a marked turnaround from twenty-five years before, when Native leaders capitalized on the Mackenzie Valley Pipeline Inquiry to garner national support for their opposition to a pipeline through their homelands, NWT Premier Stephen Kakfwi led the battle to have the NWT route selected. He and his colleagues argued that, with the settlement of land claims and devolution of authority to the territorial government, the NWT was now poised to control better the economic and social impacts of pipeline construction and to use the project to spark regional development. The Alaska Highway route appeared to have the better chance, if only because the existing road permitted faster and less environmentally harmful effects. Further, the economics of pipeline construction made it likely that only one of the competing routes would be built in the short to medium term, relegating the losing jurisdiction to economic disappointment. The Yukon government, for its part, strongly supported the Alaska Highway route, finding itself in sharp competition with Premier Kakfwi and the NWT. First Nations joined in the debate, with the aboriginal communities in the NWT corridor forming an aboriginal Pipeline Group to weigh the costs and benefits of participating in the project.

The political realities of the Canadian North were, in 2000, in the midst of a major transition. Aboriginal groups, armed with land-claims settlements and investment capital, were prepared to participate actively in resource development. The earlier alliance between environmental groups and indigenous organizations appeared significantly weakened, raising concerns among environmentalists that an unchecked resource boom was possible. Aboriginal groups argued that they would use their new powers, under devolution, self-government agreements, and treaties, to protect the fragile northern ecology, but they had nonetheless made a decisive shift in favour of properly controlled development. A new northern reality was taking shape, one with prominent and consistent aboriginal involvement, and with growing territorial flexibility and control over the pace and shape of economic development.

The federal election in the North

In a federal election year, the North also endeavoured to identify a place on the national political landscape, but largely failed in the effort to bring regional issues to national attention. The Liberal administration of Prime Minister Jean Chrétien went to the polls on 27 November, only three years into their term in office. The timing was, most observers agreed, scheduled to capitalize on selection of Stockwell Day as leader of the Canadian Alliance, formed in an attempt to reunite the conservative forces in the country. The Liberals went into the election without a clear platform, and with very little specifically designed to cater to northern voters, but with a promise to continue the established pattern of territorial self-government, regional economic development, support for aboriginal land-claims settlements, the encouragement of Nunavut, and general support for indigenous concerns. The Canadian Alliance, in turn, paid scant attention to the North, viewed for much of the decade as lost territory in the wake of the departure of long-time Yukon MP Erik Nielsen. The CA Party's criticisms of treaties and land-claims settlements, by themselves, did not rest well in the North, especially among aboriginal voters. The New Democratic Party had capitalized on the fact that their national leader, Audrey McLaughlin, represented the Yukon. But her departure in 1997 weakened the party in the region.

The largely uneventful federal election campaign in the territories ran on the back of the national campaigns. There were few unique local issues, beyond regional expectations for greater federal attention and funding for territorial governments, and support for land claims and resource development. In Nunavut, Liberal candidate and incumbent Member of Parliament Nancy Karetak-Lindell faced off against Palluq Susan Enuaraq of the New Democratic Party, Mike Sherman of the Progressive Conservatives, and Brian Jones of the Green Party. The Canadian Alliance had planned to run Agnes Poksiak-Turner of Whale Cove as their candidate. Irregularities with her nomination papers forced her to re-file, but flight delays resulted in her submitting her official papers shortly after the Elections Canada deadline. The Liberal candidate faced criticism for supporting the government's controversial gun-control legislation, but was generally well regarded for her work on constituency issues and the legislation leading to the creation of Nunavut. Ms Karetak-Lindell won over two-thirds of the vote, easily outdistancing her closest rival, Ms Enuaraq of the NDP, who secured less than 19 per cent of the ballots. Long-time Inuit leader John Amagoalik attributed the Liberal win to 'their efforts to include aboriginal people in [their] rank and file. They have an aboriginal commission within the party and they have the largest number of aboriginals running for them in these elections' (*Nunatsiaq News*, 1 December).

The campaign in the Northwest Territories attracted more attention and debate, largely because of the resource boom associated with regional diamond mines and the resolution and near-resolution of major land-claims settlements. Opposition candidates criticized the federal government for its hard line on revenue sharing, which limited the returns to the territory from major resource developments. NDP candidate Dennis Bevington attacked the government, claiming that the resource revenue-sharing policy 'allows the federal government to exploit the natural resources of the North while keeping our public government in a state of welfare dependency' (Northern News Service, 1 November). The criticism was not sufficient to derail the re-election bid of three-term incumbent MP and cabinet minister Ethel Blondin-Andrew, who returned to office with nearly 46 per cent of the vote, beating her nearest rival by almost 20 per cent. She was subsequently reappointed to cabinet as Secretary of State for Children and Youth.

The electoral battle in the Yukon Territory proved, in contrast, to be a cliff-hanger. Incumbent NDP Member of Parliament Louise Hardy, elected in 1997 when Audrey McLaughlin stepped aside, faced a tough, multi-party challenge. Ms Hardy urged Yukoners to maintain an NDP voice from the North and to work toward a minority national government. She made sharp comparisons between her work in Ottawa and the less prominent contributions of two Liberal MPs from the North, Ethel Blondin-Andrew and Nancy Karetak-Lindell. Larry Bagnell of the Liberal Party, executive director of the Association of Yukon Communities, promised Yukoners access to the governing party, a rarity for the territory over the preceding fifty years. He also campaigned on the necessity of blocking the Canadian Alliance from making a major national breakthrough. Don Cox, who stepped forward to run for the Progressive Conservatives several weeks after the writ had been dropped, campaigned for right-of-centre votes along with Jim Kenyon of the Canadian Alliance. Mr Bagnell won by only seventy votes, one of the closest elections in Yukon history, squeezing out Ms Hardy, 4,293 to 4,223. It was a bitter loss for the NDP, which surrendered the Yukon riding for the first time in five elections. Jim Kenyon and Don Cox split the conservative vote, with Mr Kenyon gaining over 3,600 votes (to Mr Cox's 991) from a campaign that focused on gun-control legislation and tax breaks and that had resulted in Ed Schultz, Grand Chief of the Council of Yukon First Nations, asking First Nations people not to vote for the Canadian Alliance candidate. As in the NWT and Nunavut, the First Nations vote appeared to go solidly for the Liberal candidates.

The federal campaign in the Yukon turned, as did the territorial election earlier in the year, on a growing urban-rural split in the territory. Larry Bagnell drew his support heavily from Whitehorse and the southern Yukon. Louise Hardy, in turn, suffered from the collapse of the population in Faro (down to a quarter of its size in the 1990s), which stripped her of a long-standing NDP stronghold. While opponents argued that electing Larry Bagnell would result in Yukon issues disappearing on the national stage, Mr Bagnell himself argued that there was merit in having a Liberal territorial government, Member of Parliament, and Senator: 'I think with a Liberal government at three levels, we'll certainly be able to work together and try and advance Yukon objectives. We all know each other' (*Whitehorse Star*, 28 November).

The Yukon Territory

The year 2000 proved difficult for the people of the Yukon, marked as it was by a continued slowdown in the mining economy (including the inability to reopen the mine at Faro) and a steady outflow of people from the territory. While transiency and mobility have long been features of Yukon life, reflecting the seasonal and resource-based economy, the long-running recession in the territory appeared to sap some of the vitality from the region. Commentators, business leaders, and citizens grumbled regularly about the government's inability to diversify the economy – something that both the New Democratic Party and the Yukon Party had been attempting in previous years – and about the malaise that appeared to grip the territory.

Demographic change

The difficult economic times are reflected in the population trends of the territory. Residents in the Yukon Territory numbered 30,663 in 2000, down from 31,084 the year previous. During this period, the Yukon had a net outflow of more than 1,400, representing a significant percentage of the population. Although the Yukon is significantly smaller than the Northwest Territories or Nunavut, more than two-thirds of the territory's population is concentrated in the capital, Whitehorse (22,545). The next two largest centres, Dawson City (1,857) and Watson Lake (1,593) are the only communities with populations over one thousand people. With the exception of Haines Junction, the twelve other communities numbered fewer than five hundred people.

Economic challenges

The Yukon Territory faces tough economic challenges, particularly in the once strong mining sector. Long known for the extraction of gold and other metals, the Yukon Territory has witnessed little activity in the mining sector since the closure of the lead-zinc mine in Faro in 1997. In fact, mining in 2000 stood at only 32.8 per cent of 1997 levels, and represented 3.7 per cent of the 2000 GDP of the territory. Nevertheless, the GDP had grown by 2 per cent over the previous year to $1,039,800,000. Public administration (excluding health care and education), by far the single largest economic sector, accounting for nearly one-quarter of the territory's GDP, continued to grow. Other sectors showed signs of strength; construction, for instance, grew by 12 per cent over the previous year.

Territorial politics

Yukon electors had their chance to pass judgment on the NDP government of Piers McDonald on 17 April. The government was widely expected to return to office with a safe, if somewhat smaller, majority. The opposition was divided. On the right was the Yukon Party, led by former Yukon government leader John Ostashek. The Yukon Party was widely remembered in the territory for tough cost-cutting measures in its last administration, and difficulties with the crucial territorial civil service, but appeared likely to draw on strong support from rural and small-town Yukon. The centrist Liberal Party, under new leader Pat Duncan, could count on strength in the Whitehorse ridings, the presence of a strong Liberal government in Ottawa, and growing unease with the NDP government. Piers McDonald, whose government struggled with the continuing difficulties in the territorial mining sector, promised economic diversification, in part through the cultivation of international trade and tourism. 'The election,' said Mr McDonald, 'is about choosing different visions of the Yukon. It's a comparison between those who express a vision of the past with a vulnerable economy tied to one resource and a forward-looking vision with an economy that's strong and diverse and flexible' (Canadian Press Newswire, 13 March). The government promised an 8 per cent cut in income taxes in their February 2000 budget and offered the territory total spending of over $500 million. Liberal leader Pat Duncan sharply criticized Mr McDonald's depiction of the territory's fortunes, arguing that high unemployment, a surge in bankruptcies, and outmigration spoke volumes about the challenges facing the Yukon.

The campaign itself produced no obvious shift in territorial preferences, and observers believed that the election would see the return of Mr McDonald and the NDP, with the governing party drawing on its mix of rural and urban support to hold off the Yukon Party and the stronger, but not dominant, Liberals. The predictions did not hold. The Liberal Party won 10 of the Yukon's 17 seats, garnering 42 per cent of the vote to the NDP's 33 per cent and the 25 per cent won by the Yukon Party. The Yukon Party was decimated, returning only one member to the territorial assembly and having party leader John Ostachek lose his seat. The New Democratic Party held onto six seats, but was wiped out in Whitehorse, where even Government Leader Piers McDonald lost his riding to Liberal Wayne Jim (the first time a government leader had been defeated). In the past, Yukon elections had typically been won by the party gaining the most rural seats (many of which had small numbers of voters). This time, in contrast, the Liberals swept all of the Whitehorse ridings, with the two opposition parties picking up the rural and small-community constituencies.

Pat Duncan and the Liberals were, like most Yukoners, shocked by the election results, albeit more excited than their opponents with the outcome. At her swearing-in, Ms Duncan indicated her plans to use the title 'Premier,' over the long-standing Government Leader. She also introduced a five-member cabinet, drawing from a caucus with limited administrative experience. The Premier reassured rural Yukoners that the government would not ignore their concerns. Ms Duncan also quickly reintroduced the NDP government's budget, with minor modifications, and indicated that no radical initiatives or changes in policy direction were anticipated. The new Premier had an eclectic background. Raised in the Yukon, she had served as constituency assistant for Conservative Member of Parliament Erik Nielsen and worked as a consultant as a manager of the Whitehorse Chamber of commerce.

The ramifications of the election were wide-ranging. John Ostachek resigned as leader of the Yukon Party and, after waiting a short time to consider his options, Piers McDonald also stepped aside. Mr Ostachek was replaced by the Yukon Party's only sitting member, Peter Jenkins; Trevor Harding, the representative from Faro, took over as interim party leader of the NDP from Mr McDonald. Mr Harding, in turn, stepped down in September and was replaced by Eric Fairclough, the first aboriginal party leader in the Yukon.

The Yukon had one further territorial political event in 2000, a by-election in Faro scheduled to coincide with the federal election. Trevor Harding, NDP MLA for the once-robust mining town, left the territory for a job with a marketing firm in Calgary. He won his seat handily in the 2000 territorial election and was touted to become the leader of the NDP after Piers Macdonald stepped down. Liberal candidate Jim McLachlan, having recently lost to Mr Harding, ran again, this time against Harold Boehm of the NDP. Mr McLachlan, a one-time MLA from Faro and long-time community activist, won the seat handily, taking two-thirds of the votes and re-enforcing the Liberal Party's hold on the territorial assembly.

Premier Duncan's government did not bring in radical changes to government policy. The NDP's 2000 budget was altered in a limited fashion and implemented. The Yukon government increased the mineral-exploration tax credit in an attempt to jump-start the important mining sector and made a renewed commitment to settle the outstanding seven land claims in the territory. The tax credit announcement came on the heels of the news that exploration in the territory had dropped to its lowest point in a quarter-century, a record the industry attributed to the Department of Indian Affairs and Northern Development's 'rat's nest of bureaucracy' (Canadian Press Newswire, 24 May).

Additional lands in the northern Yukon were made available for oil and gas exploration and prominent First Nations leader Paul Birckel was named First Nations Liaison Coordinator – Pipeline Unit to spur territorial cooperation on the competitive natural gas pipeline project.

Other issues

There were several other significant territorial issues during 2000. The Council for Yukon First Nations selected a new Grand Chief, with delegates to the February 2000 gathering selecting Ed Schultz on the second ballot. The election was held following the resignation of Albert James in the face of criminal charges. Prime Minister Jean Chrétien sparked a firestorm of protest over his decision – quickly rescinded – to rename the tallest mountain in Canada, Mount Logan, after deceased prime minister Pierre Elliott Trudeau. The change of name was viewed widely as a sign of Liberal arrogance and insensitivity to western and northern concerns, and forced the Prime Minister to backtrack quickly. The negotiation and implementation of land claims remained a prominent issue in the Yukon, particularly in the face of federal-territorial efforts to expedite the devolution of responsibility for natural resources to the Yukon government. First Nations leaders, led by the Council of Yukon First Nations, argued that they would withdraw their support for devolution if they felt that progress on land claims was being held up by the process. The land-claims process itself continued to be contentious. The controversial decision to withhold potential mining lands in the Donjek River region angered the mining industry, who argued that Premier Duncan had not consulted with them about the important decision.

Nunavut

The year 2000 was only the second in the short history of Nunavut, and the territory continued to experience the challenges associated with the long-awaited transition to regional administration. Nunavut had arrived with grand expectations, heightened by the international attention given to the establishment of a predominantly indigenous jurisdiction. Internal challenges remained, particularly over the need to increase Inuit participation in administration, high expectations of a decentralization of government services to communities other than Iqaluit, and hopes for a rapid introduction of Inuktituk services. These administrative difficulties combined with significant social and cultural issues to create a unique and very open political culture. Politicians, including Premier Okalik, spoke openly about personal difficulties that they had encountered during their lives. The speaker of the Nunavut Assembly, Leiv Barnabas, resigned after being found guilty of sexual assault. James Arvaluk, Member for Nanulik, resigned his position as Minister of Education after being charged with assault. In one of the most high-profile examples, Paul Quassa, president of Nunavut Tunngavik Inc., responsible for the Nunavut land claim, was first suspended and later reinstated to his post after revelations that he had directed significant sums of Nunavut Tunngavik Inc. funds for his personal use.

Demographic change

In contrast to the Yukon, Nunavut experienced continued population growth, due to high birth rates (more than twice the national average) rather than immigration (net inter-provincial immigration was +70 people in 2000). Nunavut's population was 27,692 in 2000, having grown by 2.6 per cent over the previous year. The relatively small population of Nunavut, however, is spread across a land mass twice the size of Ontario. The three largest communities in Nunavut (1999 data) were Iqaluit (4,627), Rankin Inlet (2,230), and Arviat (1,642). The population growth has related challenges, including significant overcrowding in most communities, major housing shortages, and overcrowded school classes. The problems were particularly acute in the outlying communities, where the comparative absence of employment prospects added to personal and familial malaise.

Economic challenges

Nunavut continued to face the long-standing challenges of dependence on government transfers, the unreliability of resource markets, and the struggle to diversify its economy. The smallest of the three territorial economies, the GDP of Nunavut stood at $811,000,000. Unemployment rates remained extremely high, with the limited exception of the government centre of Iqaluit. The two large mining operations, at Polaris and Nanisivik, neared the end of their productive lives, raising concerns about the medium-term impact of a downturn in the sector. Nevertheless, at $158.6 million, the territory's mining activity was three times the size of the Yukon Territory's. The fur trade, a stable element in the regional economy before the launch of anti–fur trade campaigns in Europe, provided little reason for optimism.

Dependence on federal payments remained the highest in Canada, with 90 per cent of territorial revenues derived from Ottawa. Despite opposition from the Canadian Taxpayers Federation – Mitch Gray said of Nunavut, 'The real question here is how much money they're spending; outrageous amounts of money, on a territorial government that may, or may not be, even necessary' (CanWest News, 23 March) – Nunavut requested an increase on the more than $553 million annual grant (or some $22,000 per person). Training Inuit for jobs in the civil service, addressing serious housing shortages, and attending to matters of health and safety presented the new government with severe fiscal challenges, particularly with the added expectation of rapid decentralization of government services.

The Government of Nunavut continued to look for economic alternatives, particularly in eco-tourism and mining. Miramar Mining Corporation identified promising finds in the Hope Bay region, raising hopes for another major resource development. Tahera Corporation announced the impending opening of a small, limited-term (eight years) diamond mine near Lupin, with expectations of over one hundred construction jobs and another one hundred ongoing mining posts. Across the territory, per capita income stood at around $11,000 per year, costs remained extremely high, and Inuit unemployment stood at around 30 per cent. Considerable effort was devoted to infrastructure matters. Nunavut signed a trade agreement with Manitoba in February, with the discussion focusing on the possible construction of road and hydro connections to Nunavut. There was growing evidence, as well, that the Inuit-controlled settlement and investment corporations were taking a more active role in the economy. Using funds provided through land-claims settlements, these companies took significant steps to improve infrastructure and services. Transport Nanuk, a joint venture between Logistec Corporation and Nunavut Umiaq Corporation, launched the M/V *Umiavut* to provide supply services through the eastern Arctic.

Territorial politics

The Nunavut riding of Quttiktuq came open in 2000, following the resignation of Levi Barnabas. He had been Speaker of the Nunavut assembly but, in accordance with territorial legislation, stepped aside following a conviction for sexual assault. (He was given a one-year suspended sentence, with a community-service requirement and a fine.) He was replaced as Speaker by Kevin O'Brien of the Arviat constituency. Mr Barnabas stepped aside '[i]n order to maintain the dignity and respect for this office and this assembly until this matter has been resolved' (Canadian Press Newswire, 16 March).

The far-flung Quttiktuq riding, which incorporates the wealthy and largely non-aboriginal mining communities of Polaris and Nanisivik, also includes the poorer villages of Arctic Bay, Grise Fiord, and Resolute Bay. The by-election attracted eight candidates (seven from Arctic Bay), including Levi Barnabas, who ran despite considerable opposition from sitting MLAs and other regional politicians. The riding was won by Rebekah Williams, who was Nunavut's second female MLA, although she secured less than 21 per cent of the vote. Mr Barnabas finished third, only thirteen votes behind Ms Williams. Importantly, the largely non-aboriginal communities of Polaris and Nanisivik once again experienced very low voter turnout.

Other issues

Nunavut continued to enjoy considerable external attention due to its unique, non-partisan, consensus-based political experiment. Southern commentators were intrigued with the idea of a predominantly indigenous jurisdiction, and found the intensely personal and small-town political culture to be fascinating. The open manner with which Nunavut politicians discussed domestic and personal concerns – often including their own – stood in stark contrast to southern political behaviour. A small number of other issues also attracted attention in 2000. The federal government's highly controversial gun-control legislation resulted in a Nunavut challenge to the Firearms Act, which they claimed failed to account for northern indigenous needs.

The Northwest Territories

Throughout 1999–2000, national and international attention focused on the newly created territory of Nunavut; the reconfigured Northwest Territories, once more carved up and reshaped by national political action, attracted scant commentary in comparison. But the Northwest Territories experienced remarkable changes during the year and appeared to be set on a very different course than the other northern territories. The NWT economy seemed destined for a prolonged boom; the government argued aggressively for massive pipeline developments down the Mackenzie Valley, and the territory's longstanding consensus government continued to function effectively. The ethnically divided jurisdiction, containing sizable numbers of First Nations, Metis, and non-aboriginal peoples, worked with considerable success to create a mutually beneficial economic and social order, providing the nation with a model for intercultural collaboration and interaction.

Symbolically, the year opened with Dene and Inuvialuit leaders from the territory officially lifting their opposition to the development of the pipeline, ending a quarter-century of opposition to the mega-project. Richard Nerysoo of the Gwich'in Tribal Council, a former NWT government leader who entered politics as a leader of the opposition to the original Mackenzie Valley Pipeline project, now encouraged aboriginal groups to capitalize on the new circumstances: 'The reality is that, what we see in the north, is a need for aboriginal leadership, and the communities to understand the importance of taking advantage of not simply jobs, but business opportunities' (Canadian Press Newswire, 28 January). This fundamental, but largely unheralded transition reflected the evolving state of aboriginal self-government and land claims, and growing territorial experience and success in joint ventures with southern-based corporations. That the Inuvialuit Regional Corporation opened blocks of land in the Mackenzie River Delta for bids on oil and gas exploration rights provided additional evidence of a continuing transition in aboriginal approaches to resource development and a growing determination to secure employment and business opportunities for their communities through active engagement in the resource sector.

Demographic change

The Northwest Territories' population continued to grow through 2000, reflecting both the high birth rate in the aboriginal population and immigration associated with the expanding mining economy. As in Nunavut, the demographic change created housing shortages and sparked demands for additional government spending in this area. Yellowknife, the territorial capital, remained the largest community at 18,028 people. Hay River (3,835), Inuvik (3,451), Fort Smith (2,625), Rae Edzo (1,864), and Fort Simpson (1,273) represented the next largest communities in the territory. The population was quite young, with 30 per cent of the people under the age of fifteen years; ironically, and importantly in terms of the costs of government services, the number of seniors continued to grow significantly.

Economic development

The Northwest Territories faced unusually positive economic prospects in 2000, based on the operations of the Etaki diamond mine, further exploration and development in the diamond sector, promising discoveries and development of natural gas fields in the Fort Liard region in the southern part of the territory, major investments in gas exploration in the Mackenzie Delta, and the renewed discussion of the potential construction of a gas pipeline down the Mackenzie Valley. The ongoing development of the Diavik diamond mine near Camsell Lake continued the high-profile diamond industry expansion in the territory, which ensured a continued surge in exploration activity. The purchase of Winspear Diamond's stake in the Snap Lake mine also brought the renowned De Beers Corporation into the Canadian market in 2000 following a long and difficult takeover bid, but when completed represented the first acquisition by De Beers outside South Africa. The Northwest Territory economy experienced significant growth, sparking additional government and corporate investment in infrastructure projects. The government lacked the resources necessary to meet the growing demand for services, and the rush of prospectors and other workers in the territories strained regional housing and other facilities. In contrast to the Yukon, where population loss was associated with a declining resource economy, and Nunavut, where economic stagnation raised concerns about the future, the Northwest Territories appeared to be on its most positive course in a quarter-century. By 2000, the GDP of the NWT stood at $2,272,300,000, representing a growth of 7.7 per cent over the previous year.

Territorial politics

The creation of Nunavut compelled the Northwest Territories to reconfigure its political structures. Stephen Kakfwi, former president of the Dene Nation and long-serving territorial cabinet minister, was selected by his legislative colleagues to become the first Premier of the redefined Northwest Territories, taking over from Jim Antoine. Mr Kakfwi brought special skills to the task, building on a track record of support for aboriginal rights, strong national connections, and extensive territorial administrative experience. One of the Dene leaders who had battled with resource developers in the 1970s and 1980s, Mr Kakfwi brought unique credibility to the challenge of negotiating with the federal government and, in particular, working with oil and gas companies on the proposed Mackenzie Valley Pipeline. He personified, in fact, the major aboriginal transformation that had occurred in the Northwest Territories: from outright opposition to pipeline construction to a commitment to carefully managed, environmentally sound, and indigenously influenced resource projects. Following now-established NWT political tradition, Mr Kakfwi was selected by the nineteen members of the NWT legislature. The non-partisan, consensus-based legislature voted on all the six members of the territorial cabinet.

Perhaps the greatest administrative challenge in the territory revolved around resource revenues. Under federal regulations and federal-territorial arrangements, the largest share of increased resource revenues went to the federal government. This meant, in turn, that the NWT did not share directly in the rapid expansion of the mining economy and found itself with increased expectations and demands for services, but without assurance of access to additional funding. The government ran a sizable deficit in 1999–2000, but expected expenditures to exceed revenues by a massive amount in the coming years. Arguing that '[i]t is possible for us to be a financially well-off government – a have territory,' Premier Stephen Kakfwi said, 'We will seek to take lands and resources from the federal government so we can become masters in our own house. We do not want to live on handouts from Ottawa' (Canadian Press Newswire, 17 January).

The transitions associated with the establishment of Nunavut, a booming economy, and uncertain revenue streams created significant budgetary problems for the NWT government, which still drew close to 80 per cent of its revenues from the federal government. The government announced a significant budgetary deficit and indicated that the future could well present more difficult challenges. The fact that the federal government held onto 80 per cent of additional personal and corporate tax revenue meant, NWT leaders argued, that the territory lacked the resources to meet the costs associated with the expanding economy. The government held off on introducing a territorial sales tax, but introduced a hotel tax.

The federal government recognized that significant changes had to take place in the management and funding of territorial resources. As Ottawa was doing with the Yukon, it launched negotiations on the devolution of resource authority to the territorial government. Led by Robert Nault, Minister of Indian Affairs and Northern Development, the federal government made strong commitments in 2000 to negotiate the transfer of powers and appropriate revenue streams to the NWT government. As Mr Nault observed in May, 'It is the intention of the government of Canada to move as fast as we can possibly move. This isn't an agenda for talk. This is an agenda for action' (7 May).

Premier Kakfwi and the NWT government also moved aggressively to encourage the territory's economic prospects in southern Canada. Long associated with opposition to unchecked resource development, the Premier became an effective promoter of exploration and investment in the North. He met regularly with southern-based corporations and made representations, in particular, to the mining and oil and gas sectors to encourage more collaborative approaches to capitalizing on northern wealth. Premier Kakfwi also enlisted corporate support for the ongoing struggle with the federal government over resource revenue sharing, arguing that the NWT government could not meet the need for infrastructure and services without a more favourable taxation arrangement in the resource sector. Mr Kakfwi devoted particular attention to the evolving competition for the northern gas pipeline, believing that the project provided a crucial opportunity for regional development. He made a particular effort to convince the federal government to support the Mackenzie Valley Pipeline, arguing that the Canadian route provided by far the best economic returns for the country. As Mr Kakfwi stated, 'When we said "No" to the pipeline in the 1970s, it wasn't in vain. Aboriginal people are no longer going to be thrown some crumbs and rolled over by industry and government' (*Maclean's*, 17 July).

Other issues

The Northwest Territories continued to cope with the evolving power of aboriginal organizations, gained through the negotiation and resolution of land-claims settlements. The eight major aboriginal groups gained additional resources and authority, particularly over settlement lands, and continued to expand their presence in territorial political life. The NWT also worked collaboratively with the Government of British Columbia, signing an economic cooperation agreement with the NDP administration. The accord focused on natural gas and forestry, and promised additional involvement in northern tourism and infrastructure development. There was continued concern about the environmental impact of major resource developments. The land-use permit associated with the Diavik diamond mine required corporate commitment to a $180 million security deposit, provided to ensure that environmental impact was minimized and that the property would be restored after the mine closed.

There was expanding commitment to ensuring the involvement of First Nations and Metis communities and organizations in northern resource development. Joint ventures expanded in scope and variety, and development companies clearly recognized that securing the cooperation of regional indigenous groups was a vital element in securing project approval. Diavik Diamond Mines, for example, struck an accord with the North Slave Metis Alliance, securing Metis endorsement of the Diavik environmental strategy in return for corporate commitments to providing employment and business opportunities in the area. On the same project, a collaboration between SNC-Lavalin, a southern engineering firm, and the Dogrib band ensured extensive aboriginal participation in the engineering and purchasing activities at Diavik. Aboriginal leaders had long argued that they were prepared to support resource development, provided that there were adequate environmental protections and sustained and appropriate opportunities for indigenous engagement. Each year brought renewed evidence that the resource companies accepted the realities and that collaborative commercial and employment opportunities were attainable.

ROBERT DRUMMOND

Ontario

Having won a second majority in 1999, the Conservative government of Mike Harris faced the question in 2000 of whether it could sustain the momentum of the 'Common Sense Revolution' that had characterized its first term. Criticism of the pace of reform had not caused Ontario voters to turn against the government in the 1999 election, but in 2000 some issues arose that cast doubt on the wisdom of the government's reduction of program expenditure and its streamlining of regulations, or at least on the speed with which they had been pursued. Conflict with teachers continued to disrupt the education system, especially at the secondary level, even as the government continued to introduce further reforms. Health remained a focus of concern, as the hoped-for reform of primary care and home care appeared stalled, and as hospital restructuring continued to put pressure on emergency rooms and surgical waiting lists. The planned opening of the energy market to deregulated pricing by private producers was scheduled and rescheduled and by year end had still not occurred. Early in the year, questions arose about the propriety of certain activities in the Ontario Realty Corporation – the agency that dealt with the purchase and disposal of government lands and buildings. Then in the late spring perhaps the most serious challenge to the government's agenda occurred when an apparent failure of water testing and treatment allowed an E. coli contamination of the water supply to occur in the town of Walkerton, eventually resulting in seven deaths and numerous instances of serious illness. Controversy immediately arose around the question of responsibility. Was the failure an issue of local malfeasance alone, or should blame also attach to the province for its reduction of resources in the environment ministry (or for the privatizing of water testing, carried out by the previous NDP government)?

In the cities of the province, debate continued on the effects of the reallocation of responsibilities (called 'downloading' by municipal critics), as well as on the amalgamation that had been pursued in a number of centres, notably Toronto and Hamilton. The plight of poor and homeless citizens was the ostensible focus of a major demonstration in mid-June at Queen's Park by the Ontario Coalition Against Poverty. When the demonstration turned violent, however, the focus of attention shifted to accusations and counter-accusations by OCAP protestors and police about who had instigated the violence.

On the partisan political front, much of the attention during the year was directed to the federal level, where the leadership of the Canadian Alliance was being contested by (among others) Ontarian Tom Long. Mr Long had been an early adviser of Premier Harris and had reportedly been one of the principal architects of the Common Sense Revolution. The Conservative caucus at Queen's Park was divided among those who supported Mr Long, those who supported a different candidate, and those who retained loyalty to the Progressive Conservative Party of Canada and eschewed involvement in the Alliance race. The Premier maintained a public neutrality, though it was assumed in many quarters that he had some private sympathy with Mr Long's candidacy. Even before Mr Long declared his candidacy, MPP Frank Klees had entered the race, backed by several of his caucus colleagues. However, he withdrew after announcing that he had been approached with an offer of financial support if he agreed to ally with another candidate. He had refused and then found himself without sufficient money to continue effectively. Federal news again crowded out provincial concerns in the press in the fall, when Prime Minister Chrétien called a federal election.

Despite the rocky patches in policy implementation, and the distraction of federal politics, the Legislature passed forty-five public bills (and seventeen private bills) during the year, in a continuation of the session commenced in 1999. Some bills were of limited scope, such as the act to establish a German Pioneers Day, or that to approve an official tartan for the province. Others were of more far-reaching significance, such as the Educational Accountability Act, the amendment of Employment Standards, and the Victims' Bill of Rights. Perhaps the most notable change in past practice was the passage of long-promised legislation to require the provincial government to submit a balanced budget each year. In the budget presented in May, Finance Minister Ernie Eves announced a planned balanced budget and indeed indicated that the government would have a surplus, part of which it would return to Ontario taxpayers in the form of a cheque of up to $200 each. Critics pointed to what they called the detrimental effects of budget cuts on the well-being of Ontarians and argued that the surplus should be spent on underfunded programs, rather than being even partly returned. Some receiving between $25 and $200 wondered if such small amounts might be more effectively used if they were combined in support of such programs. Other people told reporters they proposed to donate their refund cheques to institutions trying to deal with the fallout from government cutbacks. The government did not object and laid stress on its intent to give people back 'their money' to do with as they wished.

Early-year events

Before the Legislature reconvened in the spring, there were announcements and actions in several areas that would become increasingly significant as the year wore on. On 6 January, for example, the Social Services Ministry issued a report on Welfare Fraud Control. Of some fifty-nine thousand cases sent for investigation in fiscal 1998–9, the report indicated, benefits were reduced or terminated for almost seventeen thousand. However, despite the report's title, minister John Baird was compelled to admit that the same period had seen welfare fraud convictions in fewer than 750 cases. The minister observed the difficulty of meeting the standards of proof for a criminal conviction, but critics argued the report inflated the figures, combining instances of error and misuse with those of actual fraud. For example, about a third of those whose benefits were reduced had been ruled ineligible for full benefits in a particular month because they had spent all or part of that month in jail. Fifteen per cent of the affected cases had lost benefits because they had been deemed to be living with a 'spouse.' Just before the Legislature reconvened in September, the Ontario Court of Appeal struck down the 'spouse in the house' rule that had been applied in assessing eligibility for welfare.

Concerning the fraud control report, the *Globe and Mail*'s Richard Mackie quoted Andrew Mitchell of the Community Social Planning Council: 'They've upped the number of people they are cutting off just because of rule changes they themselves have made' (6 January). Despite criticism, the Premier announced on 18 January that by 1 April anyone convicted of welfare fraud would be denied welfare benefits for life. Critics questioned whether such a move would survive a constitutional or other court challenge.

With respect to health care, the province was set to begin negotiations with the Ontario Medical Association over increases to the medical fee schedule on 17 January (with a deadline for agreement of 31 March). As an opening salvo, the Premier mused on 12 January that doctors who refused to see patients because they had reached the 'cap' on billings (after which their fees were reduced) should be denied the right to bill anywhere in Ontario. In the end, the agreement with doctors did not come until 28 April. When it was reached, it resulted in a 2 per cent overall increase in the fee schedule, a raising of billing 'caps,' and the de-listing (effective 'privatizing') of some procedures. Despite calls for primary care reform, no departure from the fee-for-service system was pursued.

The impetus for primary care reform was strengthened when the Sinclair Commission issued its final report on 27 March. Dr Sinclair noted that the top-billing family doctor in the province had billed over $550,000, which implied that he had seen the equivalent of eighty-five patients every day. Top-billing physicians, he opined, might well be seeing the same patients too often, while other patients were unable to get to see a doctor. Dr Sinclair argued that agreement on primary care reform was essential if his 'rostering' plan for doctors (payment of primary care doctors on the basis of a roster of patients) was to be introduced on schedule. The final report contained a number of other recommendations, including an information system that would permit everyone to assess the efficiency of the health-care delivery system, a watchdog agency to enforce medicare rules, more money from Ottawa, and a long-term focus of the provincial government on health promotion, rather than on illness. When there had been no agreement with the OMA by the end of March, Premier Harris backed off his original support for radical reform of the primary care system. Opposition leader Dalton McGuinty argued for multidisciplinary clinics and physician rostering, but Mr Harris indicated his government would not now pursue rostering. The only other health initiative on the province's part early in the year was its decision in March to sue several tobacco firms for $40 billion in a New York court under U.S. anti-racketeering laws.

There were several eruptions of activity in the education sector before the Legislature reconvened. On 7 January, graduate-student teaching assistants at the University of Toronto went on strike, seeking improvements in their wages and protection against tuition increases. The strike of teaching assistants (represented by CUPE) was a forerunner of similar job actions later in the year by other CUPE locals at McMaster and York Universities. Another strike of teaching assistants at Carleton University was averted within an hour of an announced deadline.

In early March an Angus Reid poll showed that over half of Ontario residents (the most in the country) were dissatisfied with the public education system. The province promised to introduce a new 'code of conduct' for students, although criticism of the schools mainly centred on the withdrawal of extracurricular services by high school teachers in protest against alterations of their workload, and on the lack of materials, including textbooks, due to funding cuts. When the Premier spoke of a code with provision for automatic suspension or expulsion for certain offences, critics decried the loss of funds to help students with behaviour problems. The proposed legislation would give teachers the power to suspend and principals the power to expel. Heretofore the power to suspend had rested with principals and the power to expel with boards of education. Teachers were generally loath to take on the new power, believing that they functioned better as 'third parties' in a dispute between a student and the school.

On 7 March, the Windsor public school board voted to run a deficit (in defiance of provincial law) rather than cut budgets further or close more schools. After discussions with the Ministry of Education, the Windsor board agreed in May to submit a balanced budget, when the government agreed to provide some $12.3 million in additional funding for special education teachers and other improvements. Windsor Trustee Jim Cooke (brother of former NDP education minister Dave Cooke) was quoted by the *Toronto Star* on 25 May as saying he was generally happy with the agreement. 'I'm just glad we got the money we needed,' he said. 'It has pretty well solved the short-term problem we had.' However, Annie Kidder of People for Education was quoted in the same story to the effect that the Windsor decision was evidence that the province 'has boxed boards into such a corner that they can't do anything but cut.' She further worried that the government's proposed Education Accountability Act would make it even more difficult for local boards.

The focus in the area of the environment fell on air pollution in the early part of the year. In late January, then Environment Minister Tony Clement announced new air-quality regulations. Mandatory caps on nitrogen and sulphur oxides would replace voluntary limits; a 5 per cent reduction in nitrous oxides and a 10 per cent reduction in sulphur dioxides would be required, and the province would agree to accept any stricter standard imposed on the electricity sector in the United States. Critics objected that the reductions were too small to be truly useful. Companies would have the right to buy 'pollution credits' from firms who had lowered their emissions in Ontario or in parts of the U.S. sharing the Ontario 'air shed.' Critics observed that Ontario was poised to sell some two-thirds of its electricity generating capacity; making the required reductions small meant that companies purchasing the electricity generators would not face major refitting costs, which would make the sales more attractive.

On 3 March, the Premier passed the environment portfolio from Tony Clement (who retained municipal affairs) to Dan Newman. Environmentalists were not reassured when Mr Newman's first statement in office was to call for lower gasoline prices so that people could drive their cars more frequently.

In municipal politics, the City of Toronto redrew its ward boundaries in January, reducing the size of its Council from fifty-seven to forty-four seats. The new boundaries were based on the twenty-two federal and provincial ridings, with each being divided into two municipal wards. On 1 April, the city's inside workers went on strike, with the main issue being the harmonizing of salaries across the recently amalgamated city.

Amalgamation remained an issue in the Hamilton area, with the region of Hamilton-Wentworth seeking amalgamation with the city of Burlington (in Halton region). Meanwhile, Flamborough Township sought to avoid merger with the city of Hamilton by dividing into three parts, with one part seeking to join Waterloo region, a second part hoping to join Brant County, and the third applying to merge with Burlington. The plan was scuttled because, while the first two mergers were agreeable, the third was rejected by Burlington. These deliberations came to a head in late March, but in late January Hamilton amalgamation had already caused the government some grief when Conservative MPP Tony Skarica (Wentworth-Burlington) resigned his seat in the Legislature in protest against the government's municipal merger plans.

Finally, as regards municipal affairs, the city of Toronto's hope for a new opera house was squelched in March, when the province withdrew its promise of financial support, owing to the lack of funding commitments from either the city or the federal government.

In early March, Liberal MPP Dominic Agostino called for a probe of the Ontario Realty Corporation, asserting that the agency had sold some buildings in Toronto to a developer who had subsequently 'flipped' them for an enormous profit. The implication was that the provincial agency had sold the buildings too cheaply and possibly had done so in order to provide an illegitimate benefit to the developer. The Premier agreed to an independent audit to be conducted by Grant Thornton LLP, a forensic auditing firm. By the end of the month, the Ontario Provincial Police had been called in to commence a criminal investigation.

Spring sitting of the Legislature

The Legislature resumed sitting on 3 April, and the government tabled legislation intended to compel parents to pay for damages caused by their children. Opposition members pointed out that the measure duplicated existing provisions in civil and family law, but the government opted to proceed and the legislation was passed by mid-May.

The province moved in early April to place limits on municipal referenda. They had been somewhat embarrassed, though ultimately not deterred, by the referenda conducted by the various municipalities to be amalgamated in Toronto. Despite the fact that the amalgamation proceeded according to the original timetable, the government had been troubled by the publicity attendant on the referenda results, which largely opposed the move. The new legislation, ultimately passed in early June, required that a municipal referendum pose a clear question in an area of municipal jurisdiction, and it reserved for the province the right to decide what was legitimate. Furthermore, it provided that a referendum result could be binding only if a majority approved *and* turnout was 50 per cent or more. Since municipal elections routinely failed to reach the 50 per cent turnout threshold, the chance of a binding referendum being held was slim. If the answer to a referendum question were negative, the municipality would be precluded from asking it again until after the next municipal election. The legislation also provided for a maximum campaign period of sixty days and placed limits on donations to the campaign.

On 18 April, Conservative MPP Marilyn Mushinski introduced a private member's bill that called for judges to be accountable for the length of their sentences. It would have received little attention, perhaps, except that it was supported by Premier Harris and Attorney General Jim Flaherty, and it was passed at second reading and sent to committee. Critics worried about the threat to judicial independence implied by the proposal. A sense of the objections was clear in comments of Alan Gold, president of the Criminal Lawyers Association, quoted by Richard Mackie in the *Globe and Mail*: 'These people are Neanderthals when it comes to criminal justice. It is constitutionally insulting to suggest that judges should be assessed on the basis of how long their sentences are' (20 April). Ultimately, the bill met the fate of most private members' bills and died on the order paper.

Late in April the government indicated an intention to introduce legislation to permit private universities to be established in the province. There had been some interest expressed by religious institutions to get degree-granting powers for private schools, and some inquiries had been generated by out-of-province 'on-line' universities about operating in Ontario. Observers recalled as well that there had been an effort in the 1980s to develop a private degree-granting institution to be located north of Toronto. Supported at the time by cabinet minister Bette Stephenson, the proposal had not secured sufficient other support to become a reality. Both the Ontario Confederation of University Faculty Associations (OCUFA) and the Ontario Federation of Students expressed concern that such private universities would charge high tuition, unregulated by the province, but would nonetheless draw on public funds that would otherwise have been available to public institutions.

In respect of the elementary and secondary system, the province continued with a program of reform, despite the observation in mid-April by former NDP education minister Dave Cooke that 'chaos' in the schools would exist unless there was a period of relative tranquillity (as well as a salary increase for teachers) (*Globe and Mail*, 15 April). In late April, the government announced plans to require all students to sing *O Canada* each day and to recite a pledge of citizenship, including an oath of allegiance to the Queen. At the end of May they agreed that these exercises would be optional. Earlier in May they announced that teachers would be required to take mandatory professional-development courses and be tested regularly for re-certification. Principals were to be given authority to 'require' extracurricular participation by teachers, and teachers whose first language was not English or French were to be required to pass language tests. New teachers would be required to pass an exam for entry to the profession, in addition to any exams they had passed to get their education degrees. Tranquillity did not seem likely.

The government was somewhat embarrassed on 25 April when Privacy Commissioner Ann Cavoukian asserted that the government had broken its own law by giving a sensitive list of names, addresses, and account balances of Ontario Savings Office depositors to a polling firm (Angus Reid) and a management consulting firm (Wood Gundy). Finance Minister Ernie Eves conceded there had been an error, but he insisted it was an 'honest mistake.' But the Commissioner suggested the finance ministry had sought to frustrate her investigation.

In late April, the government introduced legislation to force treatment of the mentally ill. Lisa Priest of the *Globe and Mail* quoted Ted Fielding of the Schizophrenia Society of Ontario: 'This isn't about sweeping the streets. It allows people who are mentally ill to get the treatment they need and haven't been getting' (25 April). Dr James

Young, Ontario Chief Coroner, pointed out that many who should be getting treatment were winding up in jail instead. However, Erick Fabris of the No Force Coalition objected to compulsory treatment, especially forced medication, as ineffective and 'a form of chemical imprisonment.' 'You can't force people to heal,' he said (*Globe and Mail*, 25 April). The bill was finally passed just before the Legislature recessed in June.

Shortly before introducing his budget in May, the finance minister was quoted in the *Globe and Mail* as regretting the cuts to social programs, but saying that he felt he had 'no choice' (1 May). He likened himself to former federal Conservative leader (and former Nova Scotia Premier) Robert Stanfield, saying he was 'a fiscal conservative with a large social conscience.' The description was hard to square, in the opinion of some critics, with the fact that Mr Eves had resigned from the national Progressive Conservatives less than a month before in order to support Tom Long's candidacy for the leadership of the Canadian Alliance.

On 2 May, the finance minister introduced a balanced budget that included significant new expenditures in health care and post-secondary education. However, there was no increase for elementary and secondary education, and there were reductions in spending for community and social services and for transportation, municipal affairs, and housing. Expenditures on health included $1 billion for hospitals to help finish capital projects, and some $500 million through the Ontario Innovation Trust to expand research infrastructure, including cancer research facilities.

The budget also included a further reduction in personal income tax rates as well as the restoration of full indexation of tax brackets. In addition to some other minor tax reductions in the application of the retail sales tax, and a phased reduction of capital gains taxed from two-thirds to 50 per cent over four years, the minister announced a 'taxpayer dividend' of up to $200 to every Ontarian who had paid Ontario personal income tax in 1999.

Faced with the 'fiscal dividend' of a surplus, the government elected to take a balanced approach. They chose to increase spending on health – the area probably of greatest visibility and concern to citizens – to reduce the weight of public debt servicing, and to continue tax reductions. For the most part, Opposition critics suggested that the emphasis should have been greater on restoring program expenditures and less on tax cuts. Moreover, they described the 'taxpayer dividend' as a cynical ploy to distract citizens from the decline in public services by giving them a small cash payment. The government, however, was proud to point to their success in balancing the budget and to give evidence of their sensitivity to needs in the health-care system.

Soon after the budget was tabled, a number of backbench MPPs began to demand attention to their salaries and called for an increase of 10 per cent – an increase that they said fell within the government's own 2 per cent per year guidelines, as they had not had an increase in five years. In June, a commission of experts on executive compensation, appointed by the Conservatives, recommended an increase of over 32 per cent in MPPs' salaries, but Opposition critics labelled that plan a non-starter. In November the *Globe and Mail* reported that the government was considering proposing an increase of 42 per cent, seeking parity with the salaries of federal MPs (19 June). When adverse public reaction doomed that proposal, a compromise of 10 per cent was offered, but Opposition members refused to go along, and the scheme was dropped.

By the time salaries were being discussed in June, the E. coli outbreak had occurred in Walkerton, and the government's attention was immediately directed to that event. The Opposition began to demand a public inquiry, and at the end of May the Premier agreed to establish such an inquiry. Terms of reference were announced in mid-June, with a wide-ranging approach that would include assessment of possible provincial responsibility. But by then there had already been considerable comment in the legislature and in the press. The Premier and the environment minister asserted on 6 June that the town of Walkerton had failed to take advantage of provincial funds to help renew their water system; it turned out, however, that Walkerton had used federal money instead and had spent nearly $400,000 in upgrading its system. On 7 June it was revealed that an environment ministry memorandum had warned as early as 1997 that the closing of government labs for testing water could lead to a disaster like that in Walkerton. It was suggested as well that water and sewage treatment improvements had not been a priority for the province's SuperBuild Growth Fund, aimed at improving infrastructure in the broader public sector. Some critics pointed to the events in Walkerton as evidence that privatizing water and sewage treatment was not a good idea. The Premier denied that anyone in his government was promoting such privatization, but the press pointed to an earlier memorandum from Municipal Affairs Minister Tony Clement calling on cities and towns to consider public *and* private options for *all* municipal services.

Attention to the environment turned in early June to air pollution again, as Premiers across the country agreed to implement new smog-reduction targets by the end of the decade. They proposed to cut air pollution by 20 per cent by 2010 (Ontario had earlier promised to try to do it by 2015); however, the targets were not legally binding, and a plan to reach similar targets by 2005 had never been implemented. Environmental critics also attacked the agreed-upon revision in the measurement method employed. Rather than measure pollutants over a one-hour period, the new plan was to measure ozone over an eight-hour period. Critics suggested that made the targets less meaningful.

On 15 June, there was a wholesale shake-up of the environment ministry, including the shifting out of the deputy minister. Opposition critics noted that the ministry budget had been reduced by 40 per cent, and its staff by 30 per cent, before deputy minister Stien Lal had taken office. The following day, the government appointed former deputy minister Valerie Gibbons to determine whether the environment ministry needed restructuring. On 22 June, Environment Minister Dan Newman said he had never seen a sixty-one-page report (prepared by ministry bureaucrats and dated 14 March, eleven days after his appointment) that called for major changes to the ministry.

On 13 June, the Privacy and Freedom of Information Commissioner Ann Cavoukian had issued her annual report. In the shadow of Walkerton, it was disturbing to see her conclusion that the environment ministry (as well as health and natural resources) had been among the worst in the speed of reply to inquiries from her office (i.e., a low percentage answered within the thirty days permitted in law).

The Legislature was distracted from Walkerton on 15 June when a delegation from the Ontario Coalition Against Poverty marched on Queen's Park, supported by a crowd of some 500 people. They requested an opportunity to address the Legislature on the issue of homelessness, but that request was denied. Although the group could not have been surprised at the denial – no group of protestors had ever been permitted to enter and address the Legislative Assembly – they expressed considerable outrage. At some point, the protest turned violent, with people picking up broken paving stones and throwing them. Twenty-nine police officers reported being injured, and eight police horses were also said to have been hurt. Cathy Crowe of the Toronto Disaster Relief Committee reported there were 'dozens' of injuries among the protestors as well, including broken bones, and twenty-nine people were arrested. The following day, police spokesmen, including police union head Craig Bromell and Toronto Police Services Board Chairman Norm Gardiner, criticized the behaviour of NDP Toronto

Councillor (and Police Services Board member) Olivia Chow. She had been critical of the police response on the day of the riot, but Mr Bromell and Mr Gardiner alleged she had gone further and interfered with police in the performance of their duty. Ms Chow denied that allegation, but ultimately was persuaded to resign her position on the Police Services Board so as to put an end to the squabble. She was replaced by Conservative supporter Gordon Chong.

The Legislature recessed on 22 June, but not before passing legislation to return the focus of the McMichael Art Gallery in Kleinburg to a concentration on the works of the Group of Seven and to place control of the gallery in the hands of a board that included former owners Robert and Signe McMichael (who were made members for life). The government also granted the sum of $2 million for improvements and repairs to the gallery. The previous administrators of the gallery had opted to broaden the focus of the collection to include a wider range of Canadian art, but more conservative patrons had found the change disconcerting and had called for the sort of restoration the government now provided.

Also on 22 June, the government announced that the opening of the electricity market, originally slated for 1 November, would be delayed. They promised to announce a new opening date in September. The newly announced date was in 2001.

Summer recess

On 17 July, Richard Mackie of the *Globe and Mail* reported that the Premier was embarking on a wide-ranging consultation with his cabinet, caucus, and party on the potential restructuring of the Ontario government. The aim would be to develop a blueprint for what government should accomplish over the next several years. The alternative, the Premier apparently feared, was that the government would get bogged down in damage control over Walkerton, the Ontario Realty Corporation, emergency room delays, and so on. The fear was understandable, given the number of issues, large and small, that called for the government's attention in the period between the spring and fall sittings of the Assembly.

Concern with the province's water supply continued to occupy the press. Mr Justice Dennis O'Connor had been appointed to head the inquiry into the Walkerton events, and formal hearings were scheduled to begin in October. In the meantime, however, Mr Justice O'Connor announced on 5 July that he would visit Walkerton for informal talks with residents. Later in the month, the *Globe and Mail* released information from what it said was a secret government report, citing 120 cities, towns, seniors' residences, schools, and campsites with water supply problems (17 July). Towards the end of the month, Environment Commissioner Gord Miller issued a report that was critical of the environment ministry's water management, and the ministry issued a report that acknowledged some Ontario municipalities might still face serious water problems. The report noted that 241 municipal systems had been inspected – the ones that had experienced the most problems in the past – and 131 of them continued to show weaknesses. There were 389 systems remaining to be inspected. It was particularly noted in the press that two of the municipalities with water system problems were North Bay, the Premier's home town, and Parry Sound, the main centre in Finance Minister Ernie Eves's riding.

Earlier, on 11 July, the Canadian Institute of Environmental Law and Policy had called attention to another area of environmental concern. They issued a report claiming Ontario had become a 'dumping ground' for toxic waste and they blamed weak environmental laws. A spokesperson for the Ministry of the Environment expressed concern at the report's contents and suggested that some means to address the problems would be available within a month. The report identified a number of firms who had been involved in importing hazardous wastes. Since one of those firms was nearly bankrupt and another faced heavy debts, the report expressed the fear that taxpayers would wind up on the hook for the costs of any required clean-up.

Other matters continued to bubble, though perhaps not on the government's front burner. The City of Toronto, which had long complained of the consequences of amalgamation and 'downloading,' sought to have the province grant the city a Charter. Such a document would give the city greater autonomy, its proponents argued, and allow Toronto to plot its own destiny. Guy Abbate in the *Globe and Mail* quoted Brian Coburn, parliamentary assistant to Municipal Affairs Minister Tony Clement as dismissing the issue. 'We're not even going to consider it,' he said (6 July). He suggested the claim for Charter status was just a ploy to get more money from the province in a municipal election year, and perhaps to broaden the tax opportunities for the city beyond the property tax. Since there was little likelihood of the province's supporting the Charter plan, the vote by the city council could be seen as little more than a salvo in a continuing publicity battle with the Harris government.

Other summer irritants for the government included the allegation from the Ontario Public Service Employees Union that ‘workfare’ recipients were replacing Ministry of Transportation employees who had been laid off. The government, which had premised its legislation on the expectation that no workfare recipient would replace a regular employee, denied the allegation.

On 11 July, Ontario Power Generation – the generating company that had been carved out in the break-up of Ontario Hydro – announced it was leasing its Bruce Nuclear Generating Plant to British Energy PLC of Edinburgh for a period of eighteen years, with an option to extend the lease for a further twenty-five years. OPG would receive $400 million in the first year, $250 million four to six years later, and a further $150 million over the eighteen-year lease period. Some worried about the fact that a significant energy producer for the province would be controlled by an offshore company, but supporters of the deal suggested British Energy was a firm experienced in running nuclear generators and that it was desirable to get the troubled Bruce Plant out of the hands of OPG.

The government made several announcements in the course of the summer that foreshadowed legislation they would introduce in the fall. First, just after the Legislature recessed, Attorney General Jim Flaherty promised a $50 million package of programs to address domestic violence. The move came after several high-profile cases had been in the news. The bulk of the money, it turned out, would go to a project that would try to make better links between emergency shelters and rape crisis centres, on the one hand, and the justice system, on the other. The links would be facilitated by a shared computer system. At the same time, it was proposed that three thousand cell phones be issued to victims of domestic abuse, with the phones pre-programmed to dial the emergency services number, 911. Critics of this scheme suggested it would be at least equally useful to have the numbers of local help agencies similarly pre-programmed. A further aspect of the proposed reform was to enshrine the Victims of Crime office in legislation, with five full-time staff members and a budget of $1 million.

On 13 July, the Premier indicated his intention to introduce legislation in the fall that would encourage people to become potential organ donors. The announcement engendered some support in Opposition ranks, in particular from NDP MPP Frances Lankin, who had earlier introduced a private member’s bill on the subject.

Finally, on 24 July Health Minister Elizabeth Witmer confirmed a promise made in the budget – that the government would subsidize the tuition of medical students by up to $10,000 per year for four years if they would agree to practise in an under-serviced (usually remote) area of the province after graduation. This tuition assistance was in addition to some $40,000 worth of incentives already existing to lure doctors to remote areas.

On 4 August, the Premier announced that the by-election to replace Tony Skarica in the riding of Ancaster-Dundas-Flamborough-Aldershot would be held on 7 September. When the vote was held, the government suffered a fate not uncommon in by-elections – they lost the seat, this time to the Liberals.

On 10 August, the government announced a program of $240 million to upgrade water-system safety in smaller municipalities. It appeared that many of the potential problems with water safety were to be found in smaller centres, especially in rural areas where farm runoff threatened to put *E. coli* from livestock waste into municipal wells.

The continuing dispute with teachers over school reform was further fuelled towards the end of the month when the Ontario Secondary School Teachers' Federation voted to ask its members to suspend all extracurricular activities in protest against the government's revisions to their workload (and the threat to make extracurricular participation mandatory). When the Legislature reopened, Education Minister Janet Ecker said she would not intervene in the dispute, but for their part, most local boards of education did not see a means to resolve the issue without provincial help.

Fall sitting of the Legislature

The legislative session reconvened on 25 September, and the government embarked on an ambitious program of legislation. Fully thirty of the forty-five public bills passed in the session received third reading during the fall sitting. Included were several bills addressing highway traffic problems, three pieces of legislation affecting labour relations and employment standards, the victims' bill of rights, the human tissue gift amendments, and the balanced budget legislation.

The major issues of the fall sitting, however, were those that had occupied government and public attention all year – the environment, education, law and order, and the economy (including labour standards).

The Walkerton *E. coli* outbreak had been the most visible environmental issue of the year, and as hearings convened and carried on through the fall, it continued to occupy centre stage. The advisory to residents that they should boil their water was finally lifted in December, just before Stan Koebel, the manager of the town's water system, was to testify at the inquiry. Early testimony had looked at the actions of the local medical officer of health and officials of the environment ministry, but Mr Koebel reported being so distraught about the events in Walkerton that he believed he was not fit to testify. In December his claim was rejected and he was called to the stand. In the course of his testimony and that of later witnesses, it became clear that his falsifying of test results had been a significant contributing factor in the tragedy.

Criticism of the environment ministry continued unabated, however, since it was suggested that regulatory oversight of the water system – oversight that might have caught local malfeasance at an earlier stage – had been weakened by staff and budget cuts. The government's general commitment to environmental quality was also called into question in October by their refusal to sign a new federal-provincial accord on greenhouse-gas emissions and climate change. The federal government expressed disappointment and environmental activists were outraged, claiming that Ontario's refusal to take part would doom the agreement.

At the local level, the City of Toronto had long been searching for a solution to its garbage problem, caused by the filling up of nearby landfill sites. One option that had been discussed was the use of an abandoned mine shaft in Kirkland Lake, and in early October it appeared that the plan to ship Toronto's garbage north to the Adams Mine had been finalized. Within two weeks, however, the scheme was abandoned because of city council fears over liability for unforeseen costs. Instead it was decided to ship the garbage to open landfill sites in Michigan. Critics called on the city to devote more attention to reuse and recycling, and to the reduction of waste going to landfill.

On 1 November, Environment Commissioner Gord Miller issued his annual report. The report expressed concern that the province was reaching the limits of the 'carrying capacity' of the land and water in its jurisdiction. Air and water pollution were predicted to increase, and species extinction was labelled a 'certainty' within twenty years 'if present trends and mechanisms continue without attention.' Mr Miller was also critical of the Ontario Realty Corporation for selling land for development (especially on the Oak Ridges Moraine) without proper environmental assessment. The provincial auditor's report later in the month added to the government's environmental woes by signalling the auditor's agreement with those who had suggested the environment ministry was significantly understaffed.

In education, the Minister of Training, Colleges and Universities introduced in October the promised legislation to permit private universities. The legislation included a provision to require that new private universities be approved by an Education Quality Assessment Board (which would also approve new degree programs in the colleges of applied arts and technology). Critics, notably Professor Henry Jacek, president of OCUFA, suggested the move to permit private universities was an indication the province had not adequately funded its public institutions.

Unrest continued in the secondary school system. Students in a number of Toronto high schools staged brief walk-outs from classes in November to protest the lack of extracurricular activities in their schools. Neither the teachers who had withdrawn from such activities nor the province, which had sought to make participation mandatory, seemed ready to compromise, and the problem remained unresolved at the year's end.

At the elementary level, it was revealed in early November that over half the Grade 3 and Grade 6 pupils who had written the most recent standardized tests had fallen below the provincial standard in reading and writing. Predictably, these results were cited by both opponents and supporters of standardized testing as evidence for their positions.

In early December, the Education Improvement Commission established in 1997 to advise the government on education reform, issued its final report. (Its mandate was to expire in 2000.) The report noted unacceptable test results and urged the government to commit considerable additional resources to the system. They recommended spending $1 billion more each year in a variety of areas. They counselled a focus on early years and called for extending full-day kindergarten throughout the province. Observing that the private sector committed an average of 1.7 per cent of payroll to employee training, they urged that a similar percentage be committed to in-service training for teachers. The government gave no indication that it would follow any of these recommendations.

The government addressed a number of legal issues in the fall sitting of the legislature. Following reports of incidents in which replicas of firearms had been used to intimidate victims during the commission of crimes, the government moved to limit the sale of realistic toy guns. Then in December it introduced legislation ('Prohibiting Profits from Recounting Crimes Act') to capture any funds that would otherwise go to criminals who sold their stories to journalists or other authors. Existing legislation allowed the victims of crime to sue in order to recoup any profits from the sale of such stories, but the new proposed bill would allow the province to collect those funds. The legislation would not prevent a third party from making money from the story of a crime, so that it would have no impact on the group reportedly planning a movie about the Paul Bernardo/Karla Homolka sex killings. The victims' families had long sought to prevent anyone from profiting from their children's deaths, but the proposed law could not give that assurance with respect to third parties.

The same week the government introduced a bill aimed at rescuing children involved in prostitution. The law would allow police to take custody of any minor found in a strip club or prostitution venue and to go before a judge within twenty-four hours to request that the child be placed in safe custody for a period of five days for assessment. The purpose of the assessment would be to help a court to determine whether the child should be held for a further thirty days. The underlying premise of the legislation was that children in such situations were victims, rather than offenders, but that they might need to be held out of contact with pimps, and others with whom they had been associated, if they were to be permanently removed from a life of prostitution.

Earlier in December the government's zeal with respect to law and order had resulted in some embarrassment. MPP Doug Gault (Northumberland) was praising the strict-discipline 'boot camp' in his riding, and in so doing he named some young offenders who had 'graduated' from the facility. In naming youthful offenders, he had broken the law, and after apologizing for the error, he resigned his position as parliamentary assistant for agriculture, food, and rural affairs. Rob Sampson, as Minister of Corrections, was also held at least partly responsible for the gaffe and he too resigned his post.

In November, provincial auditor Eric Peters had reported that jail costs had risen although the number of offenders incarcerated had gone down. He also noted his expectation that the 'super-jails' the government was planning to introduce would be more costly than originally predicted. The auditor recommended more use of the community-release 'temporary absence' program to lower costs.

The government proceeded at the end of the session to pass new labour laws that had been heavily criticized by the labour movement. The first set of amendments seemed aimed at making it easier to decertify a union as the bargaining agent for a group of employees. Workplaces were to be required to post information about how to decertify unions. Labour unions asked when the government might require postings in non-union plants to give information on how to *form* a union. The period over which a decertification application might be generated was extended from sixty to ninety days. If a union failed in a bid to be certified in a particular workplace, there was to be a one-year cooling-off period before another attempt could be made. Unions seeking a first contract after certification were particularly targeted. In such cases, separate votes were to be held on contract ratification and on strike action. That is, a workforce was invited to be in the unusual position of rejecting a contract without undertaking to go on strike as a result. Existing law provided that a union could seek arbitration if it was unable to get a first contract from an employer in a newly unionized workplace. The new law provided decertification as an alternative, and it further provided that if there were simultaneous applications for arbitration and decertification, the Labour Relations Board was to consider the decertification first.

Unions were still reeling from these changes when the government introduced its amendments to labour standards law. The change that received the most public attention was the provision that extended the hours of the normal work week (after which overtime would have to be paid) from forty-eight to sixty hours per week. The government argued that the flexible hours in many jobs meant that someone might well work no more than an average of forty-eight hours per week over a couple of months but might occasionally work more than forty-eight hours in one week. In the government's view, employers should not have to pay overtime when the average hours worked did not exceed the weekly standard. The move was described as encouraging employers to hire workers for more flexible hours, and it was suggested that many (especially younger) workers favoured such jobs. Unions were not convinced, and it was hard to persuade many workers, when union contracts routinely set thirty-five to forty hours as the normal work week, that someone working sixty hours a week was not working overtime.

When the Legislature recessed on 20 December, with a flurry of laws passed at the last moment, the government could look back on a difficult but generally satisfying session. The environmental and educational issues continued to cause concern, but the government could point to considerable action in areas – like law and order and labour relations – with appeal to its core supporters. In addition, the government could boast of a booming economy and a balanced budget, as well as more money directed to health care – an area of wide public interest.

In early December, Finance Minister Ernie Eves announced that the economic boom (for which the government sought to take some credit) had resulted in an unexpected increase in revenues. (It had been a good year for the provincial economy, with unemployment ranging between 5.3 and 6 per cent.) As a consequence, he announced there would be some $500 million in additional money for hospitals and to provide free flu shots throughout the province. He also committed a further $1 billion to paying down the provincial debt, and he followed the federal lead in speeding up the phasing in of the capital-gains tax cut. Liberal leader Dalton McGuinty argued that more money should have been directed to education and health care, while NDP leader Howard Hampton criticized the finance minister for taking credit for a boom that was general throughout North America. In not spending on programs, Mr Hampton said, Mr Eves had squandered an opportunity, in order to provide tax cuts for his 'corporate friends.' At the end of the month, the finance minister announced a $21 million grant for emergency homeless shelters. Municipal governments, especially in Toronto, pointed out that the greatest need was not for emergency shelters but for long-term, low-cost housing, for which the province was providing no support.

One day before the Legislature recessed, Deputy Speaker (and NDP MPP) Tony Martin resigned his post. He did so, he said, because he no longer wanted to be a 'puppet' for the Conservative government.

Despite the critical reports from the Environment Commissioner, the Privacy and Freedom of Information Commissioner, and the provincial auditor, and despite the unresolved problems of air and water quality, education reform, and health-care restructuring, the government at year-end seemed as secure as it had after its renewed mandate was achieved in 1999. As long as the economy remained sound, it appeared, other problems would not resonate with enough voters to threaten the government's control. Whether that stability could be maintained until the next election was somewhat less clear.

Transitions

Several prominent political figures from the province's past died in 2000. They included former premier Frank Miller, former cabinet ministers Robert Welch and Tom Wells, former Toronto coroner and NDP legislator Morton Shulman, and Michael Starr, who had served in the federal cabinet under Prime Minister Diefenbaker and had later served as chair of the Ontario Workers' Compensation Board. The province lost TV journalist Sheldon Turcott in February and author and print journalist Sandra Gwyn, who died in May just shortly after she was named to the Order of Canada. Composer Louis Appelbaum and opera singer Louis Quilico were lost to the arts, as was cartoonist Ben Wicks. Other notable departures included former University of Toronto President Claude Bissell, former Director-General of the Ontario Science Centre James Gordon Parr, and long-time children's television star Bob Homme ('The Friendly Giant').

DANIEL SALÉE

Quebec

Quebecers greeted the new century, indeed the new millennium, with optimism. After nearly a decade of disappointing indicators during the 1990s, the Quebec economy showed strong signs of recovery, particularly in 1999. While the average annual rate of economic growth had stagnated at around 2 per cent during the previous two decades, it was 3.7 per cent for 1999. In 1998 and 1999, job creation reached levels unparalleled since the late 1980s, and the unemployment rate was at its lowest since 1976. On the eve of the new century, the outlook was good and the mood quite upbeat in Quebec.

Still, though general socio-economic perspectives remained encouraging through 2000, the year proved to be one of realignment or questioning on several fronts. Five years after the defeat of the sovereignty option in the 1995 referendum, it seemed increasingly harder for sovereignists to convince their fellow Quebecers that their idea of an independent Quebec was still worth pursuing. As the Parti Québécois reached the half-way mark of its second consecutive term in office, under the popular leadership of Premier Lucien Bouchard, it began to face mounting challenges from different segments of the population over some of its key policies. Finally, the general socio-political consensus, which had prevailed since the 1960s, over governance, over the role of the Quebec state in policy setting and management, and over the social-democratic nature of policy choices and orientations, began to meet with ever more vocal opposition. The year 2000 may well be seen retrospectively as the beginning of the end for the legacy of the Quiet Revolution.

Facing one's demons: ideological tensions around the sovereignty issue

Despite strong and stable electoral support, the perennial inability of the Parti Québécois to convince a majority of Quebecers to endorse sovereignty – its fundamental and defining political project – weighed heavily and remained a key problem of significant concern to party members and sympathizers. In the years following the 1995 referendum, with Premier Bouchard at the helm, the party vowed to hold another referendum on sovereignty, but not before 'winning conditions' were met. In essence, this meant that the Bouchard government was to put an end to deficit budgeting by the year 2000 while committing to enhancing social solidarity and improving the economic situation of Quebecers. As a result, although sovereignty continued to be an integral part of the party's objectives, the government's political energy focused more on achieving a strong record of public management than on sovereignty as such, a fact for which radical sovereignists chided Mr Bouchard.

By 2000, Quebec's fiscal situation was indeed significantly better – the zero-deficit objective had been attained the year before – and socio-economic indicators were brighter than they had been in quite some time. Good government did not, however, have expected effects on the sovereignist spirit of Quebecers: popular support for the sovereignty option had steadily declined since the referendum; the sovereignist Bloc Québécois lost several seats in the 2000 federal election; political controversies over the federal government's Clarity Act and the Quebec government's response were greeted with almost general indifference outside academic and political circles; and a Léger and Léger poll indicated that nearly three in four Quebecers believed that Canadian federalism could be renewed, and more than two-thirds of them thought that more efforts should be made to find a third way between sovereignty and current federal practices in Canada.

After forty years of intense and often divisive debates over Quebec sovereignty, it looked like the idea might well have run its course. Prominent intellectuals close to, or supportive of, the sovereignty movement, like Jean-François Lisée, publicly expressed their misgivings about the dream of an independent Quebec and proposed instead that Quebecers explore other avenues of self-affirmation within the institutional confines of Canadian federalism. Mr Lisée, a renowned Quebec journalist, was a key strategist of the 'yes' side during the 1995 referendum and one of Premier Bouchard's main advisers. He resigned from that position in September 1999. No longer confident that the sovereignist movement was steering the right course, he published in mid-winter 2000 a rather provocative, but well-documented essay entitled *Sortie de secours* (Emergency Exit), in which he argued that the referendum strategy pursued by the Parti Québécois was a mistake. The book is largely a celebration of Quebec's social, economic, and political accomplishments of the past four decades, and a reaffirmation of the importance of self-determination for Quebec, but after years of failed attempts at asserting their political sovereignty, Mr Lisée insists, Quebecers would gain more by working within the Canadian federal system.

Christian Dufour, a professor at the École nationale d'administration publique, political commentator, and high-profile pro-sovereignty contributor to public debates about the future of Quebec and Canada, echoed Mr Lisée's sentiments. In a book-length *Lettre aux souverainistes québécois et aux fédéralistes canadiens qui sont restés fidèles au Québec* (Letter to Quebec sovereignists and to Canadian federalists who remained faithful to Quebec), also published in 2000, Mr Dufour delivers a scathing attack on the Canadian political system for its allegedly inherent tendency to marginalize and keep Quebec in a minority situation. At the same time, he also suggests that the sovereignty project is dead and that it might be more productive for Quebecers to explore seriously the possibilities of asymmetrical federalism.

Mr Lisée's and Mr Dufour's position did not sit well with hard-line sovereignists, but, as polls seemed to indicate, it reflected a fairly widespread feeling among the general Quebec population. In a way, though, their respective books underscored implicitly a deeper malaise that had been brewing since then Premier Jacques Parizeau made his bitter remarks about 'money and the ethnic vote' on referendum night. Despite the appeal of the sovereignty project to a sizable portion of Quebec's French-speaking population (60 per cent supported the yes side), sovereignists have remained unable to draw sufficient numbers of non-francophones and immigrants to their ranks. They have repeatedly failed to convince them that the goal of national self-determination is a socially inclusive political project, that their dream of an independent nation is not meant only for francophone Quebecers, but for all who make Quebec their home. Beyond discussions of jurisdictional reconfiguration and administrative power-sharing between Quebec and Ottawa, beyond strict considerations of political strategy, the failure of sovereignists to persuade non-francophones and immigrants that the sovereignty project includes them as well has been a fundamental and determining factor in their inability to carry through their goal of Quebec independence.

The Bouchard government was quite aware of this reality. In order to reverse the dynamics of miscommunication between sovereignists and non-francophone and immigrant communities, it launched in June

2000 a process of general public consultation on the issue of Quebec citizenship. Though only the Canadian state can legally deliver formal citizenship status, this initiative was intended both to assert the self-determination capacity of the Quebec state and to send a strong message to non-francophones and immigrants that, in the eye of the Quebec state, they were unequivocally full-fledged members of the Quebec political community and should consider themselves as such. A two-day public forum was held at the end of September, but little came out of it as many of the ethnocultural advocacy groups involved in the process expressed thinly veiled scepticism at the whole notion of a Quebec-based citizenship. Robert Perrault, the minister responsible for the initiative, resigned from politics a few weeks later, and the issue would eventually drop from public discourse.

The inability to muster the necessary political support from all quarters of the Quebec electorate always perplexed sovereignists, as it is suffused with difficult and politically loaded questions: Who is a Quebecer? Does the prominence of French deter non-francophones from embracing the sovereignist sense of nation? Can the Québécois nation truly exist without an independent state of its own? In Quebec, such questions are not merely academic. They regularly stand at the centre of numerous and often robust political debates about Quebec nationalism; they have always troubled sovereignists in their search for the appropriate political strategy. They are fraught with contention, not only between sovereignists and other Quebecers, but also between sovereignists themselves who, since the referendum, became increasingly divided over the political status of the French language, over the ethnic (as opposed to the civic) nature of their movement, and as to whether the francophone-driven, nationalistic overtones of sovereignty should be watered down.

During most of his term as Premier, Lucien Bouchard regularly engaged in an often elusive balancing act, reassuring hard-line sovereignists that his government was still committed to Quebec independence and to the promotion of French-speaking Quebecers, all the while softening their more radical positions when dealing with non-francophone and immigrant interlocutors. It all tumbled down as the year was drawing to a close with L'affaire Michaud. This incident – which is said to have prompted Lucien Bouchard's decision to resign from politics a few weeks later in early January 2001 – exemplified with more intensity than ever before the underlying tensions that, within the Parti Québécois and the sovereignist movement in general, have regularly opposed proponents of a more uncompromising stance on matters related to the preservation and reinforcement of the French character of Quebec society and moderates, like Lucien Bouchard and René Lévesque before him, whose conception of the Quebec political community tends to be more flexible and pluralistic.

To appease hard-liners who kept voicing unequivocal concerns over what they saw as the decline of the French language in Quebec and the feebleness of the government's commitment to the promotion of French-speaking Quebecers, the Bouchard government set up in June 2000 the Estates General on language. With former Confederation of National Trade Unions president, and well-known sovereignist, Gérald Larose as its chair, the commission was to report within a year on the status of the French language in Quebec and suggest policy directions to strengthen it. On 13 December 2000, Yves Michaud, long-time independentist and Parti Québécois member, former high-ranking civil servant, adviser to René Lévesque, and businessman, presented a memorandum to the Estates General in which he lamented the gradual weakening of existing legislation meant to protect and promote the French language, the continued assimilationist and colonizing influence of Quebec's anglophone minority, the ineffectual integration of immigrants, and their tendency to vote as a bloc against the sovereignty of the Quebec people. Mr Michaud argued that immigrants are welcome to Quebec so long as they accept to live and work in French, endorse Quebec's French culture, and support the French-speaking majority in its bid to become an independent nation. To him, policies of compromise and gentle persuasion only did a disservice to the long-term interests and cultural continuity of French-speaking Quebecers. 'If we do not manage to integrate and assimilate immigrants,' he concluded, after a few gibes at the Jewish community in Quebec, 'we will fall onto the slippery slope of louisianization and of folklorization of our society.'

Mr Michaud's intervention before the Estates General came on the heels of highly publicized remarks he made on a Montreal radio show a week earlier, where he stated with unconcealed exasperation that Jews should stop acting as though they were the only people to have suffered in the history of humanity. He pointed out that the plight of the Palestinians, of the Armenians, and of the Rwandans offered other examples of terrible suffering. Mr Michaud's clearly ethnicist, us-versus-them declarations angered Jewish and immigrant advocacy groups and, on 14 December 2000, led the members of the National Assembly, without distinction of party affiliation, to condemn unanimously the sentiments and ideas he expressed in the public statement he made the previous day.

This unprecedented move by the National Assembly created a political uproar. Many felt that the censoring of Mr Michaud's opinion by the National Assembly was uncalled for and ill advised in a democratic society, for it violated the freedom of speech of a private citizen. But it soon appeared, beyond issues of democratic integrity, that the government-led action was a political manoeuvre to exclude Mr Michaud and people who shared his views from the Parti Québécois. Two days earlier, on 12 December, Mr Michaud had announced that he would seek the PQ nomination for an upcoming by-election in the Montreal riding of Mercier, a PQ stronghold. The party brass faced this prospect with alarm, and Mr Michaud's declaration the next day furthered their resolve to keep him at bay. Controversy broke out within the Parti Québécois over the suitability of Mr Michaud as a possible party representative in Mercier and over the appropriateness of the National Assembly's motion of censure. On 18 December, a few dozen prominent PQ members – among them Jacques Parizeau, former leader of the party – signed and published in several newspapers an open letter in support of Mr Michaud, chastising the National Assembly for its action. In the following days, Premier Bouchard indicated clearly that he did not want Yves Michaud to run for the PQ in Mercier: the party would have to choose between him and Mr Michaud. Mr Bouchard declared that he could not defend the position of the Parti Québécois if Mr Michaud was allowed to stand for the party in Mercier.

The year ended thus, on a note of high political drama that would spill over into the new year, leaving Quebec sovereignists more divided than ever before over the sense and nature of their political project.

Federal–provincial relations: living with the aftershocks of the 1995 referendum

As far as Quebec's relationship with Ottawa is concerned, the most noteworthy event of 2000 was without a doubt the rather tense legislative one-upmanship over Quebec's right to secede from Canada. Still reeling from the near defeat of the no side on the night of the 1995 referendum, the Chrétien government had been looking for ways to curtail the Quebec government's wish for another referendum on sovereignty. The Clarity Bill was its solution. On 13 December 1999, Bill C-20 was tabled for first reading in the House of Commons. It was passed by the House on 15 March 2000 and adopted by the Senate, in its final version, on 29 June 2000. This legislation, an 'Act to give effect to the requirement for clarity as set out in the opinion of the Supreme Court of Canada in the Quebec Secession Reference,' otherwise known as the Clarity Act, was designed to follow through on the opinion rendered on 20 August 1998 by the Supreme Court of Canada on three questions referred to it by the Attorney General two years earlier: (1) Under the Constitution of Canada, can the National Assembly, legislature, or government of Quebec effect the secession of Quebec from Canada unilaterally? (2) Does international law give the National Assembly, legislature, or government of Quebec the right to effect the secession of Quebec from Canada unilaterally? In this regard, is there a right to self-determination under international law that would give the National Assembly, legislature, or government of Quebec the right to effect the secession of Quebec from Canada unilaterally? (3) In the event of a conflict between domestic and international law on the right of the National Assembly, legislature, or government of Quebec to effect the secession of Quebec from Canada unilaterally, which would take precedence in Canada?

In answer to these questions, the Supreme Court concluded that the National Assembly, legislature, or government of Quebec does not have the right, either under Canadian or international law, to effect the secession of Quebec from Canada unilaterally. However, much to the surprise of many – the federal government in particular – the court also emphasized that the rest of Canada would have a political obligation to negotiate Quebec's separation if a clear majority of that province's population voted in favour of it.

The Clarity Act addresses this obligation by requiring that strict conditions for secession be met by the province aspiring to independence, and by imposing a process whereby the House of Commons ultimately decides whether the referendum question is clear enough and warrants that the federal government undertake negotiation in the event of a strong vote in favour of secession. According to the provisions of the Act, within thirty days of the submission of the referendum question to the provincial legislature, the House of Commons must determine whether it is sufficiently clear. On this score, the law stipulates that only a question which implies that the province would become an independent state without political link with Canada would be considered acceptable. Any other question that, for example, would call for a mandate to negotiate the terms of secession (as in the 1980 referendum), or would offer, in addition to secession, other possibilities such as an economic and political partnership with Canada (as in the 1995 referendum), would be deemed ambiguous and would therefore relieve the government of Canada of its obligation to negotiate separation. Once the clarity of the referendum question is established and a referendum held, it is again up to the House of Commons to determine whether the result of an eventual popular vote in support of secession is conclusive. To that end, the House must take into account the size of the majority of valid votes cast in favour of independence, the percentage of eligible voters voting in the referendum, the views of all political parties represented in the legislative assembly of the province, any formal statements or resolutions on the matter made by the government or legislative assembly of any province or territory of Canada, by the Senate of Canada, or by aboriginal peoples (especially those residing in the province proposing secession), and any other matters, circumstances, or views that it considers relevant. In the event that the House of Commons is satisfied that a process for the negotiation of secession can be undertaken, the division of assets and liabilities, any changes to the borders of the province, the rights, interests, and territorial claims of aboriginal peoples, and the protection of minority rights must be addressed. Finally, as there is no right under the Constitution of Canada to effect the secession of a province unilaterally, the Constitution must be amended to complete the secession process; the negotiation of such an amendment must involve the governments of all the provinces and the federal government.

The Quebec political class reacted to the Clarity Act in Quebec with a mix of indignation and disbelief. Premier Bouchard declared that his government felt that the federal law was a mere political tactic, with no legal validity, and that it did not in any way bind the province of Quebec. Gilles Duceppe, leader of the Bloc Québécois in Ottawa, said that the federal government was trying to put the people of Quebec in a straitjacket and force the National Assembly into trusteeship. Jean Charest and the Quebec Liberal Party opposed the Act on account of its imposition of a legal and judicial framework on what they considered as an essentially political issue. They deplored the fact that Ottawa was unilaterally dictating the rules of popular consultation over the sovereignty issue in Quebec, and they proposed that the National Assembly approve a formal declaration affirming the right of Quebecers to make their own decision on their political future. Others, mostly constitutional experts close to the Parti Québécois, challenged the constitutionality of the Clarity Act.

The Liberals' proposal for a motion in the National Assembly was deemed by the Bouchard government too weak and too inadequate a response. Instead, it introduced its own legislation in the National Assembly to counteract the Clarity Act. Bill 99 was adopted on 7 December 2000 as an 'Act respecting the exercise of fundamental rights and prerogatives of the Quebec people and the Quebec state.' In essence this new law states that 'the right of the Quebec people to self-determination is founded in fact and in law' and that the 'Quebec people is the holder of rights that are universally recognized under the principles of equal rights and self-determination of peoples.' As such, then, 'the Quebec people has the inalienable right to freely decide the political regime and legal status of Quebec,' and 'acting through its own political institutions, shall determine alone the mode of exercise of its right to choose the political regime and legal status of Quebec.' Countering the stringent parameters of clarity contained in the federal legislation, the Quebec law holds on the contrary that 'when the Quebec people is consulted by way of a referendum under the Referendum Act, the winning option is the one that obtains a majority of the valid votes cast, namely 50 per cent of the valid votes cast plus one.' In addition, Bill 99 reaffirms the legitimacy and sovereignty of the Quebec state 'in the areas assigned to its jurisdiction within the scope of constitutional laws and conventions,' as well as its freedom to consent to international treaties, conventions, or agreements that fall under its constitutional jurisdictions. Finally, it asserts in no uncertain terms that 'no other parliament or government may reduce the powers, authority, sovereignty or legitimacy of the National Assembly, or impose constraint on the democratic will of the Quebec people to determine its own future.'

Interestingly, this legislative battle for jurisdictional and political predominance in Quebec was restricted to political and academic circles. The Clarity Act made hardly a ripple on the pond of Quebec public opinion, and the Parti Québécois was at a loss to stir the political outrage that would have been necessary the rekindle nationalist and sovereignist fervour. Passed just a few weeks before Christmas, Bill 99 met with widespread indifference within the population; it did not create the political momentum the Bouchard government was hoping to build in order to strengthen the independentist resolve of the Quebec people. While the controversy over the Clarity Act scarcely altered the perception Quebecers have of their governments in Quebec and Ottawa, it certainly contributed to widening the divide between the Quebec government and its federal counterpart. In the end, it only worked to further embitter an already uneasy relationship.

The re-emergence of the language issue

As mentioned above, the Bouchard government set up in 2000 the Estates General on the French language, a roving commission of inquiry mandated to consult with the general population between October 2000 and April 2001 on questions related to the status and situation of French in Quebec. While, on the surface of things, this initiative may have appeared as a political move meant to contain the growing dissatisfaction among disgruntled members of the Parti Québécois and supporters of the sovereignist movement, it also seemed necessary in the mind of the government in order to take stock of what many saw as an increasingly worrisome reality. Indeed, at the end of the summer of 1999, the Conseil de la langue française published an in-depth study which showed that while 87 per cent of the Quebec population used French as their main language of public transaction, in the greater Montreal area 78 per cent did, and on the island of Montreal proper the proportion was down to 71 per cent; more than three in four anglophones in Quebec as a whole and in the greater Montreal area, and four in five on the island of Montreal, used mainly English as the language of public transaction. The study also noted that linguistic transfers among immigrants and allophones continued to favour English over French. Data indicated that 23 per cent of them chose English as the language spoken at home, as opposed to 13 per cent who chose French.

Such figures raised concern among sovereignists and defenders of the predominance of the French language in Quebec, for other experts were further arguing that French-speaking Quebecers would probably be a demographic minority within the next two decades in Montreal and that there were still a number of enterprises in Quebec where francophones encountered difficulty working in their mother tongue. The decision of a Quebec Court judge in October 1999, in a civil action filed by two Eastern township English-speaking antique dealers against the Quebec state over sign language legislation, to invalidate sections of the Charter of French language requiring the clear visual dominance of French in commercial signs was an additional source of alarm. The government appealed this decision almost immediately.

These events and expert observations fuelled sovereignists' worst fear – the decline and gradual disappearance of the French element in Quebec. Polls taken in the early months of the year 2000 showed that more than two in three Quebecers believed that the social status of French was in jeopardy, particularly in Montreal. In fact, the developments of the preceding months gave new intensity to the politics of language during the year 2000. While francophone Quebecers did not take to the streets to defend the social and political legitimacy of their mother tongue – as they did, for example, at the height of tensions over language in the 1960s and 1970s – feelings about the preservation of

French were nevertheless suffused with anxiety and alarm. The government may have breathed a sigh of relief when, in April, the Superior Court reversed the previous Quebec Court judgment and confirmed the legality of the provisions imposing the predominance of French on commercial signs. Yet, despite its attempts to contain expressions of discontent over the situation of the French language, that did not preclude the language issue from acquiring renewed visibility, or from making its way to the centre of public debates. Highly vocal Anglo-rights activists vowed to bring the case all the way to the Supreme Court.

Quite paradoxically, though, the actions of the government itself probably contributed more in the end to giving the language question new prominence in public affairs. Government officials felt compelled at different moments to reopen it and to reiterate publicly the government's commitment to safeguarding the French language, stating in essence that in the context of globalization and of the emergence of new information technologies, the attractiveness of French is reduced; it finds itself in a fragile and precarious position and needs more protection than ever. A government report titled *Les défis de la langue française à Montréal et au Québec au XXIème siècle* (The Challenges of the French Language in Montreal and in Quebec in the 21st Century) went so far as to call for the mobilization of all Quebecers (and not simply Parti Québécois members) in support of French in order to increase the language's vitality and power of attraction. Finally, the Estates General offered many an opportunity to vent their frustration at the situation of the French language in Quebec. Interventions close in content and nature to that proffered by Yves Michaud were fairly common at the hearings of the commission. By year end it was clear that the angst over the social status and political legitimacy of French in Quebec had not abated, and that language would likely remain a central policy concern for some time to come.

The winds of change: reconfiguring public management and refitting public policies

The zero-deficit commitment of the Bouchard government unavoidably entailed that the state had to reconsider its spending priorities and policy choices. Navigating an uneasy course between the social-democratic principles that the Parti Québécois has historically endorsed and the neo-liberal imperatives of market competitiveness, state reduction, and individual responsibility to which most Western governments have been compelled to conform in the last two decades, Lucien Bouchard and his colleagues struggled through most of their term in power to find the right balance between the ideals of the Quiet Revolution and the pressures for a new, more market-sensitive approach to governance and policy-making – between social solidarity and economic efficiency. In the mind of those most directly affected by cost-cutting measures, they went too far on the path of fiscal responsibility; to others who advocate significant downsizing and a redefinition of state functions, they did not go far enough. In terms of policy choices, the year 2000 was marked by this underlying and ongoing debate over the appropriate degree of state presence in social and economic life, and over the nature of the institutional restructuring that is needed to satisfy the dictates of economic efficiency. Particular developments in three key areas over the course of the year are emblematic of this latter-day conundrum: health care, higher education, and municipal reorganization.

Health care: to privatize or not to privatize?

Since the decision was made in the late 1960s and early 1970s that the Quebec state would provide Quebecers free and universal access to health care and related social services, the public health system invariably accounted for the largest expenditure of the state – nearly 40 per cent of the total budget today. By the mid-1980s, however, as Quebec faced a recessionary conjuncture, stunted economic growth, high interest rates, and declining economic opportunities, the sustainability of an increasingly expensive health-care system was seriously questioned – indeed, the viability of the whole welfare state structure put in place two decades earlier appeared problematic. In addition, the bureaucratic, rational-legal model of public administration, which guided the whole public health apparatus and ensured that fundamental standards of service delivery and basic norms of professional practice were applied and maintained, was being criticized for its rigidity, its hierarchical modus operandi, and the socio-political divide it created between clients and service providers.

In 1985, the Bourassa government (Liberal) set up a commission of inquiry on health and social services to look into possible avenues for change and reform in the administration of public health in Quebec, with a view to making it less of a financial burden on the state. The commission was chaired by Dr Jean Rochon, a public health specialist and former dean of medicine at Laval University, whose blueprint for reform included downloading certain categories of services and functions from hospitals to private clinics, community health clinics, and nursing homes, closing or merging smaller hospitals, retooling certain medical establishments to fit special needs, and significant budgetary cuts in health-care spending. Dr Rochon's suggestions would not be implemented by the Bourassa administration, but he entered politics, was elected under the Parti Québécois banner in 1994, and joined the cabinet as minister of health and social services. During his four-year tenure in this portfolio, Dr Rochon presided over an important administrative restructuring of the management and delivery of health care, and $2.3 billion worth of cuts in the state's health and social services budget, making him the most unpopular minister in the Bouchard government.

During this period, the government claimed to remain committed to the principles of universality and free access in health care. The changes that were effected by Dr Rochon were justified as attempts to democratize the management of health care and involve citizens in the delivery of services and in policy-making. In the end, though, Dr Rochon's reforms did little to alleviate the most pressing and persistent problems crippling Quebec's health-care system. If anything, overcrowded emergency wards, long waiting lists for surgeries and diagnostic tests, penury of nursing staff, insufficient numbers of doctors and specialized medical personnel in outlying regions, difficult access to family physicians, the obsolescence of some equipment and infrastructure, and budgetary crises in hospitals became even more perplexing concerns in recent years. Not surprisingly in this context, the privatization of some aspects of health-care delivery has been proposed by a number of stakeholders as a serious solution to the woes of the health-care system and touted as a guarantee of improved quality in health-care services. Insurance companies, medical entrepreneurs, wealthy patients, market enthusiasts, and neo-liberal ideologues have called with increasing insistence for the development of private medical services, the end of free access to certain services, and the possibility for patients who can afford the extra costs to bypass waiting lists and the public system in order to receive more quickly the care they need. The idea that the private sector should play a greater role in Quebec's health-care system has been gaining in support.

It is against this backdrop that Pauline Marois, Dr Rochon's successor, set up in June 2000 a special task force to look into the financing and organization of health care and social services and to recommend ways to protect, adapt, and improve the system. The task force, headed by Michel Clair, a former cabinet minister under René Lévesque, sat for several weeks in the fall of 2000, heard from 220 organizations, 6,000 individuals, and 30 international experts, and received 550 written submissions. It presented its report to Minister Marois on 18 December: a 400-page document, including 95 solutions, 36 recommendations, and 59 proposals to support them. The Clair Commission – as it was known – considered several key issues including the reorganization of service delivery, the transformation of the work environment of health and social services providers, the creation of new mechanisms of enhanced accountability for health-care and social services administrators, and the direct involvement of citizens in the policy-making process and management of public health. The commission's approach to financing, however, was the one issue, more than any other, likely to raise controversy. Indeed, Michel Clair and his colleagues stressed the important role that the private sector could play as a 'partner' in the health-care system. While they rejected the idea of a parallel private health-care network (which would lead to a two-tiered system of service delivery) and objected to user-fees (as antithetical to the solidarity of the public system), they nevertheless argued that partnerships with the private sector could provide the necessary funds to strengthen the existing health-care system. The Clair Commission suggested that the resources of the private sector could be harnessed to help solidify the provision of health care in Quebec. Subcontracting of diagnostic testing, minor day surgeries, the building of long-term-care and nursing-home facilities, and capital investment for present and future technology needs were areas in which, according to members of the commission, private-sector interventions would contribute to improve service delivery and ease the financial burden of the state.

During the commission's hearings, witnesses and participants were quite divided over the issue of privatization. Many private-sector advocacy organizations and lobby groups came out unequivocally in favour of a higher degree of private-sector involvement in health-care delivery. The labour movement and the community sector, on the contrary, warned against and even denounced any attempt at furthering the role of the private sector in Quebec's public health system. Opposing visions of society and of the role of the state, and competing interests were clearly at play here. After years of difficult policy decisions in the name of fiscal responsibility, the situation of the public health system in Quebec had not substantially improved. As bottom-line considerations continued to guide the government, the increased privatization of Quebec's health-care system might well be seen as a panacea. One thing seems certain at this stage: whether the government opts for it or not, the outcome will likely not be decided without social and political tensions.

Higher education: private-sector values as a guideline

Education in Quebec has been a pivotal and positive instrument of societal transformation. Quebec's remarkable social and economic modernization in the 1960s and 1970s was largely undergirded by the major reform of the educational system that took place in the 1960s. Universal access to high-quality and affordable education became a state priority and, like health care, a major source of state expenditure. By the 1990s, however, faced with a mounting public debt, Quebec governments resigned themselves to imposing significant and even drastic budgetary cuts on education. Universities were particularly hard hit, mostly as no government had dared to increase tuition fees in any substantial way in over two decades. (Quebec still boasts the lowest university tuition fees in all of Canada.) Although a number of federal funding programs support higher education and university research, and despite the fact that direct, private-sector contributions have been regularly solicited with appreciable success in recent years, financing Quebec's institutions of higher learning at an appropriate level remains a central public management and policy concern.

In 2000, the Bouchard government undertook to reverse the tide of underfunding by granting universities an extra $100 million towards the reduction of their accumulated debt, and by promising to invest another $600 million over the next three years. Though this was a far cry from the additional $650 million Quebec universities claimed to need annually just to maintain their competitive edge, it was welcome news nonetheless.

This financial boon came with a new vision for higher education and new parameters of accountability for universities. On 15 February, François Legault, minister of state for education and youth, released *Priorities for Our Future*, the government's policy statement on universities. With this document, the government reaffirmed the 'pivotal role' Quebec universities play in 'the development of individuals, knowledge, culture and society,' and announced its intention to formulate its policies with a view to ensuring access to university education, strengthening the quality of teaching, enhancing the excellence of research, and facilitating universities' ability to respond to the needs of society and connect to the world. In turn, universities must be prepared to 'participate in an open, attentive dialogue, with both the government and the stakeholders who formulate expectations concerning them.' They must understand that 'reinvestment in the universities will take into account the wealth of society and the government's responsibility to exercise good management,' which essentially means that the government's allocation of public money to the universities will hinge on their willingness to adhere to the government's new policy orientations and on their ability to manage rationally, cooperatively, and with transparency their resources and the services they provide: 'In any case, accountability for the results attained, in both quality of services and utilization of resources, will be an absolute requirement.' In keeping with this focus on efficient and transparent management, the minister held the universities to performance contracts negotiated on the basis of quantifiable objectives that each institution was to set for itself (with regard to program development, student retention, number of new graduates, research accomplishments, etc.). The failure of a university to meet its objectives would jeopardize its future funding.

Hardly in a position to object to these new rules, Quebec universities were generally ready to abide by the new exigencies imposed by the government. In any case, compliance seemed to hold promises of much-needed benefits after years of severe budgetary restrictions. Critics, by contrast, were quick to point out that the government's obsession with fiscal responsibility and economic efficiency forced upon the administrative process of universities management criteria derived from private-sector values. They denounced the performance contracts as instruments that coerced universities into applying a market mentality of quantification to practices and purposes that cannot and must not be quantified: the quality of an academic program does not depend on the number of students registered in it, nor is the number and size of research grants a reflection of the quality of research. In the critics' view, higher education has nothing to do with measurable performance, and they were prepared to take the government to task publicly on this score. Behind issues of funding lies in fact a deeper debate over the true, social role of the university and over how the state can help in fulfilling this role. As in the case of health care, Quebecers seem at the crossroads on the question of higher education: proponents of market-inspired managerial approaches are telling them to abandon previous, fiscally unsound ways; it is not clear as yet whether they are fully prepared to go that route.

Municipal mergers and the reorganization of local governance

In 2000 the Quebec government made significant advances toward the reorganization of local governance and municipal administration. On 16 June the National Assembly adopted Bill 124, which grants the minister of municipal affairs the power to demand that certain municipalities merge. Failure to comply can lead to a merger by ministerial decree and the end of governmental subsidies to the recalcitrant municipalities. On the same day, Bill 134 was also adopted and created the Montreal Metropolitan Community, specifying the boundaries of its territory, its organization, its powers, its jurisdictional limits, and the rules of financial accountability by which it was to abide. These two pieces of legislation were a prelude to the controversial Bill 170, which was adopted on 20 December, and which merged heretofore independent, smaller municipalities into five major urban entities: Montreal, Quebec City, Longueuil, Lévis, and Hull-Gatineau. In Montreal, where this legislation was heavily contested, the twenty-eight municipalities existing on the island of Montreal were amalgamated politically and administratively into one larger city, which would come officially into existence on 1 January 2002. This new law turned former suburban towns into boroughs under the jurisdiction of the new City of Montreal. Each borough would be represented in City Hall by a president (rather than a mayor) and two councillors. Though some powers of local decision-making of the old municipalities would remain, the new boroughs would be stripped of most of the jurisdictional latitude they once enjoyed as independent towns (not the least of which was the ability to raise taxes and administer their own, self-generated income base).

This substantial reform of municipal and territorial management must be understood as a key part of the Bouchard government's self-styled effort to redefine the role and functions of the Quebec state, ease its financial burden, reconfigure its organization, and increase the quality and economic efficiency of its services to citizens. The government established a clear connection between mergers and the importance of streamlining existing public-management practices. As its white paper on municipal reorganization, released on 25 April, argues, '[t]he merger of municipalities makes it possible to offer better services to the population, and this, at lower cost. By eliminating duplication and by making possible economies of scale, [mergers] allow municipalities to reduce costs and to reach a level of efficiency so that they can more easily provide services of better quality. The amalgamation of municipalities can also provide an opportunity to downsize and rationalize their organization.' In addition, the government also believed that mergers would foster Quebec's competitive edge and better position the province's economy to face up to new market challenges. Again, as the White paper explains, '[T]he absence of a coherent development strategy makes it difficult for our urban centres to take up the challenge of competing with the rest of the world. Indeed, there is a connection between the creation of strong socio-economic poles, able to effectively sustain competition in the context of market globalization, and the existence of a clear development strategy emanating from a decision-making role at the level of city regions.'

Reactions against the mergers were vehement. Several mayors of the municipalities slated for amalgamation were particularly vociferous in their opposition, and they succeeded in mustering support from large segments of their constituencies. For local politicians, the perspective of seeing their power base reduced was obviously not very appealing. Citizens, for their part, feared that within a larger, distant municipal entity, they would lose their ability to influence decisions that concern them directly. The strength of the bond many feel for their local community also played into their decision to join the anti-merger movement. Others offered more academic viewpoints, and challenged the government's arguments about economies of scale, administrative rationalization, and market competitiveness; they pointed to other municipal amalgamation experiments in several North American jurisdictions where similar arguments simply did not prove true.

Overall, though, it is perhaps the way in which the government forced the issue of municipal mergers and imposed its policy agenda that most irritated opponents of the initiative. Many felt that Louise Harel, the minister for municipal affairs and the metropolis, simply bullied her way through the consultative and legislative process. Bill 170 was adopted barely a month after being introduced in the National Assembly, much to the dismay of the Liberal Opposition, who lamented that debates were curtailed. A number of mayors and anti-merger activists were prompt to denounce the government as fascistic and anti-democratic. Jean Charest and the Liberal Party, riding on the coattail of the anti-merger movement, and clearly hoping to derive some political capital from it, promised that they would allow amalgamated towns to de-merge if they were brought to power in the next election.

The push for mergers and municipal reorganization was not without its proponents outside government. Pierre Bourque, the mayor of

Montreal, had originally proposed the idea of 'one island, one city' for Montreal; he was particularly active throughout the year in defence of the project. A number of well-known journalists and academics (usually close, politically, to the Parti Québécois) also supported the government. Being on the 'winning' side, however, their interventions did not seem as vocal or as forceful as the vituperations of the anti-merger movement, whose members directly felt threatened by the government legislation and managed to remain in the public light.

In the end, the municipal merger controversy raged through the better part of 2000 as a strong reminder of how divided Quebecers are over issues of public management and over the appropriate degree of transformation of state structures, of state practices, and of the policy agenda that Quebec requires.

Looking ahead ...

For all its internal disturbances and its forceful approach on key policy issues, the Parti Québécois remained fairly popular through the year and seemed to enjoy a relatively healthy amount of support in the general population. This is in no small measure thanks to Lucien Bouchard, whose personality and political acumen struck a sympathetic chord with Quebecers. Somehow Premier Bouchard had succeeded thus far conveying the sense that though the government's reforms might force the transformation of well-entrenched habits, they were well thought out and should work out for the best interests of the whole of Quebec society in the long run. Admittedly, the brighter economic performance of the past few years made it easier for people to accept changes. The government's gambit was that such good economic conditions would continue, and so it could boast of a direct correlation between economic success and its policies. These are, however, precarious and potentially shifting grounds to tread on. The coming years will determine whether the seeds of policy changes planted by the Bouchard government will take root for the benefit of all. These are crucial but fickle times; Lucien Bouchard can only take the Parti Québécois so far. The agitation within the party and the social tensions created by the government's policy have been by and large contained and reasonably well managed. They may be indications, however, that the road ahead might be bumpier than the government expects.

RICHARD WILBUR

New Brunswick

The first year of a new government's mandate is traditionally the easiest as its members get accustomed to their new roles and enjoy the perks of power. The second year brings reality, and in Premier Bernard Lord's case, that meant making some tough decisions to cope with New Brunswick's perpetually weak finances – a situation compounded by his determination to keep the last of the twenty promises to be fulfilled within his first two hundred days in office. All were completed within the allotted time except the most controversial – ending the highway tolls imposed by the McKenna government. Premier Lord had also promised to reduce the public-service sector without damaging its overall efficiency. Early in the year, the young Premier and his finance minister bit the proverbial bullet and made some hard decisions. The political fall-out was eased somewhat by three factors: the number of public servants who opted for the early retirement package; a fairly buoyant economy, especially in the south; and the weakness of the political opposition: a ten-member Liberal contingent plus Elizabeth Weir, the lonely leader of the New Democrats, who continued to raise the most pertinent questions.

Ending highway tolls

On 8 January, in his weekly column in the *Moncton Times-Transcript*, Premier Lord reaffirmed his promise to stop toll collections on the Fredericton to Moncton highway: 'We are only weeks away from a final solution.' Meanwhile, the two Opposition leaders kept the issue in public view. On 27 January, at the standing committee on public accounts, NDP leader Elizabeth Weir called for a legislative committee to investigate why the government had not collected $245,000 in late fines because of the private developer's failure to meet construction deadlines. The government refused her request. On 11 February, Liberal leader Camille Theriault, predicting that the promised toll announcement was just days away, warned that the lost toll revenue, as much as $300 million, would come from the taxpayers' pocket. On 1 March, in making his long-awaited announcement, Premier Lord claimed the cancellation deal would save the province $34.5 million – the amount left from the $67 million it would have cost to collect the tolls minus $30 million paid as compensation to the construction firm for ending the toll system. He added that the entire capital cost of the project – $850 million – would be transferred to the provincial debt. Much later, in October, Finance Minister Norman Betts admitted that an audited statement showing a increase in the province's net debt of nearly $900 million was almost totally due to the government decision to end tolls, a figure confirmed by Auditor General Daryl Wilson in his annual report in mid-December. By ending the tolls, he thought, New Brunswick's financial position had been weakened, and he could find 'no net positive contribution' from the decision.

Reducing the public workforce

After months of warning about job cuts, Finance Minister Betts made his first move on 1 February by announcing a buy-out package for 1,700 government employees eligible to take early retirement: those who had at least five years of pensionable service and were fifty-three years or older. Instead of the 1,000 he anticipated, more than 1,300, representing 13 per cent of the 57,000 public workforce, had accepted the offer by 17 March, meaning that they would retire within two years. The next day, a small but crucial group of workers, sixty-three court stenographers – all of them women – warned that court services might be disrupted if contract negotiations broke down by the end of the month. They did, and the stenographers, whose current pay scale of $29,000 was the lowest compared to their counterparts in the other three Atlantic provinces, went on strike on 25 September, eventually slowing down court business to a crawl. The finance minister refused to improve on his 1.5 per cent wage offer over the next three years, arguing, 'This isn't just about those 63 people. It's about setting a precedent for other negotiations,' a reference to the fact that in 2001 the government would start negotiating with four much larger bargaining groups (*Daily Gleaner*, 26 December).

In late October Justice Minister Brad Green announced that the twenty-six provincial court judges would be receiving pay increases of $16,000, raising their salaries to $141,202, slightly higher than the national average. By this time, the court stenographers' strike was in its eighth week, and their union spokesman accused the Lord government of being sexist. 'Had this been a predominantly male group, we would have been at the table negotiating an end to this strike. We're dealing with the Archie Bunkers of provincial politics' (*Telegraph Journal*, 1 November). Mr Green replied that New Brunswick had little choice because provincial governments were constitutionally bound to have independent boards review judges' wages and 'history has proven that provincial governments which ignore such rulings end up losing later in court' (*Times Transcript*, 31 October).

Preparing New Brunswickers for a bad-news budget

In the same week that the Lord government announced its early retirement package for civil servants, it released figures on the state of the province's finances. Based mostly on the spending program of the previous Liberal administration, they showed that almost every Liberal forecast had been off target, and instead of an $18.5 million surplus there was a $164.3 million deficit. Most departments had overspent their allocations; the health department alone was $88.7 million in the red. To no one's surprise, these figures were not raised by the Liberal Opposition during the lacklustre spring legislative session, which finally adjourned in mid-February to await the budget's presentation on 28 March. Four days before that event, Premier Lord announced a major restructuring of government departments based on recommendations of the cabinet's waste-reduction review committee. The number of cabinet ministers would remain at fifteen, but effective 1 April, there would be sixteen departments instead of eighteen. In his news conference, the Premier said that 100 of the 600 government programs would be shifted, merged, or eliminated; once the budget was presented, New Brunswickers would know which programs and services would stay. Some could be privatized, but not health or education.

In his Budget Speech to the House on 29 March, Finance Minister Betts said it met 'the test set out by New Brunswickers – to change the way government works for people. Do we fund health care or corporate welfare? Do we cut taxes or create more programs?' There would be a 3 per cent cut in personal income taxes, but it would only take effect on 1 July. The corporate tax rate for small businesses (those earning less than $200,000 a year) would be cut 25 per cent, starting in 2001. New Brunswickers would pay taxes on their income alone, rather than on a percentage of their federal tax, a change that would benefit small income earners. To help pay for these revenue losses, government program spending would be cut by $238 million; the capital budget was reduced by $152 million; subsidies to businesses would drop by $22.1 million, and unconditional grants to municipalities would be cut by $1.9 million this fiscal year and another $6.4 million in 2002. Education's allocation would be the highest in history: $999 million ($173 million more than last year), while health-care spending would increase by $143 million, although only $43 million was new money since the budget figure included $100 million that had already been allocated to health care shortly after the Lord administration took office.

Farmers were hardest hit. Although it would be weeks before most New Brunswickers would know how this first Tory budget would affect them, the impact on farmers was almost immediate. So was their reaction. 'The budget pain begins: 75 agriculture jobs lost' ran the front-page headline in the 30 March issue of the *Telegraph-Journal*. It was commenting on a meeting Food Minister Paul Robichaud had had the previous day in Fredericton with 450 agriculture and fisheries workers. The creation of the Department of Food Production out of Agriculture and Fisheries would reduce a workforce of 428 to only 120. Seventy-five, including forty veterinarians and thirty-five agriculture specialists, would lose their jobs immediately, while another 164 from the two former departments would be placed on redeployment lists or be offered early retirement. Another sixty-nine would be transferred to other departments. Mr Robichaud's response to Liberal finance critic Bernard Richard the next day in the Legislature did not help ease farmers' concerns: 'We have to make some choices and if we want to put more money in the health care system and in education, we have to take some decisions. It's a question of choices here' (*Telegraph Journal*, 30 March). When farmers in the Sussex area prepared for a protest rally, the Premier offered to go to the farming centre to hear their complaints. He got an earful from 200 citizens who packed a local hall. Two days later, on 8 April, after a seven-hour marathon meeting attended by the Premier, Mr Robichaud, government officials, and a coalition representing a wide spectrum of the agriculture industry, the government compromised. It placed a one-year moratorium on the controversial changes announced in the budget, including the elimination of veterinarians and agriculture specialists. It also agreed to rename the department to include the word 'agriculture.' After the meeting, Paul Robichaud admitted that the government should have consulted with the farmers before announcing the drastic changes. Eventually, the new department would be called Agriculture, Fisheries, and Aquaculture, and much to the relief of the farmers, the veterinarians' positions were retained. However, a number of service fees were increased sharply.

This same massive departmental restructuring prompted another protest when 150 Bay of Fundy fishers and their supporters rallied outside the Legislature to express their disapproval at the minister's decision to terminate the position of Rex Hunter, the assistant deputy minister who had gained fishers' respect during two decades in the area with the federal Department of Fisheries and Oceans (DFO). His new provincial post had been created in response to Fundy fishers' often-expressed complaints that the government was ignoring them in favour of the larger fishing region in the Acadian peninsula. Despite the support of the Tory MP Greg Thompson, the minister stuck to his decision that Mr Hunter's position had to be cut to streamline the new department. Another fisheries issue that received extensive national media coverage was totally ignored by the provincial minister and his bureaucrats. They concluded that the series of confrontations that took place in August and September between members of the Burnt Church reserve on Miramichi Bay, local non-Native fishers, DFO personnel, plus scores of RCMP was strictly a federal responsibility. Most New Brunswickers probably agreed, given their preoccupation with day-to-day concerns such as jobs, road conditions, the state and location of the nearest hospitals and schools, the rising cost of gas and power, and, as always, taxes.

Balancing highway maintenance with budget cuts

Despite the current prominence given to 'new economy' sectors like call centres and natural gas lines, the old economy represented by the forest-related industries (still New Brunswick's biggest economic generator) and highway building and maintenance was the mainstay for many, especially seasonal workers. Until now, the government of the day had released its highway capital spending estimates early in the new year, which gave a good indication of potential jobs as well as allowing contractors time to prepare their bids. This year's delay was ominous, and when Margaret Blaney, the first woman to hold the transportation portfolio, finally released her estimates in the legislature on 26 April, she admitted her department would be hiring about 200 fewer casual workers and capital spending would be cut by more than $100 million. Jim Hughson of the New Brunswick Road Builders' Association estimated this would mean a loss of 550 full-time and 1,563 part-time jobs. The industry was already coping with a massive cut-back in construction work on twinning the Trans-Canada highway, begun several years earlier by the McKenna administration but stalled since the Tories assumed office. Three weeks later, Ms Blaney confirmed another distressing rumour: the Maritime Road Development Corporation, which was building the Moncton-Fredericton highway, had awarded a $20 million grading contract to a Quebec-based firm. In July, the minister had more bad news: her department would not be paving or chip-sealing the 3,000 km of dirt roads in the province for the foreseeable future, concentrating instead on maintaining existing paved roads. In September, officials representing small municipalities, already reeling from cuts in unconditional grants, learned that this change would mean they would not be able to use government highway funds for curb and drainage work as had been the case over the past five to ten years.

Coping with mounting health-care costs

Although the latest budget had allotted more funds for health care, the sector continued to face financial challenges. The previous Liberal government's decision in 1999 to cut the cost of regular ambulance emergency calls from $275 to $120 and to make inter-hospital transfers free of any charge had sharply increased the demand for ambulances, leaving their private operators facing large deficits. In February, Dr Dennis Furlong, the health minister, announced the purchase (at a cost of $3.5 million each) of three MRI (Magnetic Resonance Imaging) machines, bringing to four the total to serve the entire province. Two would be located in Moncton and one in Saint John, while the fourth would be a mobile unit shared between Fredericton and Edmundston. The geographical inequality was obvious: no MRI for the Acadian northeast, even though the one formerly shared by Saint John and Moncton was available. Dr Furlong, the MLA for the northeastern community of Dalhousie, said the people of the north would have access to the machines in Moncton and Saint John – a four-to-five hour drive.

In July, the government's health budget suffered a $12.5 million hit – the price of a settlement of a long-running legal battle with Blue Cross of Atlantic Canada over a 'smart card' system designed by the firm that proved unworkable. The financial picture brightened a little in September with news of a $67.7 million federal grant for health-care and early development programs – a sum that fell short of the $150 million Premier Lord was hoping to get to properly fund New Brunswick's health-care system. In November, Dr Furlong announced that $46 million, to be taken from the federal grant, would be given to the hospital corporations to support the current levels until next year, when structural changes to the health-care system would be introduced pending the recommendations of the Premier's Health Quality Council. Meanwhile, the province's doctor shortage worsened: sixty vacancies existed in April compared to forty-seven when the Lord government took office. The government decision announced in May to pay for ten more medical-school seats at Memorial University would not have an immediate impact on the current situation.

On 14 September, at its annual convention, the New Brunswick Medical Society called for a 30 per cent wage increase. But Dr Furlong said the province didn't have the $57 million to cover this demand. In November, doctors in Miramichi and Saint John staged a one-day strike to get the government to sign a new working agreement replacing one that had expired nine months earlier. Other similar protests were held throughout December in major centres around the province. On 14 December Moncton physicians marched in front of Premier Lord's home constituency office. Nurses were just as frustrated, rejecting a contract offer made in late October amid rumours that a province-wide strike was a distinct possibility. A revised offer reducing the contract length from four years to three plus wage increases in line with other Atlantic-area nurses eventually brought a settlement.

Education system copes with declining enrolment, enlarged school districts

The immediate challenges facing Tory Education Minister and former principal Elvy Robichaud was not possible teachers' strikes but how to rationalize a system with fewer students, too many school districts, and demands for a return to elected school boards. Statistics released on 19 January showed that the province's student population had declined by 2,128 in 1999 to a new low of 127,000, and department officials were predicting enrolment could drop to 100,000 by 2011. One solution was obvious: close underused schools. Thus, in tabling his department estimates to the legislature on 11 April, Mr Robichaud announced that seven schools, including three anglophone schools in the Saint John area and three others in northern French areas, would be closed. A total of $34 million would be spent to improve existing facilities and supply teachers would receive their second wage increase in two years, bringing their daily stipend to $105. At the same time, union officials were charging that the government had already notified 110 teaching assistants that they would have no work in the fall.

Acting on the recommendations of a select committee on education, the Lord government decided to phase out the two language-based boards of education while restoring elected school boards. The McKenna administration had scrapped them four years ago in favour of a three-tiered parental advisory system that proved to have little influence. Premier Lord's decision came just a week before a group of French-speaking parents were scheduled to launch a court case to challenge the loss of the old elected boards. The necessary legislative changes, which would add $700,000 to the department's budget, were introduced on 29 November; the first school-board elections would take place during the May 2001 municipal elections. Under the proposed legislation, members of the fourteen new District Education Councils would be legally autonomous with all the administrative powers of school boards, including control over budgets and spending, hiring and directing superintendents, and managing school property. At the same time, the current twelve anglophone school districts would be reduced to nine, the francophones would have five instead of six, and all districts would be greatly expanded. The provincial Board of Education would be abolished, to be replaced by a provincial forum that would meet with district council chairs and officials twice a year. In August, officials at the Second Language Education Centre at the University of New Brunswick warned of an impending shortage of French teachers due to retirements, the lure of jobs in neighbouring Maine, and the steady increase in the number of students choosing the French immersion program.

Outside the classroom, the Fredericton *Daily Gleaner* noted in a 2 February article that four schools in two districts had become 'Coke schools' after having signed exclusive contracts with Coca-Cola in return for free items plus lump sums and yearly cash donations. While some students and their parents objected, Minister Robichaud was less concerned, saying that 'sometimes it makes sense for schools to partner with local companies' (*Daily Gleaner*, 2 February). In a joint announcement on 23 September, he and Premier Lord said that a two-school pilot program to provide a free nutritional program would be extended to all students from kindergarten to grade 3, starting in November. It would cost $900,000 for the current academic year and $1.03 million in subsequent years as it was extended over the full term. It would allow schools to offer food in the morning and during lunch and recess breaks, whenever the children were hungry. On the same day as this announcement, the anglophone board of education turned down a proposal from the New Brunswick Home and School Association and endorsed by the New Brunswick Teachers' Association and the Canadian Union of Public Employees for a school-bus safety program. Developed by a school bus driver and costing $100 per school, it involved taking students onto buses to learn about safety issues. Exactly two months later, a seven-year-old Grand Manan child was dragged several hundred metres when her coat drawstring became caught on the bus railing. She was uninjured, but steps were later taken to warn parents of this potential hazard.

At the post-secondary level, the biggest event was a five-week faculty strike at the Université de Moncton, which finally ended on 5 April after a thirty-six-hour bargaining session. A few days later, the university president, Jean-Bernard Robichaud, announced the details of a plan to lure disgruntled students back to the institution for the fall term: $500,000 in extra scholarships and tuition subsidies, and $700,000 in student aid. In October, U de M lost out to the University of New Brunswick in a bid to become the National Research Council's new $37 million e-commerce centre. Subsequent talks initiated by the Lord government determined that some of this money would help establish satellite centres at Moncton and UNB's campus in Saint John.

An uneven and at times confusing economic picture

Statistics Canada figures released in mid-March showed that New Brunswick's unemployment rate in February was 9.7 per cent – the seventh consecutive month it had been below 10 per cent. The thriving city of Moncton had a 5.4 per cent rate and Saint John 7.7, but for the predominantly rural area in the northeast stretching from Campbellton to Miramichi, it stood at 17.1 per cent. In May Premier Lord got a strong message from two hundred protesters gathered outside his Bathurst hotel, demanding that he 'save our jobs.' They included unemployed road crews, former provincial workers who lost their job when the government shut down a local tree nursery, plus disgruntled seasonal fish-plant workers. A few days later, the region's two cabinet representatives, Education Minister Elvy Robichaud and Agriculture, Fisheries, and Aquaculture Minister Paul Robichaud (no relation) announced that the Acadian peninsula would get 104 more jobs as a result of government help to expand several local businesses. The tourist industry, one of the seasonal mainstays for the region, reported a 10 to 15 per cent drop in visitors to the northeast, mainly because of poor weather in July – the main reason for a general drop across the province. In September Premier Lord announced that $2.2 million would be invested in the peninsula in the next fiscal year, including $546,748 for tourism projects. The funds would come from a five-year $25 million Acadian Peninsula Economic Development Fund set up the previous year. In June he was in Bathurst to help announce Can-Jet's news that it had chosen the city to establish a call centre that would employ 150 people. A few days before, the ICT group said it would open a call centre in Miramichi that would employ from 300 to 400. With more than 12,000 now working in this sector, Peter Mesheau, the minister of investment and exports, seemed to agree with a statement by his colleague, Norman McFarlane, minister of training and employment, that there was a shortage of call-centre workers by stating in November that the government was shifting its focus away from telephone contact centres to internet-based 'e-commerce' facilities like the CIBC call centre being established in Fredericton.

The north-south tug of war surfaced in two other issues: natural gas routes and airports for discount carriers. On 22 May Bathurst was the scene of yet another protest march when 225 people voiced their demands for a natural-gas line to tap the resources already moving from the Sable Island field. The Belgian firm Tractabel, which had announced in December 1998 that it and NB Power planned to build a 350-megawatt natural-gas-fired plant at Belledune, still had not settled with U.S. interests to access their transmission lines. In June, less than a month after seven cities formed a common front to negotiate compensation from Enbridge Gas for tearing up streets and sidewalks to lay its pipe, Fredericton became the first New Brunswick city to reach a deal with Enbridge whereby the firm would assume the costs for installing and operating its natural-gas system within the city. Enbridge had already agreed to pay the province $100 million over the next twenty years, and Finance Minister Betts indicated his willingness to talk to municipal representatives on how to share this revenue. By the year's end, Enbridge gas was expected to be flowing in Moncton and Saint John as well as Fredericton.

The provincial capital was less successful in the rapidly changing world of air transport, losing out to Moncton in a bid to have discount carrier CanJet use its facility. Moncton also was chosen by WestJet, but New Brunswick's three major airports all reported they were losing money after being privatized during the year.

The possible privatization of all or part of NB Power seemed a growing possibility in mid-July after the Liberal Opposition leader Camille Theriault released a leaked consultant's report that advised the government to sell off separately individual parts of the Crown-owned facility. In January, officials of two firms toured the coal-fired generators at

Grand Lake. While Premier Lord said his government was not negotiating with any possible purchaser, this didn't rule out 'hosting tours.' In March, NB Power's CEO James Hankinson admitted 'it's clearly a good option' to have a private partner to help finance a $500 million refit to extend the life of Point Lepreau, the region's only nuclear station, due for an overhaul by 2006, if not earlier (*Telegraph Journal*, 1 March). A few days later, NB Power decided to reduce its proposed rate hike from 5 per cent to 3 per cent after Premier Lord warned that if the rate jump was not kept at 4 per cent he would order a full and public review of the increase application.

Late Throne Speech a sign of the times

In the pre-McKenna era when New Brunswick had a strong opposition, the natural progression of events was a spring legislative session featuring a Throne Speech followed by a budget and then a vigorous debate. Since the advent of executive-style government, with the most important policy statements being issued early in the calendar year via carefully staged meet-the-press scenarios, the Legislature's function has rapidly diminished. Thus, in true Orwellian fashion, New Brunswickers get a Throne Speech delivered in mid-November calling for a return of 'people power.' It featured a provincial referendum on video lottery terminals, a re-establishment of elected school boards, new regional health authorities, and more public input on setting judges' salaries. As he admitted in a pre–Throne Speech news conference, Premier Lord acknowledged that 'over the past few years, there has been too much centralization of government and too much power given to one man. That will change' (*Daily Gleaner*, 15 November). As veteran political commentator Don Richardson noted, '[I]t requires as much political will to give up power as it does to accumulate it' (*Daily Gleaner*, 15 November). In their speeches, both Camille Theriault and Elizabeth Weir complained that the Throne Speech ignored the health-care system. As for the video lottery terminals, earlier reports showed that these popular gambling machines had poured $55 million into provincial revenues in the last fiscal year. Still, Premier Lord told the House on 8 December that his government would abide by the people's verdict on 14 May 2001. It would be the first province-wide referendum since the late 1960s, when citizens voted against lowering the voting age to eighteen from twenty-one, a decision that was reversed later by the Hatfield government.

PETER EDWARD BUKER

Prince Edward Island

The year 2000 in Prince Edward Island was shaped by three elections – municipal, provincial, and federal – leading to an electoral endorsement of the status quo. These results reflected the generally healthy economy of the Island, which only faltered near the end of 2000 with the U.S. import ban of PEI potatoes. There was a steady flow of progressive legislative change following the provincial election and the renewed confidence given by the overwhelming voter support shown to Pat Binns' Conservative government.

The economy

Estimated economic growth in PEI for 2000 was 2.9 per cent, with a total GDP of $3.2 billion; by comparison, the national GDP growth rate was 4.7 per cent. There was increased employment, rising personal income, and improved export performance. Island employment grew by 5.2 per cent, with an average of 64,500 people employed – a workforce participation rate of 66.9 per cent. The unemployment rate dropped 2.4 percentage points from the previous year to 12 per cent in 2000. The Island's population was 138,928 people, an increase of 0.9 per cent. Employment in the public sector, including education, health, and social services, continued to grow, accounting for 35 per cent of total PEI employment in 2000.

Consumer prices increased an average of 4.1 per cent compared to the national average of 2.7 per cent, the difference being attributable to PEI's relatively high dependence on oil that had shown significant price increases in 2000. Retail sales were over $1.23 billion, an increase of 6.4 per cent from 1999. Exports increased by 20 per cent, mostly in food products, but also significantly in machinery and equipment and forestry products. The number of tourists decreased by 7.1 per cent because of inclement weather, high gasoline prices, and the competition of Nova Scotia's Tall Ships celebration; however, total tourist expenditures remained similar to the previous year at $301 million.

Statistics Canada reported that investment in PEI increased 3.3 per cent to $534.3 million in 2000; this increase came principally from the housing, retail, and primary sectors. For example, retail development in Charlottetown was a record $43 million in issued building permits, up by over 21 per cent from 1999, housing starts were up to 710 compared to 616 in 1999, and Rodd's Crowbush Golf and Beach Resort, an $8 million deluxe hotel and cottages facility, began construction. Building permits in the Town of Montague broke a record, totalling more than $5 million, there being an estimated $30 million invested in the Montague region for new shipyard contracts and a nutraceutical operation in Lorne Valley in 2000. An $8 million Federal Addiction Research facility was also being constructed in Montague.

The total value of fish landings was $139 million, up 5.4 per cent from 1999, although revenue from lobster landings fell 3.6 per cent to $85.8 million, despite a 3 per cent increase in catch. Wood-industry production showed a decrease of 10 per cent to $55 million and primary forest products decreased by 7 per cent, attributable in part to a major sawmill reducing its production to upgrade its facility. On 29 June Prime Minister Chrétien refused to rescind the federal decisions to grant PEI a shrimp licence, in spite of opposition to Newfoundland interests; the PEI quota accounted for about 1 per cent of the total, and Newfoundland 70 per cent.

In the agricultural sector, potato receipts declined 19 per cent due to lower prices and the U.S. ban in late 2000 of potato imports; this resulted in a decline of 8.3 per cent in total farm receipts to $318 million. Livestock receipts were up 10 per cent to an all-time high of $117.3 million, and dairy receipts increased 4.1 per cent to $51 million. Cattle receipts and hog receipts both increased.

The most dramatic economic news of 2000 was the 'Potato Wart Crisis.' On 20 October potato wart was discovered in a small corner of a field in Travellers Rest, Prince County. Potato wart is a fungal disease that leaves potatoes unmarketable, and the small patch of infected potatoes was quickly isolated and contained. The detection of potato wart, however, soon became significant, as it provided reason for a U.S. ban of PEI table and seed potatoes. The crisis in the potato industry that ensued caused strident political reaction throughout November and December, as both federal Liberal and provincial Conservative politicians joined ranks to lobby Canadian and U.S. politicians and officials to remove the U.S. ban. The ban remained in place despite carefully researched scientific findings of the Canadian Food Inspection Agency that the disease had not and would not spread beyond that one small corner. The ban helped U.S. potato producers reap the lucrative rewards generated by the U.S. Thanksgiving and Christmas consumer markets. PEI Agriculture and Forestry Minister Mitch Murphy fought vehemently to have the U.S. ban lifted and demanded that the federal government retaliate by banning U.S.-produced potatoes from the Canadian market. The issue was fraught with dashed hopes of resolution; an alleged deal to lift the ban was announced on 16 December, but PEI trucks were turned away at the Maine border the next day. The United States also demanded that PEI potato producers be stopped from shipping seed potatoes interprovincially in Canada as well. A 29 December U.S. offer to drop the ban at the end of 2000 was subject to conditions that included washing potatoes to remove all dirt, treating potatoes with a sprout inhibitor, only shipping them in clearly labelled 'Product of PEI' bags of fifty pounds or less, and not shipping any seed potatoes. The U.S. ban was still in place at the end of the year. It was estimated that it had cost PEI $22 million in 2000, and could cost much more, and there was pressure in the provincial legislature to offer financial assistance to potato farmers. By the end of 2000, the province had announced compensation for some of the loss, and Ottawa was considering aid as well as retaliation. The U.S. ban was universally seen in PEI as the pursuit of a political agenda, not a scientific one. It was regarded as an opportunistic and protectionist trade ploy on the part of the U.S. potato growers' interests. The issue remained unresolved at the end of 2000.

Fiscal events

At the end of 2000, provincial finances showed a 5.7 per cent increase in total revenue to $900.4 million, leaving an annual deficit of $5.4 million and a 3.4 per cent increase in net debt to $1,024.3 million. The deficit is in contrast to a Budget Speech estimate earlier in 2000, when provincial treasurer Pat Mella's 2000–1 budget projected a modest surplus of $219,300, with $882.6 million in spending offsetting revenues of $882.8 million.

In the Legislature's spring session, agricultural tax exemptions were broadened. Treasurer Mella introduced on 23 May her first budget of the new mandate, which was essentially the same as the one presented on 17 March before the election. Ms Mella announced increased funding for education at all levels, including kindergarten. In the fall sitting, the provincial income tax rate was reduced to 57.5 per cent from 58.5 per cent and a low-income tax reduction program was introduced. This new program reduced or eliminated taxes for more than 17,000 filers, exempting 4,860 of the poorest taxpayers from the tax roll. It was based on a new structure that would uncouple the provincial income tax system from the federal system in 2001, but retain federal rates and thresholds. The resulting tax breaks, combined with the previous month's breaks given by federal Finance Minister Paul Martin, were projected to save Islanders $41 million in 2001.

Paul Martin met with the provincial finance ministers for the Atlantic Provinces on 14 January in Charlottetown. Mr Martin was asked for more money in equalization payments and transfer payments to Atlantic Canada, and urged to restore social transfer funding to 1994–5 levels. On 29 June Prime Minister Chrétien announced a five-year $700 million fund allegedly aimed at alleviating Atlantic Canadian dependency, but it was widely thought of as a pre-election strategy. Administered by the Atlantic Canada Opportunities Agency, the fund was to go into research and rural and community development.

The Legislature and politics

In 2000 the PEI electorate went to the polls three times: on 17 April for a provincial election, on 6 November for municipal elections, and on 27 November for the federal election. The generalized results of all three elections were to re-elect incumbents.

Premier Pat Binns called the provincial election for 17 April on 22 March. According to Premier Binns, the key issues were health care, education, jobs, and strengthening Island communities. Polls indicated an easy win for Mr Binns' Conservatives, who went into the election with eighteen seats, versus seven Liberal seats and one NDP. The election call followed closely on the Binns government's 17 March 'good news budget,' which included tax breaks and spending increases strategically designed to please a wide spectrum of the electorate, including the promise of a more than $12 million spending increase in health care and education.

The period leading up to the election was coloured by the booming economy and an uneventful campaign; the Tory's cautious, low-key campaign and lack of substantive issues was typified by Mr Binns' lacklustre slogan 'Let's Continue.' The 13 April televised leadership debate between Liberal leader Wayne Carew, NDP leader Herb Dickieson, and Premier Pat Binns weakly brought to the fore the ingrained

PEI phenomenon of patronage, and the wider issue of health care, especially the shortage of physicians, nurses, and other health-care professionals in PEI. In general, however, the campaigns failed to capture the electorate's imagination and did not succeed in identifying clear public-policy issues about which a meaningful election campaign could be fought.

The campaign resulted in the re-election of the Conservative government of Pat Binns with a landslide majority, the party winning all but one seat, including even the former Liberal bastion of West Prince County. Pat Binns' Conservatives trounced Wayne Carew's Liberals, but they won NDP leader Herb Dickieson's riding by only 22 votes. The one re-elected Liberal member was North River–Rice Point MLA Ron MacKinley, a colourful and outspoken fifteen-year veteran of the Legislature. The Tory victory was so complete that it took only thirty-four minutes for the CBC to proclaim the election of a majority government; thus, twenty-six of the Legislature's twenty-seven seats were won by Conservatives, making for a very lopsided house. In the aftermath of this win, Pat Binns, Premier since 1996, attributed his electoral good fortune to the buoyant economy, a drop in the unemployment rate, and sound fiscal management. Former Summerside car dealer and hospital administrator Wayne Carew, on the other hand, was widely thought to have been hobbled by inexperienced candidates and an inability to capture the electorate's interest. Mr Carew, who had been acclaimed leader of the Liberal Party in March of 1999, resigned from that position on 16 October due to mounting pressure from within his party; MLA Ron MacKinley was left as acting leader. Mr Carew was the first Liberal leader in PEI who did not become premier.

On 1 May Premier Binns announced his new cabinet; four veteran ministers were relegated to the back benches, while former minister Mildred Dover was acclaimed as Speaker of the Legislature on 11 May. Premier Binns spread cabinet posts across the province; new were Jamie Ballem as minister of health and social services, Greg Deighan as minister of tourism, Jeff Lantz in the portfolios of attorney general and education, and Gail Shea as minister of community and cultural affairs. Pat Mella remained as treasurer, and Kevin MacAdam became minister of the expanded Department of Fisheries, Aquaculture, and Environment, Mike Currie was made minister of development and technology, Don Mackinnon was minister of transportation and public works, and Mitch Murphy became minister of agriculture and tourism.

The 27 November federal election re-elected Liberals to all four ridings; incumbents Lawrence MacAulay, Joe McGuire, and Wayne Easter kept their seats, while Charlottetown lawyer Shawn Murphy replaced retiring Hillsborough MP George Proud. All Members of Parliament were elected with only moderate pluralities. The remaining votes were split between the Progressive Conservative Party and Canadian Alliance Party candidates. Canada's Solicitor General Lawrence MacAulay made PEI electoral history in Cardigan by being elected for the fourth consecutive time, narrowly defeating Morell–Fortune Bay MLA Kevin MacAdam, a high-profile cabinet minister in the Binns government, who had quit provincial politics to run against Mr MacAulay in the federal election.

The return to the status quo was also evident in the municipal elections of 6 November, in which the incumbent mayors of the municipalities of Charlottetown, Summerside, and Stratford were all re-elected. Three sitting members of Charlottetown's ten-person Council were defeated, and there were six new members.

The Throne Speech of 11 May retold the commitment to health, education, job creation, and fiscal responsibility by the provincial government. The speech confirmed the pre-election commitment to a publicly funded universal kindergarten, which began in the autumn, along with an $11 million increase in health-care funding; this funding meant that Islanders would no longer have to leave the province for Magnetic Resonance Imaging (MRI) scans. Also announced was more subsidization of nursing-home beds, a new Forest Agency, and tax measures aimed specifically at part-time farmers.

On 15 May, PEI's Premier, along with the other three Atlantic Provinces' Premiers, signed an agreement to create the Council of Atlantic Premiers, with the intent of presenting a united front to Ottawa of Atlantic regional concerns, including a desire to change the equalization formula and a need for more federal health-care funds. The newly formed Council also agreed to set up a regional process for drug approvals. Further joint efforts were made on 18 July when the five 'Eastern' Premiers met with governors from six New England states to sign a broad series of pacts for cooperation in disaster relief, allowing easier transference of students between universities, and reduction of air pollution emissions.

Treasurer Pat Mella was criticized in the Legislature for having allowed the government to pay for a $5,000 trip for her and her husband to California's wine country as representatives of PEI's Liquor Control Commission. Although a subsequent investigation determined Ms Mella's trip to be technically legal, she reimbursed the government for her husband's expenses. Premier Binns subsequently announced plans to increase accountability for government business travel.

The twenty-nine-page Speech from the Throne was read by Lieutenant-Governor Gilbert Clements on 23 November. 'Healthy children' was the focus of the speech, which introduced plans for a Premier's council on healthy child development and the intent to establish an early childhood secretariat. Also included were plans to eliminate fees for pre-natal classes, an intent to implement a children's health team, and the introduction of new child protection legislation to replace the existing twenty-year-old Child Protection Act. One provision of this legislation would be to shorten the length of time between when a child deemed at risk is taken into custody and when a judge rules on the case. The child-centred part of the speech also introduced a supported adoption program and an extension of the school milk program to kindergarten pupils. Other aspects of the Throne Speech were promises to reduce air pollution, protect natural areas, and keep the province's water supply safe. There was proposed legislation for further tax cuts for poorer Islanders. The Binns government's recurrent promise of a Freedom of Information and Protection of Privacy Act was also in the speech – PEI being distinguished as the only province in Canada without such legislation.

Other events

Thirty-six-year-old Charlottetown golfer Lori Kane won three LPGA tournaments in 2000, the New Albany Golf Classic, the Mizuno Open, and the Michelob Light Classic. In the summer Ms Kane brought some top women golfers to PEI for a televised skins game at Brudenell River Resort Golf Course, with the provincial government paying the bill for the golfers' flights, meals, and lodging. Lori Kane's contributions were recognized in her receipt of the Bobbie Rosenfield Award as Canada's Female Athlete of the Year for 2000.

The termination of art gallery director Terry Graff's contract by the administration of the Confederation Centre of the Arts created a great deal of animosity within PEI's arts community, and considerable public controversy. Later in the year, Christopher Barlow, the executive director and chief executive officer of the Confederation Centre for the past four-and-a-half years announced that he would be leaving PEI for a position in Ottawa with the Department of Foreign Affairs and International Trade.

On 13 January, in a unanimous decision, the Supreme Court of Canada mandated that the PEI government must pay for French elementary education for francophone families in Summerside. This decision finally ended the efforts started in 1995 by a handful of Summerside-area parents for a French-only school to accommodate forty-seven students of francophone background; the issue was one of constitutional rights versus the fiscal practicalities of schooling a small number of students.

Prince Edward Island became the centre of international news when, on 16 August, Prime Minister Jean Chrétien was hit in the face with a cream pie as he entered an agricultural exhibition in Charlottetown. The pie was pushed in Mr Chrétien's face by twenty-three-year-old Halifax playwright Evan Wade Brown, who claimed he was protesting for social reform on behalf of students and the poor. Mr Brown was charged with assault and released on bail; the incident embarrassed the RCMP and prompted a review of the procedures they followed to protect the Prime Minister.

In January, PEI was hit by an unusual and major tidal surge, attributed by some to the effects of global warming on Island weather. There were no injuries, but there was an estimated $1 million in damages. As a result of the surge, the PEI Emergency Measures Organization received and reviewed 133 damage claims submitted to the government for compensation. In late September, bacteria were discovered in the Charlottetown water system, and the City's 33,000 residents were told to boil their water or consume bottled water until the problem was ameliorated. The 911 emergency system was finally established Island-wide in the year 2000.

Many Islanders were saddened by the death of Angus MacLean, 85, in Charlottetown on 15 February. Mr MacLean had served as the Premier of PEI from 1979 to 1981, was a Member of Parliament from 1951 to 1976, and had been awarded the Order of Canada. His colourful life was remembered in the 1998 book *Making It Home: Memoirs of J. Angus MacLean*, published by Charlottetown's Ragweed Press. The year 2000 also saw the sale of Ragweed Press to an off-Island Canadian publisher.

A considerably public demonstration occurred on 19 May, when about 2,000 people gathered outside of PEI's CBC Television station to show their support for the spectacularly popular provincial supper-hour television news program, *Compass*, which was viewed by a majority of Islanders every weekday evening. The protest was in response to threats from CBC management that *Compass* would be axed as a cost-cutting measure. A 29 May statement by CBC president Robert

Rabinovitch announced that a new half-hour local and half-hour national program would be introduced. Despite passionate opposition to this decision in PEI, this new format was introduced in the fall with predictably large declines in CBC television viewer ratings for that time slot on PEI.

The landmark Charlottetown Forum was demolished in 2000. A $200,000 project designed to recycle excess tires by bailing them into condensed blocks to fight erosion, was introduced by Premier Binns and Public Works Minister Mike Currie in January. Strait Crossing Development was awarded the contract for the Crowbush development by the Binns government in June without a public tender or even submission of a specific proposal.

ROBERT FINBOW

Nova Scotia

Nova Scotia entered the new millennium in festive style with fireworks and the decorative lighting of the refurbished MacDonald Bridge in Halifax. More quietly, but significantly, on New Year's Eve the first natural-gas exports flowed from the offshore fields to markets in New England. Mi'kmaq spiritual leader Noel Knockwood was named the provincial legislature's Sergeant-at-arms, the first Native Canadian to hold this post. Jean Chrétien appointed Myra Freeman as the first female lieutenant-governor. These appointments appeared a fitting way for the increasingly diverse province to enter the new millennium. But the new era began with old problems unresolved, as the new Conservative government of John Hamm struggled to balance the budget and slow the rise in the massive provincial debt. The government's restraint program generated considerable popular anger and made 2000 a turbulent political year.

Health care continued to be a hot-button issue, as a new report showed citizens' frustration with funding restraint, doctor shortages, and wait times. At public meetings in thirty-two communities, the Provincial Health Council heard a general lament of chaos in health care. Long waits in emergency rooms left many frustrated and without essential care. Delays of six weeks to see a family doctor or six months to see a specialist were common. Many communities experienced difficulties, including Truro where obstetricians and pediatricians threatened to withdraw services when experienced nurses were reassigned from the pediatric ward. The recruitment of doctors to rural areas remained a priority, but progress was elusive. Up to four hundred people a month sought new general practitioners, many unsuccessfully. The province lost nursing graduates to other provinces and U.S. states where they received better offers. The federal Liberals promised new funds for health care, but with little immediate impact. Yet a report on Nova Scotia's heavy smoking rate, the highest in Canada, showed the costs of illness could be under citizens' control.

The province's Mi'kmaq asked a provincial court to recognize their right to use all resources on Crown land, which they had never ceded in treaties. The case, involving thirty-five Native loggers charged by forestry officials, drew upon the Supreme Court's Marshall decision, which gave Mi'kmaq the right to fish in provincial waters. Centuries of continuous habitation in the wilderness, and court precedents upholding treaty rights to forests, fish, animals, and land, were cited. This case had implications for the development of oil, minerals, and forestry across the province, but remained unsettled at year's end. Mi'kmaq from Indian Brook came into conflict with non-Native lobster fishers after the Marshall decision. The band wanted to set 5,000 lobster traps off southwestern Nova Scotia, but federal officials feared this would threaten conservation. Fisheries officers seized two Mi'kmaq vessels that were allegedly catching snow crab outside their licence zone. Authorities also investigated complaints that band councillors and chiefs in two Nova Scotia communities received exorbitant salaries and benefits.

Retired judge Fred Kaufmann reported on the problem-plagued prosecutions in the 1992 Westray mine disaster in which charges against company managers and officials were stayed. Judge Kaufmann concluded that a lack of funds for Crown attorneys and the failure of police to protect the site as a crime scene made a successful prosecution impossible. While the province had changed safety rules to prevent a repeat of the disaster, workers in the offshore sector complained of loopholes in federal and provincial regulations that still required employees to work in unsafe conditions. Simulations of the crash of Swissair flight 111 in 1998 indicated that the plane may have been able to fly, but that the pilots lost control in the darkness after electrical systems failed. The aircraft could likely have landed safely if it had not turned back to sea to dump fuel; the airlines revised procedures to allow for quick emergency landings when smoke was detected. The cause of the fire was unclear, despite reconstruction of the wreckage. Swissair paid fishers who had lost income when barred from coastal waters during the lengthy recovery efforts. Relatives of 229 victims and crew gathered near Peggy's Cove to mark the second anniversary of the crash.

The Premier refused calls for an inquiry into the $56 million fund to compensate alleged victims of abuse in provincial youth centres, despite a new Justice Department report refuting claims of widespread abuse. The report criticized the government program for encouraging false claims with promises of up to $120,000 in compensation. The government ran into trouble for trying to conceal the Justice Department report. Premier Hamm appointed Judge Kaufmann to conduct an informal inquiry as police investigated whether fraudsters had claimed compensation based on false claims. The NDP claimed the issue needed a judicial inquiry to determine the actual extent of abuse, and to address possible fraudulent claims. The union representing youth-centre workers wanted a public inquiry to restore reputations and provide restitution to those falsely accused, many of whose lives had been ruined (*Chronicle-Herald*, 27 October).

Politics

Premier Hamm pursued a moderate version of the 'common sense revolution.' He presided over cuts to health-care and education spending, and sliced 1,000 jobs from the civil service. The Premier insisted that spending restraint was needed to provide balanced budgets since the province trailed most others in deficit fighting and debt reduction. But Premier Hamm's was a compromised version of restraint, leading one commentator to refer to his 'reign of ambiguity' (*Chronicle-Herald*, 23 December). A task force suggested a moderate approach, relying on attrition and slower deficit and debt reduction, while avoiding the painful 'shock therapy' used in Ontario by Mike Harris. The government backed off some of its commitments on privatization and eliminated the private-public partnerships in school construction, blamed for cost overruns.

The government announced the amalgamation or elimination of five of fifteen departments, and privatization of some provincial enterprises. Several recently created departments, once touted as examples of government modernization, were eliminated or merged, including Environment, Aboriginal Affairs, Human Resources, Housing and Municipal Affairs, the Petroleum Directorate, and the Technology and Science Secretariat. The government sought to eliminate many 'optional' programs and shore up critical services like health and education. A leaner civil service would be more in keeping with the province's means, but job cuts would focus on administrators, not front-line service providers. In June the government reported plans to reduce or eliminate one-third of its 1,126 programs. Cuts to student employment and loan programs were assailed for reducing access to higher education when tuition was increasing rapidly. Critics complained that family violence-prevention programs were cut while transition houses remained strapped for cash. Insurance companies were asked to pick up costs for artificial limbs and for drugs for cancer, diabetes, and cystic fibrosis. Also controversial were cuts in rural agricultural offices, jails, and courts. Premier Hamm had pledged to preserve rural services in any restructuring. Polls showed increased dissatisfaction with the Premier's performance (*Chronicle-Herald*, 14 June).

With the Conservative majority solid, both Opposition leaders decided to step down. Former premier Russell MacLellan announced that he would resign as leader on 30 June. The Liberals selected MLA Wayne Gaudet as interim leader. Facing a mandatory leadership review and coming off a poor showing in two election campaigns as leader, Mr MacLellan retired from the House in the fall. The Liberals were briefly forced out of their shared status as Official Opposition when a judge ruled that irregularities in Cape Breton East required a by-election, though he exonerated Liberal campaign workers on charges of intimidation of voters in a special-care group home. In the April by-election, Liberal Dave Wilson again took the seat.

In 1997 Robert Chisholm had led the NDP to a record nineteen seats, tied with the governing Liberals and in Official Opposition status for the first time. However, the party dropped to eleven seats in the June 1999 election, prompting Mr Chisholm's unexpected resignation. The NDP selected former MLA Helen MacDonald, a long-time party activist from Cape Breton who had lost her seat by only 100 votes, as its new leader. She did not ask any of the sitting NDP MLAs to surrender their seat so she could seek election to the House in a by-election, though party activists feared this would weaken her political presence. Cape Breton MLA John Macdonnell served as acting leader on the floor of the House. The NDP lost Halifax-area MLA Eileen O'Connell to cancer, but cabinet minister John Chattaway recovered after eleven hours of surgery for a brain aneurysm.

On the federal scene in September, Progressive Conservative Leader Joe Clark won a by-election in Kings-Hants when MP Scott Brison resigned to make way for his leader. The Liberals sought to improve their standing over the 1997 election, when they lost all of their seats in the province. The Chrétien government announced a string of spending initiatives to help the party recover in a region where they had lost twenty-one of their thirty-one seats in the 1997 contest. Liberal activists spoke off the record about a return to pork-barrel politics in announcing spending for employment creation in Cape Breton and other popular initiatives. Proposed Employment Insurance changes restored benefits to seasonal workers, reduced clawback for higher earners, gave more tolerance to repeat claimants, and reduced premiums. These amendments were long called for in the region, reversing earlier changes by the Chrétien government, but the late date of introduction of the bill prevented passage before a fall election.

In the federal election in November, the Liberal strategy met with some success. Two ridings in Cape Breton were won from the NDP by Liberal rookies. Notable newcomers included Robert Thibault, an Acadian lawyer, who won the close race in Western Nova, defeating a Tory incumbent. Geoff Regan, son of the former premier Gerald Regan, took back Halifax West from the NDP. But former provincial minister Bernie Boudreau, now federal minister responsible for the Atlantic Canada Opportunities Agency, who took the risky step of resigning from the Senate to run as a parachute candidate in the Dartmouth riding, was defeated. Despite their losses, both the Tories and the NDP managed to hold on to official party status by winning enough Nova Scotia seats. The new Canadian Alliance made little impression in a region it alienated through stereotypical comments on regional dependency; one party strategist criticized the region's 'lazy' residents who were always looking for 'handouts' (*Chronicle-Herald*, 7 October).

The Legislature

The legislative agenda was dominated by the fiscal restraint program. In his April budget, Finance Minister Neil LeBlanc was forced to admit to a worse fiscal situation than predicted, as Canada's most debt-ridden province could not join others in cutting taxes or restoring spending to health and education. Instead of a $2.3 million surplus forecast by the Liberals, the new government expected a deficit of $767 million, once Crown corporation losses were included. The government claimed that it had to cut 1,600 civil service jobs, reduce other spending by $295 million, and sell off assets. This included partial privatization of the liquor commission: eight private rural outlets and private specialty stores were planned. Most job cuts would come through attrition, with severance packages to be paid out of an $88 million restructuring fund. Critics assailed the government for failing to provide details of the job cuts, which Premier Hamm said would be available only after employees were notified.

Mr LeBlanc aimed to slash the deficit to $268.1 million in this fiscal year, and promised a balanced budget by 2003. Cuts would average 10 per cent across departments, though health and education would be cut only 3 per cent. Opposition leaders claimed the government was exaggerating its fiscal problems to pave the way for spending cuts. By the fall, Mr LeBlanc's efforts were buoyed by the strong economy, which resulted in an additional $105 million in tax revenues and equalization payments. But the added revenues only reduced the deficit by $8 million, as higher costs for health, hospital, and school boards, losses at Nova Scotia Resources Ltd, and higher debt repayments from the low value of the dollar eroded the gains. The province overspent by $97 million compared to spring estimates, with an embarrassing $30 million accounting error in education.

The government also increased service fees for the 911 system, ambulances, and prescription drugs for seniors to bring in an additional $20 million annually. Opposition critics assailed the drug levy, which might force some seniors to forgo essential medicines. Mr LeBlanc claimed these hikes did not violate the pledge not to raise taxes, since income taxes were left unchanged. But seniors groups complained that seniors would have to choose between prescriptions and heat as high oil prices hit hard; some seniors feared that they would have to sell their homes to make ends meet. The government resisted calls by the NDP to refund the windfall in Blended Sales Tax revenues coming from higher prices for gas and heating fuels, but eventually decided to continue a $50 rebate to low income earners to compensate for high fuel-oil costs.

The Conservatives' restraint policies generated frequent protests, including a day of action in late April that saw record numbers of protesters mass at Province House. Public-sector workers protested at proposed cuts of $200 million from department budgets and the loss of jobs. Demonstrating jail guards interrupted House debates to demand a resumption of contract talks in June. Highway workers picketed against a rumoured privatization of highway maintenance. Eventually the government backed off the plan to privatize Transportation department activities. The nurses' union complained that the six hundred health administrative job cuts would increase nurses' workloads. The Premier defended the cuts, which he said would avoid hundreds of millions in debt servicing charges from accumulated debt. Despite protests, the Conservatives stuck with restraint in the spring session, passing bills extending provincial control over health and education boards, and extended sittings to fourteen hours a day to overcome Opposition stalling.

Angry protests also greeted proposed cuts to education, which threatened teacher layoffs and cuts to popular programs such as art, music, theatre, and French immersion. The government said cuts were needed because of declining birth rates and enrolment in many school districts. Students, parents, teachers, and staff joined demonstrations against the reductions, which school boards estimated would result in seven hundred layoffs and increased class sizes. The government eventually admitted an error in budgeting for teachers, and restored some $33 million to school boards, but this fell short of the $53 million the boards said was required. Some 250 jobs would still be lost through retirements and resignations. The government took over some $20 million in school-board debts, adding to the provincial debt of $11 billion. Legislation also added one seat for a black representative on each school board, to improve relations between the boards and the black community, and to help alleviate racial tensions at schools. While critics rejected a race-based voting system, Mi'kmaq leaders sought similar representation. The government extended free high school completion to adults though a new Nova Scotia School for Adult Learning, to combat adult illiteracy and lack of skilled labour in the knowledge-based economy.

The welfare reform bill, dubbed the Employment Support and Income Assistance Act, combined family benefits and social assistance with increased incentives for recipients to seek employment or training. Benefit rates were reduced and welfare recipients were encouraged to re-enter the workforce, possibly by volunteering. Long-term family benefits for those on social assistance were also reduced. To encourage welfare recipients to return to work, the government allowed them to keep some child benefits while employed. Supporters saw the bill's incentives to work as necessary to reduce dependence on social assistance, but critics termed the provisions mean-spirited, given the difficult struggle to maintain housing and essential services for many low-income families. The Opposition noted the lack of job openings, problems of single parents, and lack of child care, which would remain obstacles to people seeking jobs after this 'punitive' bill took effect. The government was embarrassed when its members accidentally approved giving phones to welfare recipients, which would have cost $12 million; a second vote reversed the mistake.

It was a relatively scandal-free year in provincial politics. But the government caucus faced division when the NDP leaked a confidential letter from backbench MLA Mark Parent objecting to government plans to move Department of Health offices to property owned by the Sobey family; Mr Parent left the Legislature temporarily after the embarrassing leak. A secretive process on the classification of Crown lands as protected areas drew criticism as well. When an independent commission awarded MLAs a 3 per cent raise, the Conservatives announced they would give theirs to charity. A controversial bill allowing municipal bylaws to empower police to seize the vehicles of persons attempting to pick up prostitutes was reintroduced, despite concerns over legal rights. A bill extended parental leave to one year to match a federal extension of benefits, and another gave alimony and maintenance rights to same-sex couples, as mandated by the court.

The economy

A Conference Board of Canada report said that Nova Scotia's economy trailed all provinces in economic growth in 2000, at 1.9 per cent. This sluggishness was attributed to a 43 per cent drop in non-residential construction, mostly owing to the completion of several major offshore energy-related projects. When the Sable projects were factored out, growth rates of 3.8 per cent placed Nova Scotia at the middle of all provinces. Economists believed the delay in income tax cuts relative to other provinces also contributed to weaker growth, but the government insisted that deficits must be eliminated before taxes could be reduced (*Chronicle-Herald*, 23 November). Still, the province performed better than expected. Construction on consumer distribution systems for natural gas provided some stimulus. A boom in apartment and condominium construction in Halifax sustained employment, though the housing market slowed later in the year and overall employment in Metro dropped by some 5,200 jobs. Exports also performed well, led by natural gas, fish, and forest products, though shipments slowed in the second half. Tire exports were helped by recalls of rival American products. Consumer purchases tailed off, as elsewhere in Canada. However, the slowdown did not reverse the decline in unemployment, now nearing 9 per cent as 11,000 new jobs were created. Though high gasoline prices limited growth in tourism, the low Canadian dollar continued to make the province an attractive destination (*Atlantic Report*, Winter 2001). The millennium parade of tall ships in Halifax and Sydney boosted tourism.

Economic activity was dominated by the long-awaited arrival of natural gas. An economic milestone was reached when a power plant in Dartmouth, the first local customer, began burning offshore natural gas. Most of the gas, produced in higher volume than expected, was exported to U.S. markets by Maritimes and Northeast Pipelines. This company paid $5,000 in fines and restoration after construction of a river crossing fouled fish habitats during heavy rains. High demand and increased prices encouraged Sable Offshore Energy Inc. and its partner Shell Canada Ltd to plan increased production and further exploration.

But higher prices brought only marginal royalty increases for the province, with greater windfalls expected in the near future. Consumer distribution was held up by a dispute with Sempra gas, which wanted to build rural pipelines on highway shoulders despite concerns about safety and the environment. Continuing losses led the government to plan the sale of its offshore company, Nova Scotia Resources Ltd. Offshore development near the Cabot Strait continued to be delayed by a boundary dispute between Nova Scotia and Newfoundland. Federal Natural Resources Minister Ralph Goodale appointed a three-member arbitration panel to rule on the dispute, which some feared would drive exploration and development to the small French territory of Saint Pierre and Miquelon. Premier Hamm's offer of joint management of the area to allow development while a boundary was decided was rejected by Newfoundland Premier Brian Peckford.

Opposition critics assailed the deal to sell the Sydney steel mill (the fourth such announcement in six years), arguing that the terms were too generous. The government promised to allow the Swiss-based company Duferco to have $21 million in Sysco's account, plus a loan of $4.5 million, which critics said broke an election promise not to pour more public funds into the troubled mill. The company would pay between $10 and $25 million for the plant, which taxpayers had supported at a cost of hundreds of millions. If Duferco met employment and production targets for five years, it would not have to pay a $15 million performance fee, which would reduce the province's take to $7.6 million. Employment would drop from 500 to between 215 and 400; the United Steel Workers had backed a rival plan that they claimed would maintain current jobs. Provincial taxpayers had to fund severance and pension benefits, and the environmental cleanup of the Sydney tar ponds. The bill's provisions overriding provincial laws and restricting the rights to sue for environmental and health effects were called dangerous precedents by the Opposition. Duferco was still negotiating with Nova Scotia Power on electricity rates at year's end.

The government aimed to avoid such political boondoggles in the future, and take politics out of the process, by creating a private-sector board to oversee grants to industry. Under the plan, an independent Nova Scotia Business Inc. would be created with a private board to dispense government assistance to business in a non-political fashion. But Opposition critics feared the private-sector appointees would have too much power, and simply provide more economic largesse to insiders. In this light, a $3.5 million tax rebate to the grocery giant Sobey's raised eyebrows, though it helped to attract new jobs (*Chronicle-*

Herald, 16 November). The Halifax Airport Authority took over the province's largest airport from the federal government as a non-profit, private agency, despite having to absorb the costs of environmental impacts from pyritic slate runoff. Halifax's port facilities were modernized to deal with Post-Panamax vessels, a new generation of large container ships. New call centres boosted employment in Halifax and other centres.

Intergovernmental relations

Premier Hamm pressed his 'campaign for fairness' in search of more revenue from the federal government for health, education, and highways. The Premier called for fairer equalization payments to address the province's fiscal needs, worsened as a result of up to $1 billion in reduced federal transfers under the Chrétien Liberal government. As well, he wanted to revise the deal on offshore oil and gas revenues, which clawed back royalties against the province's equalization entitlements, meaning that 70 per cent of offshore revenues flowed to Ottawa. Premier Hamm felt that future projects would make this arrangement quite lucrative, though basing some royalties on profits rather than production allowed companies to juggle costs to minimize royalty payments. He also complained that the Liberals had found money for a highway outside of Montreal beyond the infrastructure commitments made to the provinces, and so should be able to afford $135 million for twinning the dangerous Highway 101 through the Annapolis Valley. The federal government was also criticized for its failure to make good on promises to strengthen its support for families and alleviate child poverty. A Nova Scotia report concluded that almost one in five children lived in poverty, with a rate of 77.5 per cent in families of single mothers. The rate had increased 16 per cent in the past decade, despite federal promises of national action. However, the province did welcome the $700 million Atlantic Innovation Fund announced by Ottawa in the run-up to the fall election.

Nova Scotia decided to set its income tax rate independently of Ottawa to make independent fiscal decisions and avoid a loss of revenues as federal taxes were reduced. Opposition leaders called this move a disguised tax increase, since provincial residents would not benefit from inflation adjustments on tax brackets. Premier Hamm argued that the province's high deficits made this revenue essential, since Ottawa was not restoring transfers to sufficient levels despite its surpluses. However, federal tax cuts were expected to help the province as these targeted lower- and middle-income families, and included more generous child tax credits. Despite a campaign pledge, the Tories also decided that pulling out of the blended sales tax with Ottawa and its Atlantic neighbours was not viable. Premier Hamm still sought flexibility on rates and taxable items, but felt that re-establishing a separate tax would be costly and cumbersome for business.

Nova Scotia joined with New Brunswick, Prince Edward Island, and Newfoundland to form the Council of Atlantic Premiers, to help the region speak with one voice in negotiations with Ottawa and other provinces. The Council addressed a range of issues, including cuts to CBC regional news programs and reduced service by national airlines. While earlier cooperation efforts had foundered on disputes over lottery funds, location of joint police training facilities, and other issues, the Premiers pledged more durable cooperation to promote prosperity. Joint tourism promotion and trade missions to the United States were among the avenues for regional cooperation. Costs of services could be reduced through joint school curricula, textbooks, and other economies of scale. The province resolved a dispute with its neighbours over the Atlantic Lottery Corporation, and announced that the Nova Scotia Gaming Corporation would control ALC local activities.

The Council joined other provinces in advocating restoration of health-care funds, and its members cooperated on drug approvals and purchases, to help offset climbing costs. Premier Hamm called for a larger health transfer from Ottawa because of Nova Scotians' aging population, which was more prone to illness and needed more medical care. Health Minister Jaime Muir argued that the province could not find sufficient administrative savings and that Ottawa had to invest more resources. However, he sounded a conciliatory note in agreeing with federal Health Minister Allan Rock that future spending should be used in innovative ways. The province applied for funds to train rural physicians in mental health issues to compensate for the lack of psychiatric practitioners. Nova Scotia welcomed federal support for home care, community health centres, and long-term-care facilities. Premier Hamm felt a deal that would transfer $626 million more over five years was inadequate, as it would still not permit equal access to health care across the country.

The Council of Atlantic Premiers pressed the Chrétien Liberals to review equalization payments to help have-not provinces provide service levels comparable to those in wealthier regions. The current formula did not meet the constitutional guarantee of equitable services, and Premier Hamm sought the removal of caps on equalization increases and a recalculation of entitlements based on the fiscal capacity of all ten provinces, not just the middle-ranking five. He requested as well $120 million in additional equalization under a fair scheme recognizing the province's unique costs in health, post-secondary education, and other services. Federal Finance Minister Paul Martin would only commit to relax the overall $10 billion cap on equalization, because of stronger revenues from Ontario's high growth rate, which would provide an additional $5 million. Premier Hamm stressed the importance of making the constitutional guarantee on equalization more meaningful in practice, and argued that inequality between rich and poor provinces was a greater threat to national unity than Quebec separatism (*Chronicle-Herald*, 22 November).

PETER NEARY AND MELVIN BAKER

Newfoundland and Labrador

In Canada the millennium year 2000 began, as all years begin, in Newfoundland. To mark the occasion the government sponsored a First Light Celebration throughout the province. On the waterfront in St John's there was a televised Debut 2000 event on 31 December, featuring a Countdown Concert. The St John's celebration attracted international attention and gave the province a unique opportunity, which was not missed, to show itself to advantage. In the same spirit, Newfoundland and Labrador joined enthusiastically in various international celebrations during 2000 to mark the one thousandth anniversary of the voyage of the Viking adventurer Leif Ericsson to the region. The high point, on 28 July, was the arrival of the *Islendingur*, a replica of a Viking longship, at L'Anse aux Meadows, Newfoundland, the site of a Viking settlement ca. AD 1000. This was an occasion made for the television camera. 'Vikings! 1000 Years: Make the Journey,' the name given to the overall celebration, featured a Web site, enjoyed federal, provincial, and corporate sponsorship, and exemplified the growing importance of heritage for tourism. From 15 to 24 September the Viking International Millennium Symposium was held at St John's, L'Anse aux Meadows, and the Labrador Straits.

Politically, the year began quietly. On 13 January Kelvin Parsons (Burgeo and La Poile) joined the cabinet as minister of justice and four other ministers changed portfolios. On 17 February Premier Brian Tobin visited Corner Brook for the launch of the government's Strategic Social Plan for the region. According to a news release, the purpose of the plan was to promote 'a new way of working together at the regional level' and 'a long term approach to addressing social and economic development, together, on a community and regional basis' (Executive Council, *News Release*, 17 February). By contrast, Municipal Affairs Minister Joan-Marie Aylward announced on 22 February that 130 elected local officials, twenty-one of them mayors, had been removed from office for being in arrears on their own local taxes. On

28 February, Premier Tobin sought to draw the curtain on some old business when he welcomed the decision of the Newfoundland Court of Appeal upholding the constitutionality of the amended Term 17 of the 1948 Terms of Union with Canada. The amendment had made possible the ending of denominational education in the province. 'Now is the time,' the Premier ventured, 'to put this chapter behind us' (Executive Council, *News Release*, 28 February).

The Forty-Fourth General Assembly, elected in 1999, began its second session on Tuesday, 14 March. The Speech from the Throne, read by Lieutenant-Governor A. Maxwell House, reaffirmed the government's commitment to reduce income tax and obtain favourable agreements for the province in relation to the development of the nickel deposit at Voisey's Bay and the waterpower of the Lower Churchill River, both in Labrador. When it got down to business, the House, which initially sat until 13 April and then from 1 to 11 May and 4 to 14 December, passed forty-one bills on a wide range of subjects, including collective bargaining in the fishing industry, mining, labour standards, and urban and rural planning. By an Act given assent on 14 December the Legislature established a Holocaust Memorial Day in the province. The budget speech was delivered by Finance Minister Lloyd Matthews on 22 March. He forecast a deficit of $34.7 million on a current account gross expenditure of $3,447.1 million, a capital account gross expenditure of $261.9 million, and provision for a contingency reserve of $30 million. The 2000–1 budget increased health-care funding by $87.5 million, further reduced payroll taxes, and froze post-secondary tuition for a second year.

On 25 April the Liberals retained Trinity North in a by-election occasioned by the resignation of Doug Oldford. The result was Ross Wiseman (Liberal), 2,654 (48.1 per cent); Bruce Stagg (Progressive Conservative), 2,463 (44.7 per cent); and Perry Feltham (New Democratic Party), 398 (7.2 per cent). Then, on 15 May, in a close and hard-fought contest, Loyola Hearn managed to hang on to St John's West for the Progressive Conservatives in a federal by-election. This seat had become vacant through the resignation of Charlie Power; the by-election featured as a candidate the professional wrestler Sailor White. Mr Hearn's principal opponent, however, was the actor Greg Malone, of *Codco* fame, who ran for the New Democratic Party. The final result was Loyola Hearn (PC), 11,392 (35.5 per cent); Greg Malone (NDP), 11,036 (34.4 per cent); Anthony G. Sparrow (Liberal), 8,032 (25 per cent); Frank Hall (Canadian Alliance), 1,315 (4.1 per cent); and Sailor E. White (no affiliation), 332 (1 per cent). No sooner had the dust settled from this battle than Ed Byrne, citing family responsibilities, announced on 12 June his resignation as leader of the provincial Progressive Conservatives. From Calgary, where he was attending the World Petroleum Congress, Premier Tobin praised the outgoing Tory leader as a 'tough competitor ... and hard-hitting Leader of the Opposition,' but someone who had brought 'fairness and decency' to even the most heated of their House of Assembly debates (Executive Council, *News Release*, 12 June). On 4 August the Conservatives announced a leadership convention for 6–8 April 2001, in St John's. However, by the end of the year only one candidate had announced for the position: the St John's lawyer and businessman Danny Williams, who had done well in federally licensed cable television.

Economically, there was much good news for the province in 2000 but cautionary notes were also sounded. Oil production led the way in economic growth, with impressive gains also again being made in tourism. In April Human Resources and Employment Minister Julie Bettney welcomed the news from Statistics Canada that in 1999 the population of the province had grown for the first time in seven years, mainly because of in-migration. In June Premier Tobin announced that Convergys Corporation of Cincinnati, Ohio, would open a 575–seat call centre – the largest such facility in the province – in a former department store building on Torbay Road, St John's. This would create 1,000 jobs and showed that Newfoundland and Labrador had 'an excellent work force, a business friendly environment and a competitive business location' (Industry, Trade and Technology, *News Release*, 8 June). Important progress was also made during the year in the rebuilding of the fishing industry following the groundfish moratorium of 1992. In December it was reported that the value of seafood production had exceeded $1 billion for the second consecutive year and that direct and indirect employment in the fishing industry stood at 28,000 persons.

On the other hand, the breakthroughs long sought by the province in negotiations with Inco Ltd about Voisey's Bay nickel and with Quebec about Lower Churchill power failed to materialize in 2000. On 11 January, following a round of meetings with Inco officials, Premier Tobin announced that the province had decided to suspend negotiations with the company. 'We have come to the mutual conclusion,' he pronounced, 'that – for now – discussions on the development of Voisey's Bay during the 2000 construction season will be suspended ... At this time the elements we require to make this deal viable for the province are just not there. We require a commitment to full processing in the province, from ore to finished nickel metal ... At this point, Inco cannot make that commitment, and we will not agree to less' (Executive Council, *News Release*, 11 January). On 2 February the Premier commented that the stumbling block in the recent round of talks had been the company's retreat 'from its plans to build a smelter and refinery in the province using proven technology' (Executive Council, *News Release*, 2 February). On 17 February Inco upped the ante on the province by scaling back its office in St John's. There was also talk of the company shifting its development focus from Voisey's Bay to New Caledonia, but none of this made any difference. In September Mines and Energy Minister Paul Dicks said that no talks with Inco had taken place since January and that no further talks were scheduled.

Negotiations with Quebec about the Lower Churchill development, in progress since 9 March 1998, also followed a tortuous course in 2000. On 10 May, having earlier expressed optimism about a possible agreement, Premier Tobin told the Legislature that the province was prepared to work with another partner 'if the deal on the table with Quebec' was 'not acceptable to the people of Newfoundland and Labrador' (*Hansard*, 10 May). On 16 May, however, he and Premier Lucien Bouchard issued a conciliatory joint statement that described the Lower Churchill project as 'a very interesting and competitive opportunity for both parties.' On the other hand, rapid changes in the electricity market brought on by deregulation had made it 'difficult to lock in a pricing arrangement which would be satisfactory for both parties over the long-term.' Accordingly, fieldwork would be scaled back while the parties continued 'to work on solutions to this issue' (Executive Council, *News Release*, 16 May). In sum, there was no deal but the provinces would remain in touch. On 10 November Mr Dicks announced that the province, while keeping its options open, was now also considering a much smaller Churchill River development, which would require Hydro-Québec not as a business partner but as a customer for power.

In federal–provincial and interprovincial relations the year produced mixed results for the province. In February Premier Tobin joined with the other Atlantic Premiers in issuing a statement naming health care their top priority at the Premiers' meeting to be held in Quebec City on 3 February. Another continuing interest of the province in 2000 was an improved national employment insurance program. On 28 February, Intergovernmental Affairs Minister Walter Noel asserted that federal-government employment insurance reform had 'been crippling to individuals and communities' in the province and had 'caused tremendous individual hardship related to the increased entrance requirements associated with the hours-based approach, as well as the combined impacts on their benefits rates of the intensity and divisor rules' (Executive Council, *News Release*, 28 February). There was an urgent need for the federal government 'to find long-term solutions to seasonal unemployment and to make available ... employment insurance funds to finance new measures to extend employment opportunities for seasonal and part-time workers.'

In May the province welcomed the announcement by the federal minister of natural resources of the appointment of an arbitration tribunal to establish a maritime boundary between it and Nova Scotia. Former Supreme Court Justice Gérard La Forest was named to chair the tribunal, to which Leonard Legault and Dr James Crawford were also appointed. Premier Tobin likewise welcomed remarks made in St John's in April by federal Finance Minister Paul Martin that he would look at the possibility of a ten-year holiday on the equalization clawback imposed on the poorer provinces when their resources revenues increased. 'Where is the benefit for Canada,' the Premier asked, 'in keeping Newfoundland dependent on a kind of federal welfare' (*Canadian News Facts*, 6043). With this issue to the fore, on 15 May the Atlantic Premiers signed an agreement in Moncton, New Brunswick, establishing a new Council of Atlantic Premiers and committing the four provinces to 'a strategic cooperation agenda' (Executive Council, *News Release*, 5 May). In September, at the first ministers' meeting, Prime Minister Jean Chrétien committed the federal government to a review of the equalization program; in December the Council of Atlantic Premiers called on Mr Chrétien to hold a first ministers' meeting on equalization in January 2001.

The most abrasive issue for the province vis-à-vis Ottawa in 2000 was fishery policy. The year got off to a good start on 31 January when provincial Fisheries and Aquaculture Minister John Efford and federal Fisheries and Oceans Minister Herb Dhaliwal signed a memorandum of understanding on emerging fisheries development. This display of goodwill, however, did not survive subsequent federal regulatory actions, especially Ottawa's decision (announced in June) to allocate a shrimp quota off Newfoundland to a Prince Edward Island consortium. 'This is a resource that belongs to Newfoundland and Labrador,' Mr Efford publicly protested on 15 June, 'and we've given enough away' (*Canadian News Facts*, 6068). 'The province's rural economy,' he said the next day, had 'been gutted by federal mismanagement of the groundfishery' (Fisheries and Aquaculture, *News Release*, 16 June). In

July the Newfoundland minister strongly criticized the federal department for its failure to tackle the problem of the presumed adverse effect on fish stocks of seal overpopulation. In September he took his case against Ottawa to Toronto, where he addressed the Rotary Club at the Royal York Hotel.

If the province's relationship with Ottawa was occasionally testy during the year, its relationships with the governments of other countries continued to move in promising directions. Building connections abroad had been a provincial priority for some time, and in 2000 notable advances were made in this regard. In April Premier Tobin announced that ten provincial companies would participate in the Team Canada Atlantic Trade Mission to New England scheduled for May, and in July he attended the Conference of New England Governors and Eastern Canadian Premiers in Halifax. On 26 September, during a visit to St John's, Iceland's Minister of Industry and Commerce, Valgerdur Sverrisdóttir, announced that her country would establish a trade office in the province. In October Industry, Trade and Technology Minister Sandra Kelly led a delegation of twenty-three companies and organizations to Ireland. During the delegation's stay there, Taoiseach Bertie Ahearn and Ms Kelly were present for the signing of four agreements between Irish and Newfoundland and Labrador organizations.

In June Prime Minister Chrétien announced an Atlantic Investment Partnership, which would involve the spending of $700 million over five years in support of the region's developing technology economy. Included in the initiative was a $300 million Atlantic Investment Fund to augment university and other research efforts. Then, in October, the federal government announced changes to the employment insurance program that addressed the continuing complaints from the Atlantic region. In the minds of many, all this beneficence could only mean one thing – that a general election would soon be called. On 16 October, with speculation about this at fever pitch across the country, Brian Tobin announced his resignation as Premier of the province at a news conference in St John's. His decision, he said, had been made 'after much soul searching' (Executive Council, *News Release*, 16 October). Later in the day he would be going to Bay Roberts to announce his intention to seek the Liberal nomination in the federal constituency of Bonavista-Trinity-Conception. Thereafter he would immediately travel to Ottawa to be present the next morning as Prime Minister Chrétien continued 'to put forward a vision and a program for Canadians to consider.' The cabinet and caucus, Mr Tobin reported, had unanimously recommended to the lieutenant-governor that Beaton Tulk (Bonavista

North) become Premier until the Liberal Party chose a new leader. In keeping with this advice, Mr Tulk was sworn in as Premier the same day in a ceremony at Government House in St John's. On 17 October Mr Tobin was named federal Minister of Industry.

The announcement of a federal general election followed on 22 October, with voting day scheduled for 27 November. The seven seats to be filled in the province were contested by thirty-two candidates (including three women), with the Liberals, Progressive Conservatives, New Democrats, and Canadian Alliance fielding candidates in all constituencies. Going into the election the Conservatives held St John's East and West and the Liberals the other five seats. The result on 27 November was exactly the same. The popular vote in the province was as follows: Liberals, 103,103 (44.9 per cent); Progressive Conservatives, 79,157 (34.5 per cent); New Democrats, 29,993 (13.1 per cent); Canadian Alliance, 8,837 (3.9 per cent); others, 8,404 (3.6 per cent). Mr Tobin was an easy winner in Bonavista-Trinity-Conception, where he commanded 54.4 per cent of the popular vote. Among the Liberals defeated in the election was Charles Furey, the former provincial minister of tourism, culture and recreation. One of his last acts in this office, on 4 October, was to attend the official ground-breaking ceremony at Fort Townshend, St John's, for the construction of The Rooms, the imaginative $40 million arts centre announced in 1999.

While the federal election campaign was in progress, Premier Tulk was kept busy reorganizing the government and establishing himself in the office that had so unexpectedly come his way. On 1 November he made known that ministers seeking to lead the party – the leadership convention was scheduled for Mount Pearl, 2 and 3 February 2001 – were free to stay in the cabinet provided specified guidelines were followed. By the end of the year three candidates had declared their intention to contest the leadership. They were Mr Efford, Mr Dicks, and Health Minister Roger Grimes.

As Premier, Beaton Tulk retained the post of minister responsible for aboriginal affairs. Much had happened in relation to this portfolio during the year. In January the province was granted standing in the lawsuit of the Nunavik Inuit (Quebec Inuit represented by the Makivik Corporation) against the federal government in the Federal Court. The purpose of the action was to prevent the federal government from ratifying the 1999 Labrador Inuit Association land claims and self-government agreement in principle until overlapping claims were settled. In June Premier Tobin announced that agreement had been reached between the province and the Labrador Inuit Association with respect to 'interim measures to protect lands for a proposed park reserve in the Torngat Mountains area' (Executive Council, *News Release*, 14 June). In September provincial leaders of the Anglican, Presbyterian, Roman Catholic, and United Churches issued an apology for abuse of aboriginals in the past by church officials, but the year closed on a tragic note when five members of one family in the Innu community of Sheshatshiu lost their lives in a house fire in late October. On 26 November, the day before the general election, the federal government made a commitment to open a detoxification centre to treat children in need in Sheshatshiu and Davis Inlet. In making this announcement, Brian Tobin also confirmed Ottawa's commitment to extend the Indian Act to the Innu. On 14 December, after meeting with Chief Simeon Tshakapesh in Ottawa, Indian Affairs and Northern Development Minister Robert Nault announced that he would make a two-day visit to the Labrador Innu in 2001. This was hopeful, but as the year ended, a corrosive Canadian social and economic problem was far from resolution.

Overall, 2000 in Newfoundland and Labrador was a year of cultural celebrations, political surprises, and more shocking revelations about aboriginal life. As the province geared up for two leadership conventions and the one hundredth anniversary of Guglielmo Marconi's reception (on Signal Hill, St John's) of the first transatlantic wireless message, 2001 promised more of the same.

Obituaries 2000

APPLEBAUM, LOUIS (20 April, age 82). Oscar-nominated composer; recipient of a special achievement award at the 1995 Juno Awards ceremony in recognition of his leadership in a host of Canadian arts initiatives.

BAROOTES, EFSTATHIOS (29 July, age 81). Medical doctor and former Conservative senator.

BERGERON, HENRI (10 July, age 75). Radio-Canada broadcaster who opened the network's first television broadcast.

BISSELL, CLAUDE (21 June, age 83). Former president of the University of Toronto and Carleton University; also served as chair of the Canada Council.

BLACK, WESLEY (10 January, age 89). Former British Columbia cabinet minister in the Social Credit government of W.A.C. Bennett.

CAMERON, ROBERT B. (17 February, age 80). Prominent Nova Scotia entrepreneur whose business holdings included steel and newspaper interests.

CHEVALIER, LEO (16 June, age 65). Famed Montreal fashion designer; first designer to be named to the Order of Canada.

CORNELL, WARD (5 February, age 75). Former host of CBC's Hockey Night in Canada, who later served as a senior provincial bureaucrat in Ontario.

COULTHARD, JEAN (9 March, age 92). Renowned composer who taught at the University of British Columbia; recipient of the Order of Canada and the Order of British Columbia.

DESCHENES, JULES (10 May, age 76). Former Quebec Superior Court judge who headed a royal commission on war criminals in Canada; companion of the Order of Canada.

DEWOLF, HARRY (18 December, age 97). Retired vice-admiral and former chief of naval staff in Ottawa.

DOMM, BILL (8 January, age 69). Controversial former Conservative

MP known for his outspoken opposition to some of his own party's policies.

DONAHOE, RICHARD (25 April, age 90). Former senator and Nova Scotia cabinet minister.

FULTON, E. DAVIE (22 May, age 84). Former federal cabinet minister in the Conservative government of John Diefenbaker; later a British Columbia Supreme Court judge.

GHERMEZIAN, JACOB (3 January, age 97). Founder of Triple Five Corporation, whose holdings include the West Edmonton Mall.

GWYN, SANDRA (26 May, age 65). Author and journalist who won the Governor General's award for non-fiction; awarded the Order of Canada.

HÉBERT, ANNE (22 January, age 83). Celebrated Quebec author; winner of three Governor General's awards for literature.

HENNING, DOUG (7 February, age 52). Emmy Award–winning magician who became the most prominent member of the Natural Law Party of Canada.

HODDER, WILSON (4 July, age 51). Gay-rights activist involved in the successful challenge of Nova Scotia's definition of marriage; died of AIDS after he and his partner won access to survivor benefits under the Canada Pension Plan.

HOMME, BOB (2 May, age 81). Known to generations of Canadian children as CBC-TV's Friendly Giant; recipient of the Order of Canada.

LAMBERT, MARCEL (24 September, age 81). Former Conservative cabinet minister and Speaker of the House of Commons.

LEVESQUE, GEORGE-HENRI (15 January, age 96). Inspirational figure in Quebec's Quiet Revolution of the 1960s; awarded the Order of Canada, the Order of Quebec, and the Pearson Medal for Peace.

LITTLE, STANLEY (16 May, age 89). Founding president of the Canadian Union of Public Employees.

MACEWAN, GRANT (15 June, age 97). Former Alberta Liberal leader who later served as the province's lieutenant-governor.

MATTHIAS, JOE (10 March, age 56). Squamish Chief for three decades; founding member of the First Nations Summit and the Union of BC Indian Chiefs.

MCLEAN, ANGUS (15 February, age 85). Former Conservative premier of Prince Edward Island; awarded the Order of Canada.

MILLER, FRANK (21 July, age 73). Former Conservative premier of Ontario.

MILLER, MARY BETH (2 July, age 24). Medal-winning biathlete who died after being mauled by a bear while training alone at a Canadian Forces base in Quebec.

MILLER, RICHARD (2 May, age 75). Justice of the New Brunswick Court of Queen's Bench who headed an inquiry into sexual abuse at a Fredericton centre for troubled youth.

MURPHY, CHUCK (25 May, age 66). Dominion president of the Royal Canadian Legion who led efforts to return Canada's Unknown Soldier from France to Canada.

PAPINEAU-COUTURE, JEAN (11 August, age 83). Composer and former dean of the music faculty at the University of Montreal.

PARR, JAMES GORDON (5 April, age 72). Scientist, university professor, and broadcaster; served as the head of TV Ontario and the Ontario Science Centre.

PÉPIN, MARCEL (5 March, age 74). Former head of the Confederation of National Trade Unions and the World Confederation of Labour who was once imprisoned for leading a strike against back-to-work legislation.

PURDY, AL (21 April, age 82). Winner of two Governor General's awards for poetry; appointed to the Order of Canada.

QUILICO, LOUIS (15 July, age 75). World-renowned Canadian opera star; companion of the Order of Canada and recipient of the Governor General's Performing Arts Award.

RANKIN, JOHN MORRIS (16 January, age 40). Member of the Celtic music ensemble the Rankins; killed when he drove his truck into the frigid waters of the Gulf of St Lawrence.

REAY, GORDON (21 December, age 57). Retired lieutenant-general and former commander of Canadian land forces; died following a traffic accident in Zagreb, Croatia, where he was serving as a special adviser on landmines to the Canadian ambassador.

RICHARD, MAURICE (27 May, age 78). Better known to hockey fans as Rocket Richard of the Montreal Canadiens; set numerous records and won eight Stanley Cups in his eighteen-year NHL career.

SCHMIRLER, SANDRA (2 March, age 36). Three-time world curling champion and Olympic gold medallist; inductee in the Canadian Curling Hall of Fame; died of cancer.

SHULMAN, MORTON (17 August, age 75). Former Toronto chief coroner; later served as an NDP MPP in the Ontario legislature; author of best-selling investment books, newspaper columnist, and television host.

SMITH, MELVIN (2 September, age 66). British Columbia public servant and constitutional affairs expert who vocally opposed both the Charlottetown Accord and the Nisga'a Treaty.

SMITH, MICHAEL (4 October, age 68). Nobel Prize–winning biochemist and director of Vancouver's Genome Sequence Centre; companion of the Order of Canada.

STARR, MICHAEL (17 March, age 89). Former mayor of Oshawa and cabinet minister in the Conservative government of John Diefenbaker.

TRUDEAU, PIERRE ELLIOTT (28 September, age 80). Former Liberal prime minister; best remembered for introducing official bilingualism, for invoking the War Measures Act during the 1970 October Crisis in Quebec, and for giving Canada its own constitution and Charter of Rights.

TURCOTT, SHELDON (18 February, age 64). Long-time CBC television news correspondent and anchor.

VAUGHAN, COLIN (1 January, age 68). Architect, former municipal politician, political commentator, and broadcaster.

WELCH, ROBERT (29 July, age 72). Minister in a dozen different cabinet portfolios under three Conservative Ontario premiers; later represented Canada on the International Joint Commission.

WICKS, BEN (10 September, age 73). Well-known Canadian cartoonist whose humanitarian work on behalf of children in developing countries earned him the Order of Canada.

Index of names

Index of subjects

Note: Page numbers followed by ‘t’ indicate a table.